Energy Subsidies

Lessons Learned in Assessing their Impact and Designing Policy Reforms

Edited by Anja von Moltke, Colin McKee and Trevor Morgan

ANJA VON MOLTKE, Economic Affairs Officer at the Economics and Trade Branch in Geneva, is responsible for managing projects of the United Nations Environment Programme in the field of environmental economics, including research and policy analysis, country studies and capacity building. Recently, her focus has been on the impact of subsidies and the use of economic instruments for sustainable development. Prior to joining UNEP in 1999, she worked for the German Environment Ministry on climate change. She received a MPhil in Environment and Development from Cambridge University (UK).

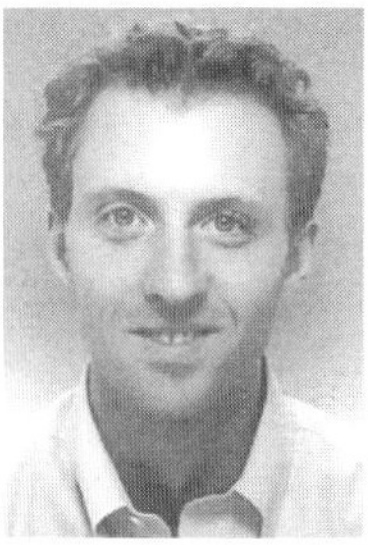

COLIN McKEE is a consultant for the Economics and Trade Branch of the United Nations Environment Programme. He assists the Branch on projects related to the use of economic instruments in environmental policy-making and the impacts of subsidies on the energy and fishery sectors. He received his BA degree in economics and international relations from Colby College (USA).

TREVOR MORGAN is the Paris-based Director of Menecon Consulting, an independent firm he set up in 1999 which advises energy companies, organisations and governments on energy strategy, policy and economic issues. Previously, he spent seven years as Senior Economist at the International Energy Agency. During that time, he was responsible for leading and contributing to a number of energy policy reviews, several studies of energy market reform and the Agency's flagship report, *World Energy Outlook*.

UNEP

UNITED NATIONS FOUNDATION™

ENERGY SUBSIDIES

LESSONS LEARNED IN ASSESSING THEIR IMPACT AND DESIGNING POLICY REFORMS

EDITED BY
ANJA VON MOLTKE,
COLIN McKEE
AND
TREVOR MORGAN

WITH A FOREWORD BY
KLAUS TÖPFER

Greenleaf
PUBLISHING
2004
The Work is published for and on behalf of UNEP

First edition 2004

The designations employed and the presentation of the material in this publication do not imply the expression of any opinion whatsoever on the part of the United Nations Environment Programme concerning the legal status of any country, territory, city or area or of its authorities, or concerning delimitation of its frontiers or boundaries. Moreover, the views expressed do not necessarily represent the decision or the stated policy of the United Nations Environment Programme, nor does citing of trade names or commercial processes constitute endorsement.

Published by Greenleaf Publishing Limited
Aizlewood's Mill
Nursery Street
Sheffield S3 8GG
UK

Printed on paper made from at least 75% post-consumer waste
using TCF and ECF bleaching.
Printed and bound by William Clowes, UK.
Cover by LaliAbril.com.

British Library Cataloguing in Publication Data:
A catalogue record for this book is available from the British Library.
ISBN 187471911X

Contents

Acknowledgements

This report was commissioned by the Economics and Trade Branch (Division of Technology, Industry and Economics) of the United Nations Environment Programme (UNEP). The Branch is headed by Hussein Abaza. Anja von Moltke, Economics Affairs Officer, was responsible for managing the project, assisted by Colin McKee, Consultant. Martina Otto, Associate Expert, of the DTIE was also involved in the project.

This report builds largely on presentations and discussions held during a series of regional workshops on reforming energy subsidies, organised jointly by UNEP and the International Energy Agency (IEA) in 2000 and 2001. The workshops were largely financed by voluntary contributions from Austria, Canada, Denmark, Germany, the Netherlands, Sweden, Switzerland and the United Kingdom. Both UNEP and the IEA would like to place on record their appreciation to these governments as well as the workshop participants for their contributions. Additionally, UNEP would like to express its formal appreciation to the United Nations Foundation, whose funding made this publication possible.

Whereas the compilation of papers presented in this study addresses a number of important issues related to energy subsidies and their reform that arise in a variety of countries and regions, it does not strive for a common or comprehensive approach. Furthermore, the views expressed in the following chapters are those of the authors and do not necessarily reflect those of UNEP. The principal authors are as follows:

- Chapter 1 (introduction): Trevor Morgan of Menecon Consulting, United Kingdom
- Chapter 2 (analytical framework): Trevor Morgan, Professor Anil Markandya and Alistair Hunt of Bath University, UK
- Chapter 3 (OECD): Trevor Morgan
- Chapter 4 (Czech and Slovak Republics): Jirina Jilkova of the University of Economics in Prague, Juraj Krivosik, SEVEn, the Energy Efficiency Centre,

Prague, and Tomas Chmelik from the Ministry of Environment, Czech Republic

- Chapter 5 (Russia): Igor Bashmakov of the Centre for Energy Efficiency, Russia
- Chapter 6 (India): Trevor Morgan
- Chapter 7 (Indonesia): Hoetomo of the State Ministry of Environment, Indonesia
- Chapter 8 (Korea): Myung-Kyoon Lee from the UNEP Collaborating Centre on Energy and Environment, Denmark
- Chapter 9 (Iran): Mostafa Tavanpour Paveh of the Ministry of Energy, Iran
- Chapter 10 (Senegal): Youba Sokona from ENDA-TM, Senegal, and Pape-Alassane Deme from PROGEDE, Senegal
- Chapter 11 (Chile): Raul O'Ryan and Sebastian Miller (University of Chile), Jorge Rogat (UNEP) and Carlos de Miguel (ECLAC), Chile
- Chapter 12 (country analysis): Trevor Morgan
- Chapter 13 (policy design and implementation): Trevor Morgan
- Annex (methodological approaches): Professor Anil Markandya and Alistair Hunt of Bath University, UK

Anja von Moltke, Colin McKee and Trevor Morgan were responsible for reviewing and editing all chapters.

The report also benefited from comments and suggestions from Ronald Steenblik from the Organisation for Economic Co-operation and Development (OECD), R.K. Batra, Meeta K. Mehra and Divya Datt from The Energy and Resource Institute (TERI), Kai Schlegelmilch from the German Ministry for the Environment, Nature Conservation and Nuclear Safety (BMU), Doug Koplow from Earth Track, Inc., Kristi Varangu from the International Energy Agency (IEA), Roberto Kozulj and Hector Pistonesi from the Instituto de Economía Energética/Fundación Bariloche (IDEE/FB), and Slav Slavov from the United Nations Economic Commission for Europe (UNECE). Their help is gratefully acknowledged.

For more information about UNEP's work on subsidy reform and economic instruments, please contact:

Anja von Moltke
Economics and Trade Branch (ETB)
Division of Technology, Industry and Economics (DTIE)
United Nations Environment Programme (UNEP)
11–13, Chemin des Anémones
CH-1219 Châtelaine/Geneva
Tel.: (41-22) 917 81 37
Fax: (41-22) 917 80 76
E-mail: etb@unep.ch
Internet: www.unep.ch/etu

Foreword

The need to reform energy subsidies was one of the pressing issues highlighted at the World Summit on Sustainable Development held in Johannesburg in September 2002. Many types of subsidy, especially those that encourage the production and use of fossil fuel, and other non-renewable forms of energy, are harmful to the environment. They can also have high financial and economic costs, and often bring only few benefits to the people for whom they are intended.

Removing, reducing or restructuring such energy subsidies is helpful for the environment and the economy at the same time. Potential social costs in terms of employment in the conventional energy industry or reduced access to energy could be addressed by redirecting the money formerly spent on subsidies to income support, health, environment, education or regional development programmes.

Of course, subsidies can have certain positive consequences, particularly where they are aimed at encouraging more sustainable energy production and use. Temporary support for renewable energy and energy-efficient technologies to overcome market barriers, and measures to improve poor or rural households' access to modern, commercial forms of energy, for instance, could be positive measures in support of sustainable development.

I hope that this book will be successful in raising awareness of the actual and potential impacts of energy subsidies and in providing guidance to policy-makers on how to design and implement energy subsidy reforms. It provides methodologies for analysing the impact of subsidies and their reform and reviews experiences with energy subsidies in a number of countries and regions. Drawing on these case studies, it analyses the lessons learned as well as the policy implications, and provides guidance on how to overcome resistance to reform.

Klaus Töpfer
Executive Director
United Nations Environment Programme

The United Nations Environment Programme

The United Nations Environment Programme (UNEP) is the overall co-ordinating environmental organisation of the United Nations system. Its mission is to provide leadership and encourage partnerships in caring for the environment by inspiring, informing and enabling nations and people to improve their quality of life without compromising that of future generations. In accordance with its mandate, UNEP works to observe, monitor and assess the state of the global environment, and improve our scientific understanding of how environmental change occurs, and, in turn, how such changes can be managed by action-oriented national policies and international agreements. UNEP's capacity-building work thus centres on helping countries strengthen environmental management in diverse areas including freshwater and land resource management, the conservation and sustainable use of biodiversity, marine and coastal ecosystem management, and cleaner industrial production and eco-efficiency, among many others. UNEP, which is headquartered in Nairobi, marked its first 30 years of service in 2002. During this time, in partnership with a global array of collaborating organisations, UNEP has achieved major advances in the development of international environmental policy and law, environmental monitoring and assessment, and our understanding of the science of global change. This work has, and continues to support, successful development and implementation of the world's major environmental conventions. In parallel, UNEP administers several multilateral environmental agreements including the Vienna Convention's Montreal Protocol on Substances that Deplete the Ozone Layer, the Convention on International Trade in Endangered Species of Wild Fauna and Flora (CITES), the Basel Convention on the Control of Transboundary Movements of Hazardous Wastes and their Disposal (SBC), the Convention on Prior Informed Consent procedure for Certain Hazardous Chemicals and Pesticides in International Trade (Rotterdam Convention, PIC) and, most recently, the Cartagena Protocol on Biosafety to the Convention on Biological Diversity as well as the Stockholm Convention on Persistent Organic Pollutants (POPs).

Division of Technology, Industry and Economics

The mission of the Division of Technology, Industry and Economics (DTIE) is to encourage decision-makers in governments, industry and business to develop and adopt policies, strategies and practices that are cleaner and safer, use natural resources more efficiently and reduce pollution risks to both human beings and the environment. The approach of DTIE is to raise awareness by fostering international consensus on policies, codes of practice and economic instruments through capacity-building and information exchange and by means of pilot projects.

Economics and Trade Branch

The Economics and Trade Branch (ETB) is one of the Branches of the Division of Technology, Industry and Economics (DTIE). The work programme of the Branch consists of three main components: economics, trade and financial services. Its mission is to enhance the capacities of countries, particularly developing countries and countries with economies in transition, to integrate environmental considerations in development planning and macroeconomic policies, including trade policies. UNEP's mission in the field of environmental economics is to promote the internalisation of environmental costs and enhance the use of economic instruments for environmental policy, at national, regional and international levels, including in the specific context of multilateral environmental agreements.

Executive summary

In principle, any measure that keeps prices for energy consumers below market levels, or for energy producers above market levels, or that reduces costs for consumers or producers may be considered a subsidy. An energy subsidy can take several different forms. Some subsidies can have a direct impact on price. These include grants, tax reductions and exemptions or price controls. Others affect prices or costs indirectly, such as regulations that skew the market in favour of a particular fuel, government-sponsored technology, or research and development (R&D).

Energy subsidies are widespread, but they vary greatly in importance and type according to the fuel and country. In the OECD, most energy subsidies are still concentrated on the production of fossil fuels and nuclear power, although the amount of these subsidies appears to have declined in recent years. In many European countries, subsidies to oil are often offset by special taxes and levies intended mainly to raise money for the national treasury. Remaining subsidies are aimed at protecting local industries from competition from imports for reasons of regional employment or energy-supply security, or both. The coal industry still benefits from large subsidies in a small number of countries, notably Germany, although these subsidies are being reduced gradually in most cases. Subsidies in support of transport projects that facilitate road, rail and water transit can also be substantial with direct benefit to the oil industry as they drive up the demand for oil products. They are not, however, considered in this report.

At the same time, subsidies to renewables and energy-efficient end-use technologies are growing in response to environmental concerns, particularly climate change and local pollution. In some cases, governments subsidise these technologies to enhance access to electricity in remote areas, to diversify the fuel mix or to promote decentralised generation. Certain countries are also seeking to obtain an early lead in the international market for such technologies. The most common forms of this type of subsidy are favourable tax treatment, grants and soft loans, regulations that favour a particular technology and R&D funding.

Energy subsidies in developing countries and countries with economies in transition considered in this report are generally much larger net of taxes than in

OECD countries, and take markedly different forms. The majority of them are aimed at consumers. Government price controls, which hold prices below the full economic cost of supply, remain the most widespread means of providing subsidies. They are most common for electricity, but are still important in some countries for oil products, coal and gas. The extent of under-pricing is generally bigger in countries where the energy sector is state-owned. State companies are usually treated as public-service entities and are not required to maximise profits. Energy subsidies are especially pervasive in energy-producing countries such as Iran and Indonesia, where the prices of almost every form of commercial energy are well below competitive market levels. India has taken important steps to raise oil and coal prices to economic levels in recent years, but massive electricity subsidies remain.

Economic theory says that social welfare is maximised when the price of each good and service is freely determined by the interaction of buyers and sellers in open, competitive markets. In practice, however, free markets in energy services left to their own devices do not work perfectly. In particular, they do not take account of any environmental and social benefits and costs that might be associated with certain types of energy activity. Barriers to market entry—for example, for demand-side technologies—may also cause markets to fail. So it can be argued that there exists a justification for governments to intervene in energy markets in pursuit of environmental and social objectives.

Subsidies can be justified if overall social welfare is increased. This situation occurs when the social gain or environmental improvement exceeds the economic cost. But experience in the countries analysed in this report provides evidence that, in many instances, the net effects of subsidies are negative. In other words, overall social welfare would be higher without subsidies. This may be the case if the rationale for the subsidy is invalid: for example, because too much emphasis is put on a particular policy goal to the detriment of others. The way in which the subsidy is applied may also be ineffective. Even where the net benefits are positive, energy subsidies may not be the most efficient way of achieving policy goals. Table I summarises evidence of the kinds of economic, environmental and social effects from the country case studies in this report.

The country case studies demonstrate that the economic costs of energy subsidies can be significant. They can place a heavy burden on government finances, weaken the foreign trade balance and stunt the potential of economies. These costs are especially large in Indonesia and Iran, where energy is very heavily subsidised. Depending on how they work, they can also undermine private and public investment in the energy sector, impeding energy conservation and the expansion of distribution networks. Electricity subsidies in India, for example, by undermining the financial health of the state electricity boards, undermine investment and the quality of electricity service. Subsidies to specific technologies can also hinder the development of competing technologies that might be more economic in the longer term. In other words, subsidies can 'lock in' inappropriate technologies. And, very often, it is more affluent socioeconomic classes that end up with the largest share of subsidies intended for the poor.

Many energy subsidy schemes are also harmful for the environment. Subsidies that encourage the production and use of fossil fuels inevitably have some harmful

Country/region	***Types of subsidy assessed***	***Economic effects***	***Environmental effects***	***Social effects***
OECD	All types	Studies show that removing fossil fuel subsidies would boost trade and economic growth.	Since most subsidies go to fossil fuels, removing them would reduce noxious and CO_2 emissions.	Significant short-term distributional effects, mainly due to impact on employment and household spending on energy.
Czech and Slovak Republics	All types	Subsidies have held back economic restructuring and hindered innovation, resulting in high energy intensity and low energy efficiency.	Have exacerbated the harmful environmental effects of energy supply and consumption, including local and regional air pollution and CO_2 emissions.	No detailed studies of social effects have been carried out even though household income support is primary reason for subsidising energy.
Russia	District heat	Large consumer subsidies, together with lack of metering and payment problems, cause waste and undermine investment and efficiency.	By encouraging over-consumption, under-pricing contributes to pollution and greenhouse gas emissions.	Heat is a vital service to most households. But savings from subsidy removal can finance welfare payments to the poor and improved metering and billing.
India	Electricity	Subsidies encourage waste and hold back investment in the power sector—a major constraint on economic development. Removing subsidies would trim demand in the long run by 34%.	Removing electricity subsidies alone would cut CO_2 emissions by 99 million tonnes, equivalent to a third of current power-sector emissions.	Subsidy removal would raise cost of service to households, but would improve quality of service and enhance utilities' ability to extend and expand capacity.
Indonesia	All types	Net economic cost of subsidies to kerosene, diesel, gasoline and heavy fuel oil amounted to $4 billion in 2001.	Subsidies exacerbate pollution, especially particulates and lead.	Reducing subsidies would free up resources to support the poor in more effective ways.
Korea	All types	Coal subsidies of around $500 million per year and large cross-subsidies in electricity and gas, together with the tax system, distort energy-use patterns.	Subsidies to coal and to industrial users of electricity and gas encourage over-consumption of fossil fuels and consequently boost emissions.	Removal of coal subsidies would have serious economic and social consequences for mining communities.
Iran	All types	Subsidies cause inefficient energy use, are a major burden on public finances and have resulted in poor energy-sector performance.	Excessive energy use has aggravated local and regional pollution, a major public health issue.	Mainly benefit higher-income groups, which consume larger amounts of subsidised energy. But eliminating subsidies would have a dramatic impact on household budgets.

Table 1 **Summary of findings of country case studies: main effects**
(continued opposite)

Country/region	Types of subsidy assessed	Economic effects	Environmental effects	Social effects
Senegal	LPG	Subsidies have successfully stimulated LPG use, bringing some economic benefits but at a significant financial cost.	Growth in LPG use has resulted in savings of about 70,000 tonnes of fuelwood and 90,000 tonnes of charcoal per year, relieving defor-estation pressures and reducing pollution.	Subsidies have Improved household comfort standards and safety, and have enhanced incomes.
Chile	Oil and coal	The elimination of coal subsidies in 1995 was economically beneficial. Removing remaining oil subsidies would incur short-term economic costs.	The environment clearly benefits from subsidies reform in both cases through large reductions in CO, particulate and CO_2 emissions.	Removing oil subsidies completely would have a slightly larger negative impact on richer household incomes.

Table 1 (continued)

environmental effects. Consumer subsidies that lower the price paid for those fuels or the cost of using them almost always result in higher consumption levels. This can lead to higher emissions of noxious and greenhouse gases as well as other forms of environmental damage, such as water contamination and spoiling of the landscape. Recent international legal frameworks, such as the 1997 Kyoto Protocol, explicitly require a reduction of subsidies that encourage greenhouse gas emissions. In many developing countries, such as Iran, India and Indonesia, the more pressing environmental cost of subsidies relates to the health impacts of local pollution.

But the overall impact of fossil fuel and other energy subsidies on the environment is not always negative. For example, encouraging the household use of oil products can reduce pressure on forests in poor rural areas of developing countries otherwise dependent on firewood. Subsidies to oil products and electricity in poor countries can also reduce indoor air pollution, if they encourage a shift away from traditional biomass fuels, such as wood, straw, crop residues and dung. Similarly, the environmental effects of subsidies to nuclear power and renewable energy sources are mixed. By reducing the use of fossil fuels, they would normally lead to lower airborne emissions. But nuclear power production results in radioactive waste and the small but nonetheless real risk of contamination from accidental releases of radioactive substances. Some types of renewable may have adverse environmental consequences, too, such as the disturbance to regional ecosystems caused by dams. The production of biofuels, subsidised by several OECD countries, can also be harmful for the environment, since they usually result in greater use of mineral fertilisers and pesticides. Nevertheless, subsidies to other forms of energy such as wind and solar can often have positive environmental impacts.

Evidence from the case studies in this report of the net environmental effects of introducing or removing energy subsidies is generally qualitative. This reflects the immense practical difficulties in estimating quantitatively the different effects, expressing them in consistent monetary terms and aggregating them. Nonetheless, partial analyses suggest that there is considerable scope in some countries for reducing environmental degradation by eliminating energy subsidies. In India, for instance, carbon dioxide (CO_2) emissions could be cut by around 100 million tonnes a year—equivalent to more than 10% of the country's total emissions—by removing electricity subsidies. Similarly, the removal of oil subsidies in Chile could lower sulphur dioxide (SO_2), nitrogen oxides (NO_X), particulate and CO_2 emissions each by around 5% in the short term.

Removing subsidies that are both economically costly as well as harmful to the environment would be a win–win policy reform. As many fossil fuel subsidies fall into this category, governments should prioritise removing them. But governments are often faced with awkward trade-offs between the economic and environmental benefits of reforming those subsidies and the social costs of higher fuel prices or of lower employment in indigenous energy industries. In some poor developing countries and transition economies, removing subsidies to modern household cooking and heating fuels has had a dramatic short-term impact on living standards. This factor has deterred the Russian government from addressing heat subsidies. And removing subsidies to coal can have a devastating effect on employment and incomes in local communities that depend heavily on mining.

But these subsidies have to be paid for—often out of general tax revenues. At the least, governments should think seriously about the opportunity costs of energy subsidies. The money saved by removing subsidies could be spent on other social welfare programmes, such as direct income-support payments, health and education. Moreover, it is doubtful that one could ever find overall net social benefits from protectionist policies aimed at maintaining employment in domestic energy industries such as coal mining. Such subsidies can hold back innovation and efficiency gains, and thus cost reductions. They furthermore can restrict economic growth and reduce employment in other sectors of the economy. And even the local communities concerned may not benefit in the long run. Experience in Europe shows that redirecting coal subsidies to retraining and regional economic development aid can boost higher-paid, safer and more desirable jobs to replace the jobs lost in the coal industry.

Not all energy subsidies are bad, however. There may be a good case for retaining subsidies in specific instances, especially where they are aimed at encouraging more sustainable energy use. Examples might include temporary support for new renewable and energy-efficient technologies to overcome market barriers, and measures to improve poor or rural households' access to modern, commercial forms of energy. But the way in which a subsidy is applied is critical to how effective it is in meeting policy objectives and its cost.

In practice, governments need to take account of national and local circumstances in reforming subsidy policies or designing new ones. These include the country's own policy objectives and priorities, its stage of economic development, market and economic conditions, the state of public finances, the institutional framework and the state of the country's environment. Nonetheless, there are a number of basic principles that countries need to apply in designing subsidies and implementing reforms to existing programmes. Experience shows that, when applied, subsidy programmes and their reform should meet the following key criteria:

- **Well targeted.** Subsidies should go only to those who are meant and deserve to receive them.
- **Efficient.** Subsidies should not undermine incentives for suppliers or consumers to provide or use a service efficiently.
- **Soundly based.** Subsidies should be justified by a thorough analysis of the associated costs and benefits.
- **Practical.** The amount of subsidy should be affordable and it must be possible to administer the subsidy in a low-cost way.
- **Transparent.** The public should be able to see how much a subsidy programme costs and who benefits from it.
- **Limited in time.** Subsidy programmes should have limited duration, preferably set at the outset, so that consumers and producers do not get 'hooked' on the subsidies and the cost of the programme does not spiral out of control.

In practice, public resistance to reform can be very strong. Reforming existing energy subsidies requires strong political will to take tough decisions that benefit society as a whole. Certain approaches can also help. Implementing reforms in a phased manner can help to soften the financial pain of those who stand to lose out and give them time to adapt. This is likely to be the case where removing a subsidy has major economic and social consequences. The pace of reform, however, should not be so slow that delaying its full implementation involves excessive costs and allows resistance to build up. The authorities can also introduce compensating measures that support the real incomes of targeted social groups in more direct and effective ways. That goal may be considered socially desirable. It may also be the price that has to be paid to achieve public and political support for removing or reducing the subsidy. Whatever the precise design of reform policies, politicians need to communicate clearly to the general public the overall benefits of subsidy reform to the economy and to society as a whole, and consult with stakeholders in formulating reforms to counter political inertia and opposition. Stakeholder consultation ensures transparency and adds legitimacy to the proposed reforms, thereby increasing the chances of the policy being accepted.

1 Introduction

1.1 Background

Natural resource subsidies have a number of perverse consequences: among others, they send false price signs that encourage overuse of resources; they inhibit the development of substitutes that are more environmentally friendly; they distort international trade; and they divert scarce financial resources from other social purposes. Yet they persist. In some cases, subsidies still serve legitimate social goals, benefiting poor or marginalised consumers while, in others, governments are reluctant to undertake reform for fears that their removal may adversely affect competitiveness and employment in certain sectors.

Fossil fuel subsidies offer a good illustration of these linkages. Fossil fuels are the principal cause of climate change, mainly in industrialised countries, but increasingly in developing countries. While considerable political and legal progress has been undertaken in negotiations to control greenhouse gas emissions and mitigate climate change, many countries around the world continue to subsidise fossil fuel production, processing, transportation and consumption. This impedes more efficient energy use and conservation as well as the development and deployment of renewable energy sources. The 1992 UN Framework Convention on Climate Change (UNFCCC) and the 1997 Kyoto Protocol, which aim to stabilise greenhouse gas emissions, both recognise the key role that removing harmful subsidies could play in achieving this goal. However, while general agreement has been reached on the need to reform energy subsidy programmes, implementation of subsidy reform has so far been limited—in a large part due to the difficulty in understanding their complexity and scope. Among the factors that hinder reform are a lack of transparency, disagreement on how to define and measure subsidies and their effects and vested interests.

There is thus the need to better understand the uncertainties surrounding fossil fuel subsidies, to develop policy options that address the economic, environmental and social impacts while helping governments to ease the transition for those who currently benefit from such subsidies.

UNEP, with the IEA, conducted a series of regional workshops on energy subsidy reform and sustainable development in late 2000 and early 2001. They were financed by voluntary contributions from Austria, Canada, Denmark, Germany, the Netherlands, Sweden, Switzerland and the United Kingdom. The primary aims of the workshops, at which the findings of UNEP and IEA analyses of energy subsidy issues were presented, were to:

- Provide a platform for dialogue at the regional level for government representatives, experts, non-governmental organisations and industry participants to exchange ideas and policy experiences on specific regional issues.
- Further the dialogue between developed and developing countries on the opportunities and challenges in reforming subsidies.
- Review and develop methodologies for identifying and assessing quantitatively the effects of energy subsidies.

UNEP and the IEA subsequently prepared a synthesis report, *Energy Subsidy Reform and Sustainable Development: Challenges for Policymakers*, setting out the key issues discussed during the workshops and the main findings and conclusions. That report was submitted to the ninth session of the United Nations Commission on Sustainable Development held in New York in April 2001. A booklet, *Reforming Energy Subsidies,* describing in non-technical language the central messages and findings of the synthesis report and the background analytical studies was published in April 2002.[1]

1.2 Objectives and structure of this report

This report analyses in more detail issues related to energy subsidies and their reform. It aims to raise awareness of these issues among stakeholders, to highlight the impact of subsidies and the barriers to reform, and to provide guidance to policy-makers on how to go about designing and implementing reforms.

The next chapter, describing the analytical framework, aims to set the scene for the detailed discussion of energy subsidy issues at the country level. It considers how subsidies are defined, how they can be measured, how big they are and how their effects can be assessed. A more detailed discussion of methodological approaches to the assessment of the economic, environmental and social effects of subsidies and their reform is contained in the Annex .

Chapters 3–11 contain country case studies from contributing authors, which review various experiences and issues related to energy subsidies in selected countries, but do not strive for a common approach. They are organised along geographical lines, beginning with a review of energy subsidies generally in OECD

1 UNEP/IEA 2002. Information about the workshops and the synthesis report can be found at www.uneptie.org/energy/act/pol/wokshops/sub_ws.htm [*sic*].

countries. Case studies of energy subsidies in transition economies—the Czech and Slovak Republics (Chapter 4) and Russia (Chapter 5)—follow. Three studies of Asian countries focus on the costs of different types of energy subsidy: electricity subsidies in India (Chapter 6), oil subsidies in Indonesia (Chapter 7) and energy subsidies generally in Korea (Chapter 8). Chapter 9 reviews the effect of energy subsidies in Iran and suggests a pragmatic approach to reforming them. This is followed by an assessment of the LPG subsidy programme in Senegal (Chapter 10) and an analysis of the effects of removing coal and oil subsides in Chile (Chapter 11).

Chapter 12 analyses the lessons learned from these case studies, focusing on the economic, environmental and social effects and their implications for policy. Finally, Chapter 13 discusses the implications of these findings and makes practical recommendations for designing and implementing policy reforms.

2
Analytical framework

This chapter presents various principal issues surrounding energy subsidies, as well as an introduction on how to analyse the economic, environmental and social impacts of subsidies and their reform. Subsidies come in both direct and indirect forms, such as tax exemption and price controls, or as regulations that may skew the market. Such diversity has led to difficulty in defining their exact nature, but it is generally agreed that subsidies can be any government action that keeps the price below or above what the market level would normally determine. Global estimates of fossil fuel consumption subsidies have been placed at around $230 billion. In understanding subsidies' impacts, as well as the benefits of reform, it is essential that the economic, environmental and social factors be considered together. Such integrated assessment can therefore highlight the trade-offs stemming out of government policy impacts, while also accounting for the overall well-being of both individuals and society. Methodologies to undertake such analysis are introduced with further discussion provided in the Annex.

2.1 Defining energy subsidies

There is enormous confusion surrounding the terminology and definition of energy subsidies. Government intervention, assistance, transfers and support measures can all generally be considered as a form of subsidy. The narrowest and perhaps most commonly used definition of a subsidy is a direct cash payment by a government to an energy producer or consumer. But this is just one way in which governments can stimulate the production or use of a particular fuel or form of energy. Broader definitions attempt to capture other types of government intervention that affect prices or costs, either directly or indirectly. For example, an OECD study defined a subsidy in general terms as *any measure that keeps prices for consumers below market levels, or for producers above market levels or that reduces costs for consumers and producers* (OECD 1998). In a similar way, the IEA defines an energy subsidy as *any government action that concerns primarily the energy sector that lowers the cost of energy production, raises the price received by energy producers or lowers the price paid by energy consumers* (IEA 1999). This report does not adopt any specific definition but works broadly within these ideas of what a subsidy is.[2]

An energy subsidy can take several different forms. Table 2.1 sets out the principal sources of subsidies based on the IEA definition. Some subsidies have a direct impact on price, such as grants, tax exemptions and price controls. Others affect prices or costs indirectly, such as regulations that skew the market in favour of a particular fuel or government-sponsored technology research and development.

		How the subsidy usually works		
Government intervention	***Example***	**Lowers cost of production**	**Raises cost of production**	**Lowers price to consumer**
Direct financial transfer	Grants to producers	✓		
	Grants to consumers			✓
	Low-interest or preferential loans to producers	✓		
Preferential tax treatment	Rebates or exemptions on royalties, sales taxes, producer levies and tariffs	✓		
	Tax credit	✓		✓
	Accelerated depreciation allowances on energy supply equipment	✓		
Trade restrictions	Quotas, technical restrictions and trade embargoes		✓	
Energy-related services provided directly by government at less than full cost	Direct investment in energy infrastructure	✓		
	Public research and development	✓		
Regulation of the energy sector	Demand guarantees and mandated deployment rates	✓	✓	
	Price controls		✓	✓
	Market-access restrictions		✓	

Table 2.1 **Main types of energy subsidy**

Source: UNEP/IEA 2002

2 It is important to note the distinction between a consumer subsidy as defined above and the 'rent' that a consumer receives from using energy. The latter is the difference between what is paid for the commodity or service and what it is worth to the consumer. A subsidy lowers the price to the consumer below what it would otherwise be, thus allowing him to obtain a greater rent.

How governments choose to subsidise energy depends on a number of factors. These include the overall cost of the programme, the transaction and administration costs it involves and how the cost of the subsidy affects different social groups. A per-unit cash payment to producers or consumers is the simplest and most transparent form of subsidy, but can involve considerable accounting and transaction costs. It also involves a heavy direct financial burden on the national treasury. Governments generally like to keep subsidies 'off-budget' for political reasons; on-budget subsidies are an easy target for pressure groups interested in reducing the overall tax burden. For this reason, subsidies often take the form of price controls that set prices below full cost, especially where the energy company is state-owned, or a requirement on energy buyers to lift minimum volumes from a specific, usually indigenous, supply source at above market prices. Subsides may be aimed at producers, such as a grant paid for each unit of production, or to consumers, such as a rebate or exemption on the normal sales tax.

Subsidies to indigenous energy production, usually aimed at protecting sectoral employment and reducing exports, remain common throughout the world. They have, nonetheless, been declining in many countries over the last decade with the shift towards more market-oriented economic and energy policies and liberalisation of international trade. Subsidies to coal producers, for example, have fallen sharply in recent years, although they remain important in several countries, including a handful of OECD countries—notably Germany. On the other hand, subsidies designed to encourage the uptake of renewable energy technologies are growing, driven mainly by environmental and energy-security concerns and, in some cases, by regional employment objectives. For example, several OECD and non-OECD countries subsidise the production of fuels derived from agricultural products.

It is important to make a distinction between gross subsidies and subsidies net of taxes in measuring both their size and their impacts on energy supply and use. Energy taxes reduce the effect of subsidies on price. In some cases, energy subsidies are more than offset by special taxes and duties that raise the final end-use price to above free-market levels. However, this price rarely accounts for full external costs. What matters in practice is the overall impact of all subsidies and taxes on the absolute level of prices and costs and the competitiveness of each fuel or technology.

To achieve an economically efficient allocation of resources in a market economy, producers and consumers should pay for the full costs associated with their activities.[3] Therefore, in principle, one can argue that an uninternalised external cost, such as environmental damage, constitutes a subsidy.[4] However, defining subsidies in this way is challenging because of the practical difficulties in measuring those costs and assigning monetary values to them (see Section 2.4.4). Unless otherwise stated, the quantitative estimates of subsidies cited in this report do not take this approach.

3 An economically efficient economy is defined as one where the allocation of resources is such that no one can be made better off without someone else being made worse off. In economics, such an allocation is also referred to as 'Pareto efficient' or 'Pareto optimal'.

4 See IEA 1999: 56-58 for a discussion of this issue.

2.2 Measuring energy subsidies

Much of the work on identifying and measuring government interventions has been carried out by organisations concerned with international trade and comparisons of trade policies. The **effective rate of assistance (ERA)** is a basic measure of a subsidy, covering any direct or indirect action that affects the price of the good in question. While it has the virtue of capturing the full extent of the subsidy, such a measure is difficult to use in practice because it requires information on subsidies to industries upstream of the good being examined.

A more limited yet practical indicator is the **producer subsidy equivalent (PSE)**, which was developed by the OECD and has been used by the IEA to quantify coal subsidies (see IEA 2002). The PSE defines the nominal cash transfers to domestic producers equivalent to the total value of existing support, provided at current levels of output, consumption and trade. PSEs do not, however, capture all subsidies since they focus solely on the supply side. Other interventions, which have the effect of reducing end-user prices and thus raising energy use and related emissions, are picked up by the **consumer subsidy equivalent (CSE)** indicator. A CSE is defined as the algebraic sum of the difference between domestic and world prices times the quantity consumed plus any direct financial payment to consumers that reduced the price paid for domestic consumption.

The **price-gap approach** involves comparing actual end-user prices of energy products with reference prices, defined as those prices that would prevail in undistorted markets in the absence of subsidies. The difference between the two is the 'price gap'.[5] Combining the percentage change in prices (the price gap divided by the reference price) with the elasticity of demand yields the change in consumption that would result from the complete elimination of subsidies that cause the price gap. This approach has the attraction of conceptual and analytical simplicity. But it also has limitations. It only captures the effects of subsidies on economic efficiency to the extent that they lower or increase the end-use price of the good. Moreover, the price gap measures only the net price effect of all the different subsidies; a mix of subsidies may result in a zero net price gap but still involve significant efficiency losses. Because it relies on simple assumptions, it cannot take into account the effects that, for example, rationing may be having on the consumption of energy at the current price. This approach is, therefore, mainly suitable for producing a broad estimate of the impact of subsidies on consumption levels and, therefore, the potential reduction in greenhouse gas emissions from subsidy removal.

2.3 The size of energy subsidies

Energy subsidies are widespread, but they vary greatly in importance and type according to the fuel and country. Estimating their size depends heavily on defini-

5 See Annex, Section A1, for examples of studies that have used this approach.

tions and methodologies. Big differences in definitions make comparisons of individual studies of the impact of energy subsidies in specific countries or regions difficult and complicate discussions of issues relating to subsidies and their reform. Very few studies have attempted to quantify energy subsidies for the world as a whole, because of data deficiencies and the sheer scale of the exercise. The most well-known global study, carried out by Larsen and Shah in 1992, put world fossil fuel consumption subsidies from under-pricing alone at around $230 billion per year. The Former Soviet Union accounted for around two-thirds of that and developing countries for most of the rest. An OECD study, published the same year, estimated net global consumption subsidies at $235 billion per year, with $254 billion of net subsidies in non-OECD countries offsetting $19 billion in net energy taxes in the OECD. A more recent multi-country study analysis by Myers and Kent (2001) estimated fossil fuel subsidies worldwide at $133 billion. Other recent studies confirm that energy consumption subsidies are much bigger in non-OECD countries. A 1997 World Bank study estimated annual fossil fuel subsidies at $48 billion in 20 of the largest countries outside the OECD and $10 billion in the OECD, although the scope of the subsidies considered was narrow. A related OECD study looks at ending coal-production subsidies as part of a broader assessment of the environmental effects of liberalising trade in fossil fuels (OECD 2000). This study is discussed in further detail in the Annex.

The overall size of energy subsidies has fallen sharply since the 1980s, mainly due to economic reform and structural adjustment programmes in the former communist bloc and other non-OECD developing countries. Subsidies dropped by over half in the five years to 1996 according to a 1997 World Bank study (World Bank 1997a; Fig. 2.1). A 1999 IEA study, which examined eight of the largest non-OECD countries covering almost 60% of total non-OECD energy demand, put the total value of energy subsidies in those countries at around $95 billion in 1998 (IEA 1999). End-use prices were found to be about a fifth below market levels in those countries. This study is described in more detail in the Annex.

Producer subsidies, usually in the form of direct payments or support for research and development, are most common in OECD countries. By contrast, most subsidies in developing countries and transition economies go to consumers—usually through price controls that hold end-user prices below the full cost of supply. In all regions, the fossil fuel and nuclear industries get the lion's share of subsidies. In the United States, for example, renewables and energy conservation together receive only 5% of total federal energy subsidies, according to studies carried out by the government in 1999 (US DOE/EIA 1999). However, the trend in OECD countries is towards an increasing share of support for renewable and alternative-energy technologies.

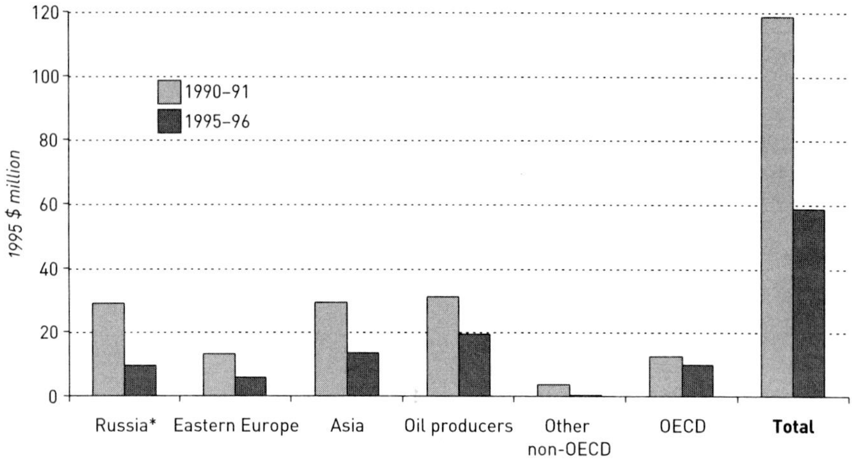

* Estimates for Russia are for 1990 and 1994 in purchasing power parities.

Figure 2.1 **Fossil fuel subsidies in selected countries, 1990–91 and 1995–96**

Source: World Bank 1997

2.4 Analysing the impact of subsidies and their reform

The underlying principle of policy-making for sustainable development is to take into account the overall well-being of both individuals and society as a whole. Progress towards integrated assessment of the impact of government policies is therefore essential so that the different determinants of well-being can be considered together. The economic, environmental and social changes that result from reform of energy subsidy policies, therefore, need to be identified and evaluated within a common framework. In practice, however, that is by no means straightforward. Estimates of the effects of reform should, therefore, be treated with caution.

2.4.1 Economic, environmental and social effects

The measurement of the economic impacts of removing subsidies can be conducted in two ways. The first, based on a partial equilibrium approach, looks at the net gains in consumer and producer 'surplus', which broadly measure the net benefits of consuming and supplying energy after accounting for the price paid by consumers and the production costs paid by producers. The second uses a more general equilibrium (GE) approach, taking account of how markets are linked, so that the effects of energy price changes on the labour and product markets are accounted for. In this case the measured effects of the changes in subsidies are usually reported in terms of changes in gross domestic product (GDP).

Both approaches have been widely used for a considerable period of time in estimating various policy impacts, to also include those of energy subsidies and their reform. The first approach is limited in that it does not take account of inter-sectoral linkages and does not measure changes in the distribution of income, which have to be addressed separately. In using it to measure changes in economic welfare, it is important to allow for market imperfections. For example, if the market supplier has market power, this must be accounted for in the measurement of surplus.

The second approach does address inter-sectoral linkages but not, generally, the income distribution issue. It has the disadvantage of being considerably more complex and the data demanding to use (if the data is not available, its use based on estimated values may be less accurate than the partial equilibrium approach).[6] The complexity of what happens with energy subsidies is better understood with specific examples. It is often argued that energy subsidy reform may be expected to result eventually in higher market prices to consumers. This, in turn, would normally result in lower demand for the energy source in question and, therefore, lower output. Employment levels would fall in that sector as a consequence. This fall in production and in revenue could result in a lower GDP and lower economic welfare. However, the picture is usually more complex. The money previously spent on maintaining the subsidy would now be free to be used in other ways. It could, for instance, be returned to firms or individuals in the form of support for environmental protection programmes or tax cuts, which would free up income for them to spend on other goods. Thus, while the composition of GDP may change, it is not certain whether the total would rise or fall.

There are also a variety of distortions to economic efficiency that may be reduced as a result of subsidy reform. One such distortion, experienced in a number of OECD countries, involves subsidies to specific technologies reducing the rate of development of competing technologies that might be more economic in the longer term. In other words, subsidies can 'lock in' inappropriate technologies.

The changes in output within the energy sector may have significant environmental consequences. Less demand for the use of exhaustible resources such as coal, oil or gas would ensure that the stock of natural resources is depleted less rapidly. In addition, a reduction in energy production and use would, in most cases, result in lower emissions of pollutants from combustion processes.

This is described in Figure 2.2. Assuming that the supply and/or use of a particular fuel results in some form of air pollution or climate-destabilising emissions, the introduction of a per-unit subsidy on fuel production shifts the supply curve down from S to S_{ps}. This causes the price to drop to P_{ps} and the quantity of the fuel sold to rise to Q_{ps}, corresponding to an increase in environmental damage from E

6 It is a common misperception that the GE approach assumes perfect markets and perfect information. It does not, and indeed many of the models now available allow for failure in market clearance, when this is critical. Moreover, if one sector has monopoly power, this can and has been modelled with success. A further discussion of results from such models is given in the Annex.

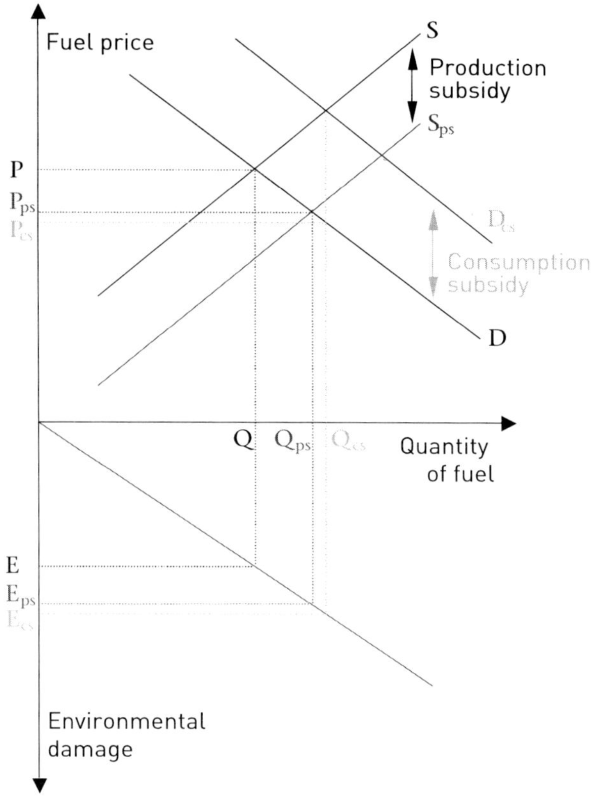

Figure 2.2 **The environmental effects of subsidies**

Source: UNEP/IEA 2002

to E_{ps}. Similarly, a per-unit consumption subsidy shifts the demand curve up from D to D_{cs}. This results in a drop in the net price paid by consumers to P_{cs}, an increase in the quantity consumed to Q_{cs} and an increase in environmental damage to E_{cs}.

The precise impact of any production or consumption subsidy depends on demand for and supply of the fuel in question and the relationship between consumption of the fuel and environmental damage. The less sensitive supply and demand are to price, the less impact subsidies have on the environment. Inter-fuel substitution will determine the overall environmental impact of a subsidy on a given fuel, since that subsidy will normally affect the use of other fuels.

Economic changes can result in the deterioration of social conditions as a consequence of energy-sector workers being made redundant. However, an increase in public investment in healthcare or education that could result from a redirection of public expenditures could lead to improvements in well-being, both in the present and in the future. Alternatively, the reduced need to raise taxes could enable better targeting of welfare support to low-income groups through tax benefits. Nonetheless, in undertaking such an integrated assessment, it is important to note that the net changes in social welfare are sensitive to the weights assigned to costs and benefits as they accrue to different economic groups or stakeholders.

2.4.2 Identifying linkages

A framework for capturing and quantifying the type of environmental, economic and social effects of subsidy reform outlined above is presented in Figure 2.3. Implementation of the framework begins with a fiscal 'incidence analysis'. This involves identifying the ultimate recipients—sectors or groups—of the subsidy under investigation, and assessing how subsidy reform would affect prices, the quantity of energy produced and consumed and incomes (the composition and level of production in the economy).

The starting point of integrated analysis is, therefore, the economic dimension. At a macro level (i.e. in terms of aggregate well-being, growth, etc.), previous analyses have shown the effects of the removal of energy subsidies to be generally beneficial. For details, see the Annex. This does mean, however, that these economic impacts will be the most important, or that they are the key to the problem. There are also important environmental and social effects that do not necessarily work in the same direction as the economic impacts and that must be included in any integrated assessment.

On the environmental side, the changes in the volume of production will directly affect natural resource input requirements and emissions of pollutants to air, water and land. The extent of these changes will depend on, among other things, environmental policies. If a recipient sector is subject to strict environmental standards, then the magnitude of *actual* changes in emissions resulting from subsidy reform may be mitigated. However, pollution control regulations rarely result in zero emissions. Indeed, many countries set emission limits based on best available abatement technology for coal-fired power plants that are less stringent than those for gas-fired power plants. Removing a subsidy that favours electricity generation from solid fuels, even if the affected plants are subject to 'strict environmental standards', could still result in a shift towards much cleaner power generation.

The economic and environmental impacts described above will also have social implications. Hence a social assessment is a critical part of any overall integrated assessment. This should look particularly closely at how the changes in prices affect the use of energy by vulnerable groups and how the mix of fuels they use changes. For example, a reduction in subsidies to commercial fuels (gas, kerosene, LPG [liquefied petroleum gas], etc.) can make them so expensive that households resort to non-commercial fuels, such as wood, which cause environmental degradation and increase exposure to indoor air pollution. Estimates of worldwide premature deaths due to indoor air pollution are put at 2 million (Smith and Metha 2000). Other important social impacts include: (a) employment (reduced demand for the less-subsidised energy resulting in loss of jobs and hardship); (b) education

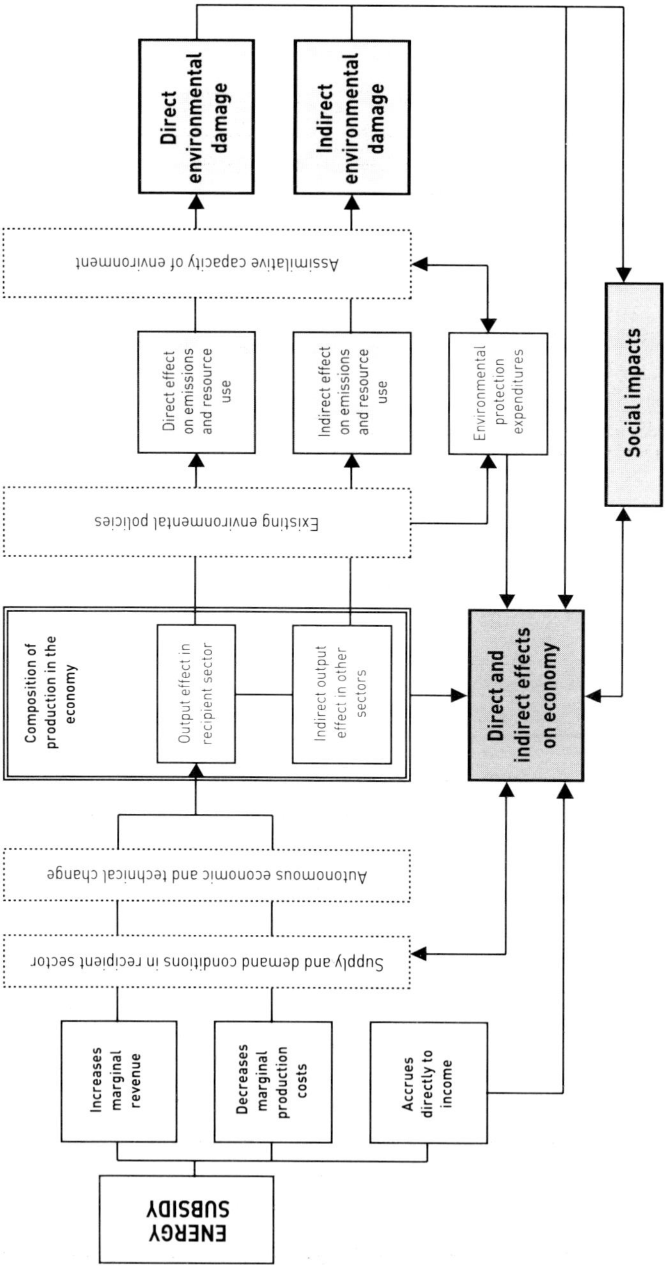

Figure 2.3 Integrated assessment framework

(poor households whose use of electricity may be so reduced that children cannot use enough of it for homework); (c) infant mortality (a recent World Bank study looked at demographic and health data from over 60 low-income countries and found that in urban areas linking households to electricity is the only key factor reducing both the infant mortality rate and the under-five mortality rate, and that this effect is large, significant and independent of incomes [Buys *et al.* 2003]); and (d) problems of cold among poor elderly households (a World Bank study has shown a strong correlation between low indoor winter temperatures and illness in Eastern Europe [World Bank 2002]). These impacts, especially health-related, are clearly important and have major social implications, especially in developing countries. Indeed any programme of subsidy removal would need to track them with great care, additionally paying special attention to urban–rural differences.

While the focus of the impacts of subsidy removal in the previous paragraph has been on the poor, it is also important to note that there can be big effects on the better-off as well. Often it is they who have benefited most from the subsidies and who will have most to lose as subsidies are removed. For examples, see the Annex.

Once the effects of the policy reforms and their interlinkages have been established, the task of an integrated assessment is to weigh up the different outcomes against one another. This is far from straightforward if the changes are very different in nature. For example, changes in income cannot easily be compared to a fall in the emissions of SO_2 that may result from a reduction in coal subsidies due to the difficulties in assigning a monetary value to an environmental improvement. Likewise, an increase in the share of expenditure on energy in poor households and an increased use of non-commercial fuels have impacts that can be quantified but not easily compared with the changes in budget expenditures and other economic impacts.

2.4.3 Measuring welfare in a common unit

Measuring and expressing welfare effects in common units helps integration of the analysis of the different types of effect resulting from energy subsidy reform. The most common unit of measurement is financial, as it is easily understood. Moreover, financial units are commonly used to measure economic welfare. The monetisation of welfare changes brought about by environmental changes is more problematic and controversial. Since environmental changes are generally not expressed directly in market prices, these values must be imputed in other ways. The methodologies used for this imputation are still developing and are not, as yet, widely accepted, and there are numerous environmental effects that economists have not so far been able to monetise. Nevertheless, progress is being made in this area and estimates of this kind are being used in policy-making, especially in OECD countries.

The monetisation of social effects is complicated by the fact that changes in income distribution that result from energy subsidy reform relate to different levels of welfare for different social groups. One way to deal with this is to apply different weights to the income changes of the poor versus those of the rich. Thus, for example, if a scheme to remove subsidies reduces the real income of both a poor person and a rich person by one euro, society may value the first loss greater by giving it a weight of 2 and the second loss less, by giving it a weight of 0.5. In this way the total loss would add up to $(1 \times 2) + (1 \times 0.5) = 2.5$ instead of 3. Techniques for doing this have been developed some time ago and used in cost–benefit analysis.[7]

Changes in access to electricity can, in principle, be estimated by calculating the present value of the additional income derived from the changes in livelihoods within the population that gains access to electricity; and by the changes in the health and other impacts, such as education. Other dimensions of social effects, such as the impact on social capital, can usually only be described in qualitative terms.

The quantification of environmental and social effects in financial terms allows for decisions about subsidy reform to be based on cost–benefit analysis, whereby the costs of the reform are weighed against the benefits. The standard decision rule is that, if total benefits of the reform are greater than the total costs, then the reform will lead to an improvement in welfare. In this case, reform should proceed. However, as mentioned above, taking into account all the effects, particularly environmental and social, in monetary terms, may not always be possible and raises a number of moral concerns (see e.g. Pearce and Barbier 2000; UNEP 1997). It may, however, be possible to describe many effects in physical units or in qualitative terms only.

An assessment of conflicting, incommensurate and incompatible views and values would therefore have to be undertaken within a decision-making framework such as multi-criteria analysis (MCA). MCA methodologies entail a participatory approach to the identification of multiple criteria and the ranking of options (see e.g. Saaty 1980). Since stakeholders will, in any case, use their preferred methodologies to analyse energy subsidy reform, MCA could be used as an instrument for encouraging dialogue among them and negotiating a compromise. This approach has greatest merit where estimated values of different effects diverge significantly or where important effects are not amenable to monetisation.

2.4.4 Methodological approaches

The various analytical approaches available for assessing the effects of energy subsidy reform can be broadly divided into two main categories:

- Those that rely on equilibrium modelling, such as economic techniques that quantify changes in incomes—i.e. *flows* of money, goods or pollution—while looking at impacts independently of each other (e.g. the impacts in the markets for electricity, gas, etc.). These are called partial equilibrium approaches.
- Those that look at the impacts through models that recognise the linkages between the demands and supplies of the products. These are referred to as general equilibrium approaches.

7 For a recent study using such weights, see Markandya and Halsnaes 2002.

Both methodologies can be applied to estimating the welfare effects in the current time period as well as in future time periods. They are discussed in more detail in the Annex.

2.4.5 Stakeholder consultation

Involving stakeholders from the outset in the design and implementation of reform packages is an essential determinant of their success. The principle aim of stakeholder consultation is that all individuals or groups affected either directly or indirectly by proposed changes in a subsidy should have an opportunity to express their views. Furthermore, it is thought to be preferable for these stakeholders to be involved in each stage of policy development. Stakeholder consultation ensures transparency and adds legitimacy to the proposed policy reform, thereby increasing the chances of the policy being accepted.

Ideally, stakeholder consultation involves a democratically appointed government developing and introducing policy reforms with public participation. In many countries, stakeholder representatives are asked to participate in policy meetings and other related discussion forums. The consultation process could first involve identifying all the economic, environmental and social effects of the proposed reform and an agreement—or at least a discussion—on the methodologies to be used to measure these effects. The process could then focus on the implementation of the reforms.[8]

While stakeholder consultation is important, it is also necessary to recognise its limitations. In many cases the reason why the subsidies were introduced in the first place was to benefit specific groups of people who have political power and who can capture the rents associated with the goods they control through subsidies. For example, domestic owners of high-cost coal would be unable to sell much of it without a producer subsidy. By pushing through such a policy they stand to benefit directly and often in a very significant way. Stakeholder meetings for the removal of such subsidies would then operate only at a symbolic level, while policy reforms are blocked by the groups that control the political process. It may then need more direct political action to get the necessary changes made.

More generally, the political economy of subsidies is important and has to be taken into account in the design of any policies that deal with subsidies and their reform. This is not to say that all parties gaining from the status quo have to be satisfied with the proposals, but that their position and interests must be understood by policy-makers. Gainers and losers need to be identified and any options for the phase-out need to track the welfare of these groups over time.

8 For discussion on the stakeholder process, see UNEP 2004.

3

Energy subsidies in OECD countries

This chapter reviews the prevalence of energy subsidies in OECD countries and analyses the possible economic and environmental effects of their removal. Most OECD countries have reduced energy subsidies over the past two decades as part of a general move away from heavy government intervention in energy markets and other sectors of the economy. Examples of this include cuts in direct grants and payments to consumers and producers, the lifting of price controls, cuts in research and development programmes and the removal of trade barriers. Most of the energy subsidies that remain are intended to protect domestic industries and employment in them, redistribute income to poor people or, increasingly, to protect the environment. Often, subsidies that encourage the production and consumption of fossil fuels by lowering prices are offset by taxes, such that net subsidies are in many cases small or negative. The scope for CO_2 emission reductions through the removal of subsidies to fossil fuels may be large in some countries but is probably modest for the OECD as a whole. The scope for reducing emissions by increasing subsidies to low carbon-intensive or carbon-free fuels or increasing taxation of carbon-intensive fuels appears to be larger. However, subsidies may not be the most efficient way of achieving emission reductions.

3.1 Overview

OECD governments intervene in the energy sector for a variety of reasons and in a variety of ways. Many instances and types of intervention are explicitly designed or intended to support certain energy policy objectives and are specific to energy production and supply industries or the use of energy. Other actions, designed to support broader economic or social goals, also affect the supply and use of energy indirectly. The rationale for government intervention is usually based on theoretical arguments concerning market failures (see Chapter 12).

Most OECD countries have reduced or eliminated direct and indirect subsidies over the past two decades as part of a general move away from heavy government intervention in energy markets and other sectors of the economy. Examples include cuts in direct grants and payments to consumers and producers, the lifting of price controls, cuts in direct financing of R&D programmes, privatisation and deregulation of energy companies, and the removal of trade barriers. Few OECD countries now use price controls to achieve social, economic or environmental goals, preferring in general to use grants, taxes, regulatory instruments and support for R&D. These trends largely reflect a profound shift in government attitudes resulting from the perceived failure of past interventionist policies and from broader structural economic reforms and changes. This stems from an assessment that in many cases the economic and sometimes environmental costs outweigh any social or environmental benefits.

There are three main reasons why governments continue to subsidise energy in OECD countries:

- **To protect domestic energy industries and employment in them.** This is particularly the case with subsidies for coal mining in Germany, Japan and Spain; for peat in Finland and Ireland; and biofuels in France, Italy and the United States. R&D programmes for energy technology may also fall into this category. Such protectionist objectives are nonetheless generally declining in importance across the OECD. Security of supply is sometimes cited as a reason for support programmes.
- **Industrial policy.** A major motivation of subsidies to renewable energy technologies is to develop a technological lead over competitors in other countries.
- **To protect the environment.** This goal is typically pursued through measures that seek to encourage the development and deployment of more environmentally friendly technologies and energy sources, including renewables. This is an increasingly important goal in most OECD countries.
- **To redistribute income to poor households.** Most OECD countries now prefer to use means other than energy subsidies, such as social welfare payments or tax benefits, to achieve this goal. But several countries still explicitly seek to redistribute income through energy policy: for example, through low tax rates on heating fuels.

The most common forms of energy subsidy in the OECD include the following:

- **Grants and credit instruments.** These may take the form of soft loans and interest-rate subsidies applied directly as government transfers to producers or consumers of energy. Grants for energy services or appliances commonly encourage the use of energy-efficient technologies. Such an approach is practised extensively in some countries, notably Denmark. The Danish government offers subsidies of up to 30% for investments in energy efficiency or conservation in industry and commerce, in addition to tax rebates on such investments for energy-intensive firms. A number of countries, including the United States and Australia, use tax credits to foster industry research and development. Several countries, including Australia and Denmark, offer cash subsidies to producers of renewables.

- **Fiscal instruments.** Differential taxation, involving exemptions or rebates, is sometimes used to encourage or discourage the production and use of certain fuels or to lower the effective cost of heating fuels to end-users. In the latter case, such subsidies are intended to benefit most the poorest end-users, for whom heating represents a significant proportion of household expenditure.[9] Some countries, such as the United States, continue to offer tax benefits to oil producers. Canada has traditionally differentiated royalties on oil and gas production to encourage development of resources in specific regions. Several OECD countries have restructured their energy taxes to penalise the most carbon-intensive fuels, in some cases through an explicit carbon tax. All the Scandinavian countries have introduced carbon taxes and many other European countries have introduced new energy and environmental taxes as part of a so-called Ecological Tax Reform (ETR). The aim of ETR is to shift the burden of taxation from labour to energy consumption (EEA 1996, 2000). In this vein, the European Union recently agreed to establish minimum excise duties on all energy products from 2004. Several countries such as Germany have discussed extending ETR to a Green Budget Reform or Environmental Fiscal Reform (EFR). This aims to bring all public spending and taxation into line with environmental objectives (Schlegelmilch 1999).
- **Regulatory instruments.** Regulations requiring or encouraging consumers to purchase a given fuel from a particular source, usually domestic, sometimes at a regulated price, have been introduced in several countries. Denmark, for example, requires utilities to burn minimum quantities of straw or wood in power stations. Subsidised tariffs for wind-generated electricity have made Germany the world's largest wind-power producer. France is also implementing an aggressive wind-power programme involving an obligation on the state-owned utility to purchase such power at prices set high enough to induce investment. Most countries have adopted energy-efficiency standards for a range of energy-using equipment and appliances.
- **Public funding of research and development.** The governments of almost all OECD countries undertake energy R&D, either directly or indirectly through support for private-sector programmes. Generally, publicly funded R&D is directed to those sectors where the country has a strong domestic production capability or to more environmentally friendly technologies. Although much of R&D funding goes to fossil fuels and nuclear power, programmes are often aimed at improving combustion efficiency and therefore lowering fossil fuel use and related emissions. The total level of energy R&D funding has been declining in recent years: total reported energy R&D budgets in IEA countries fell by more

9 In practice, however, better-off consumers who tend to consume more energy may benefit more in absolute financial terms.

than 13% in real terms over the period 1990–2000, although spending rebounded slightly towards the end of the 1990s (Fig. 3.1). Large cuts in overall spending on coal and nuclear research have been offset to a small extent by increases in end-use energy efficiency and conservation R&D. But nuclear power still accounts for just over half of total spending, due mainly to large programmes in France, Japan and the United States.

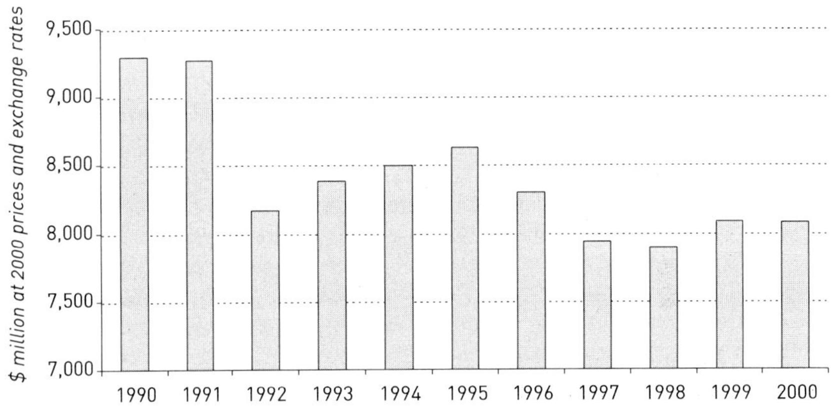

Note: 1999 and 2000 are estimated.

Figure 3.1 **IEA government R&D budgets**

Source: IEA 2001a

OECD countries in general levy substantial taxes on oil products (in addition to general sales or consumption taxes), more than offsetting the effect of any subsidies on the final price in most cases. Table 3.1 shows aggregate tax revenues from oil product sales alone, excluding general sales taxes in selected OECD countries for 1998. In almost all OECD countries, tax revenues from the sale of oil products and other forms of energy over and above those from general sales taxes far exceed public spending on direct financial subsidies, such as grants, soft loans and interest rate credits, and energy R&D. This is particularly the case with road transport fuels. The share of taxes in the final pump price of unleaded gasoline across the OECD currently varies from 13% in Mexico to 80% in the United Kingdom (IEA 2002b).

Some countries also impose special taxes such as excise duties or local taxes on other forms of energy, including natural gas, coal and electricity. However, in almost all cases the rate of taxation is lower than for oil products used in transportation. This is largely because of the low price elasticity of demand for oil-based transport fuels, which provides a stable source of tax revenue, concerns over the international competitiveness of industry and distributional considerations, which limit the extent to which governments tax household heating fuels. Favourable taxation of non-oil energy sources aimed at promoting switching away from oil has also been motivated in most OECD countries by concerns over energy

Country	Revenues ($ million)
Canada	4,482
France	26,718
Germany	37,906
Italy	57,604
Japan	25,095
United Kingdom	34,556
United States	35,148

Note: Revenues exclude general sales-tax receipts.

Table 3.1 **Revenues from special duties and levies on sales of oil products in selected OECD countries, 1998**

Source: OECD databases

supply diversity and oil security. For example, relatively low taxes on natural gas have been used in several European countries to promote rapid switching from other fuels.

3.2 Quantitative assessment of subsidies and impact of their removal

A number of recent studies have attempted to identify and quantify energy subsidies in OECD countries. Some have attempted to calculate the economic and environmental effects of their removal. Most studies have focused on specific countries or sectors. The IEA uses a PSE approach to estimate objectively the level of subsidy to producers of coal in member countries. Two OECD studies, one in collaboration with the IEA, have attempted to quantify the level of subsidies in the OECD and the impact of their removal on real GDP and carbon emissions. The results of the above and other recent studies of OECD energy subsidies are reviewed below.

3.2.1 IEA coal PSE analysis

Because of the historical and social importance of coal-mining activities to local economic activity and employment, several OECD countries have traditionally intervened heavily in the coal industry.[10] The extent of this intervention has declined considerably, but subsidies remain significant in a number of countries,

10 Coal subsidies in the case of Korea are discussed in Chapter 8.

notably the Czech Republic, France, Germany, Japan, Spain and Turkey. Very few OECD countries impose taxes on the production or sale of coal. In those countries that do, such as the United States, where special taxes and levies are imposed at the federal and state levels, the level of taxation is generally very low compared with oil products.

The IEA monitors the level of hard-coal industry subsidy on an annual basis in those countries (excluding the Czech Republic) as part of its policy of encouraging an early removal of such aid. PSE estimates cover assistance to current production only, although the IEA also monitors other subsidies, such as grants for colliery closures and workforce retraining. In 2000, the member countries of the IEA[11] produced 1.3 billion tonnes of coal equivalent (tce) of hard coal.[12] Of this, 92 million tce (around 7%), in six OECD countries—France, Germany, Japan, Spain, Turkey and the United Kingdom[13]—received state aid (Fig. 3.2).

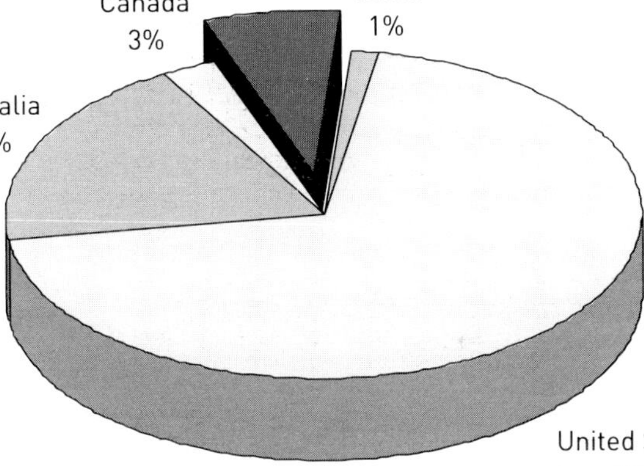

Figure 3.2 **IEA hard coal production, 2000**

Source: IEA 2001b

The amount of IEA hard-coal production receiving government financial assistance, as measured by the PSE, has been declining over the last decade, both in absolute and in percentage terms. Subsidised production has fallen by 55% since 1991. The main reasons for the reduction are the programmed decreases in domestic production in these countries. Total PSE assistance has dropped more slowly

11 The IEA is made up of all the OECD countries except Iceland, Mexico, Poland and the Slovak Republic.

12 Tonne of coal equivalent (tce) is a standard unit of measurement with an energy value of 29.3 GJ/tonne or 7 000 kcal/kg. 1 tce is equal to 0.7 toe (tonne of oil equivalent).

13 State aid for coal was reintroduced temporarily in the United Kingdom in April 2000 and ended in July 2002.

than production, by 53% in nominal terms since it peaked in 1992 to a total of $5.8 billion in 2000 (see Fig. 3.3). Germany accounts for around 68% of this assistance and Spain for a further 13%.

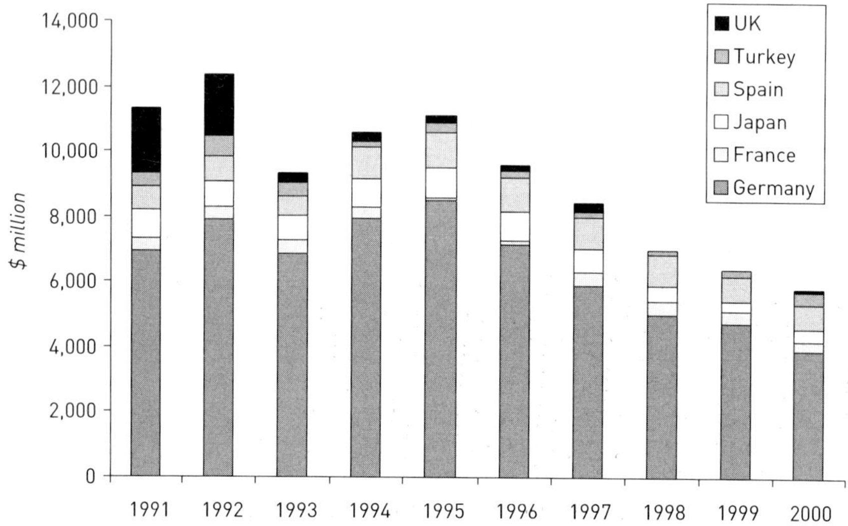

Figure 3.3 **IEA hard coal production, 2000**

Source: IEA 2001b

The form of aid varies considerably between countries (Table 3.2). In all countries bar Japan, subsidies are almost entirely in the form of direct aid. For example, in Germany a special grant to promote sales of thermal coal accounted for 99% of total subsidies in 2000 while in Spain subsidies take the form of aid to cover operating losses. In Japan, production is subsidised mainly through price support for coal consumed by power generators.

The impact of coal-production subsidies on the environment, and particularly on greenhouse gas emissions, is difficult to estimate. Most of the remaining coal-production subsidies do not lead to subsidised end-user prices. Thus the removal

	France	*Germany*	*Japan*	*Spain*	*Turkey*	*Total*
Direct aid	307	3,917	27	730	304	5,285
Indirect aid	0	0	0	0	65	65
Price support	0	0	348	0	0	348
Total	307	3,917	375	730	369	5,698

Table 3.2 **PSE estimates of assistance to coal producers, 2000 ($ million)**

Source: IEA 2001b

of subsidies would not lead to direct increases in prices paid by consumers of coal, and thus may not lower consumption. An indirect effect could result from the loss of this production from world coal markets leading to a tightening of supply and hence an increase in price. However, the quantity of subsidised production is relatively small—less than 2% of world production and about 10% of internationally traded coal. As a result, the effect on hard-coal prices from the removal of this production would most likely be small.

The impact of subsidy removal would depend on country-specific circumstances. These can vary enormously: for example, with respect to energy policy, the type of subsidy in place, the quality of the coal being subsidised, including sulphur, ash content and calorific value, the degree of competition in the electricity supply industry and the structure of energy demand:

- In the United Kingdom, the elimination of the obligations of the large power producers to purchase domestic coal led to a rapid increase in gas-fired generation at the expense of existing coal-fired generation. However, the conditions under which the market was liberalised and increases in nuclear output also played a role in the rapid decline in coal use.
- In Spain, many of the existing coal-fired generation stations using domestic coal would incur significant transportation costs to use imported coal and may not be competitive with other generation sources. The share of natural gas in generation will most likely continue to grow as coal subsidies are reduced. Increased output at existing coal-fired plants using imported coal can also be expected if domestic coal requirements are reduced. The emission benefits of replacement of the domestic coal plants by gas-fired generation may be offset to a limited degree by a reduction in electricity prices, as electricity consumers would no longer be paying incentives to utilities to use domestic coal.
- By contrast, the situation in Germany appears quite different. There, consumers of coal are already free to choose suppliers. So the effect of eliminating the subsidies on demand for coal is not obvious since coal consumers might be expected to switch to imported coal. However, the money saved by removing these subsidies could be spent on measures to promote energy efficiency, conservation and renewables. Germany is also the only country in Europe still applying a tax on natural gas and mineral oil used for electricity generation. This leads to a favourable treatment of nuclear fuel and coal, which thus hinders investment in generation natural gas, the cleanest fossil fuel.

3.2.2 OECD study using the GREEN Model (2000)

A 2000 study by the OECD looks at ending coal-production subsidies as part of a broader study of the environmental effects of liberalising trade in fossil fuels (OECD 2000). The study uses a price-gap approach together with the OECD's in-house general equilibrium model, GREEN. It demonstrates that trade liberalisation and policy reforms involving the elimination of subsidies that distort end-user prices in both OECD and non-OECD countries would result in a net reduction in energy-related CO_2 emissions. This would be brought about by a major shift in energy consumption and international trade patterns. The study also shows that, if these reforms occur solely in the OECD, fossil fuel demand would marginally increase in the long run due to a fall in prices and some substitution of high-priced domestically produced coal with cheaper imports in Japan and Europe. In this case, CO_2 emissions and economic welfare would increase slightly. The results are summarised in Table 3.3.

		OECD only liberalises	*Non-OECD only liberalises*	*All countries liberalise*
Global CO_2 emissions	2000	−0.1	−1.8	−1.9
	2010	+0.1	−6.3	−6.2
Global real income	2000	0.0	0.0	+0.1
	2010	+0.1	0.0	+0.1

Table 3.3 **GREEN model simulations (percentage change from business-as-usual scenario)**

Source: OECD 2000

Interpretation and use of the study's results should be undertaken with care. The authors argue that the impact on energy-related CO_2 emissions could be underestimated because of data limitations, and the fact that the study covered only the industrial and power generation sectors (which account for just 40% of OECD emissions). In addition, the results are very sensitive to estimates of reference prices; the price gaps calculated for several OECD countries appear to be much bigger than IEA data would suggest.

3.2.3 OECD/IEA study on reforming coal and electricity subsidies (1997)

The OECD together with the IEA conducted a study in 1997 for the Annex I Expert Group on the UNFCCC as part of a major project entitled 'Policies and Measures for Possible Common Action'. The study attempts to quantify the impact of removing various types of government intervention that can be classed as subsidies in the coal and electricity sectors in selected OECD countries. A range of energy-market, energy-system and macroeconomic models were used. The study concludes that it is not possible to generalise about the environmental and economic effects of removing subsidies, but it does identify particular types and combinations of policies whose removal or reform would probably reduce greenhouse gas emissions (Table 3.4). For example:

	Subsidies removed	Monetary equivalent of distortion ($ million)	Reduction in CO_2 emissions relative to reference scenario in 2010 (million tonnes)
Australia	State procurement/planning	133	0.3
	Barriers to gas and electricity trade	1,400	0.8
	Below-market financing cost	NQ	NQ
Italy	Net budgetary subsidies to electricity supply industry	4,000	12.5
	VAT below general rate	300	0.6
	Subsidies to capital	1,500	3.3
	Tax exemptions on fossil fuel inputs to ESI	700	5.9
Norway	Barriers to trade	NQ	8.0 (Nordic region)
United Kingdom	Grants/price supports to coal/nuclear producers	2,500	0.0–40.0
	Below-market required rate of return in ESI	NQ	NQ
	VAT on electricity below general rate	1,200	0.2

Note: Subsidies are defined in different ways and so results are not strictly comparable.
NQ = not quantified ESI = electricity supply industry VAT = value-added tax

Table 3.4 **Summary results from OECD/IEA case studies of energy subsidy removal in the OECD**

Source: OECD 1997

- **Removing coal-producer grants and price supports.** These measures include removing market entry barriers and preferential conditions in the regulation and financing of the electricity supply industry. This option appears from the OECD case studies to offer a large potential for greenhouse gas mitigation. Hundreds of millions of tonnes of CO_2 per year would be avoided by 2010 if implemented throughout the Annex I region. Methane emissions would also most likely be reduced.

- **Removing sales-tax exemptions for electricity and other energy forms.** This appears to offer a small potential for greenhouse gas mitigation, amounting to less than 1 million tonnes of CO_2 per year by 2010 in the case studies where the issue was examined.

- **Eliminating electricity supply obligations and subsidies to supply in remote areas.** This probably offers a small potential for emission reduction, perhaps in the region of a few million tonnes of CO_2 per year by 2010 in the Annex I region.

- **Removing electricity subsidies for energy-intensive industries.** Again, this option appears to offer a small mitigation potential, perhaps in the region of a few million tonnes of CO_2 per year by 2010.

Greenhouse gas mitigation as a result of reforming these policies is likely to be larger beyond 2010. Removing market distortions would lead to changes in investment choices by electricity suppliers and consumers, with increasing effects on the generating mix, energy efficiency and greenhouse gas emissions.

3.2.4 Other studies

A 1992 study by Burniaux *et al.* at the OECD focuses on the effects of policies that artificially maintain domestic end-use prices for energy below comparable prices on world markets. Neither market-price support to production nor budgetary support to either production or consumption are considered. The study estimates global transfers to consumers of primary fossil energy through lower prices at $235 billion. Such consumption subsidies are concentrated in non-OECD countries, where they amount to $254 billion, though the United States is found to have a small net subsidy for oil and gas. Small net taxes, i.e. negative subsidies, on primary energy in the OECD amount to $19 billion.

The authors use the OECD GREEN model to estimate the impact of removing distortions that keep prices below world levels (over the 1990–2000 period) on real GDP and carbon emissions. The no-price distortion case also re-prices energy to world prices in countries with domestic primary energy product prices higher than world prices. Results are derived relative to a business-as-usual case, where existing subsidy levels are maintained. Simply removing existing energy-price distortions improves cumulative discounted world real income by 0.7% over the period 1990–2050 and reduces carbon emissions in 2050 by 18%. This results mainly from a 16% fall in energy use.

The 1994 DRI study referred to in Chapter 2 uses IEA estimates of PSEs to model the effect of removing coal-producer subsidies on coal consumption and CO_2 emissions in Japan and five European countries. The study concludes that, under a scenario in which all subsidies are removed by 2010, production would fall by a cumulative 80 million tce over the period 1994–2010 and demand by 13 million tce, mainly due to substitution of coal by natural gas. As a result, imports are projected to increase by 67 million tce. Annual CO_2 emissions are projected to fall by 0.8 million tonnes in 2000 and 10.3 Mt in 2010. Although not modelled by DRI, the 1997 IEA/OECD study discussed above contends that the removal of subsidies in Europe and Japan, by raising the international coal price by 20% by 2010, would reduce global emissions by at least 55 Mt in 2010.

An earlier study by Okugu and Birol (1994) models retrospectively the impact on CO_2 emissions of phasing out OECD coal subsidies. The study concludes that the complete removal of subsidies in Germany, Spain and the United Kingdom alone would have resulted in emission reductions due to lower coal consumption totalling 49 Mt, or 28%, in the year 1990.

A 1995 study by Steenblik and Coroyannakis showed that one major effect of the way that coal subsidies were being provided, especially in Europe (through government-brokered contracts) was that old, inefficient coal plants were being kept operating simply to dispose of locally mined coal. Meanwhile, new, heavily subsidised 'demonstration' plants were being built in coal-mining areas, thus ensuring a continued market for high-cost—and often high-sulphur—domestic coal.

A 1997 Greenpeace study of European energy subsidies claims that more than 90% of direct subsidies from European governments to the energy industry over the period 1990–95 went to fossil fuels (63%) and nuclear power (28%). Just 9% of total direct subsidies, or $1.5 billion a year, were directed to renewables. In the European Union alone, renewables accounted for 12% and fossil fuels and nuclear energy 88%. The study defines direct subsidies as government spending, including R&D, and tax exemptions and reductions.

Other studies have focused on individual OECD countries. A 1992 US Department of Energy (DOE) study, commissioned by Congress, attempts to identify and quantify in monetary terms federal subsidies in the energy sector. The study concludes that there exists a wide range of direct and indirect subsidies but they are not large in relation to the total value of energy production. Subsidies are put at $5–10 billion, equivalent to 1–2% of total energy production. However, the DOE estimates that the impact of energy regulation, for which a subsidy equivalent was not calculated, could be much larger. The cost of just those programmes considered in the study is put at as much as $50 billion. The study does not consider the potential economic or environmental impact of subsidy removal.

The DOE study was updated in 1999 and 2000. The value of total federal energy subsidies for fiscal year 1999 (to September) amounted to $6.2 billion—equivalent to just over 1% of the total value of energy supply in the United States. Fossil fuels received nearly half the total. Renewables accounted for about $1.1 billion—mostly through the excise tax exemption on corn-based ethanol blended into gasoline. The 2000 report estimates that total subsidies calculated on an equivalent basis declined by 16% in real terms compared with 1992.

A 2000 study by Koplow and Martin, commissioned by Greenpeace, estimates the cost of federal subsidies to the US oil industry in 1995 at between $5.2 and $11.9 billion, excluding the costs of defending Persian Gulf oil supplies. The largest single elements are stockpiling of oil in the Strategic Petroleum Reserve to protect against supply disruptions and tax breaks for domestic oil exploration and production.

A 1995 study by Böhringer at the University of Stuttgart examines the effects on CO_2 emissions of reducing subsidies to German coal production, using a general equilibrium model. His study evaluates income and other economic effects of various possible modifications of the then current coal support system, subject to different national emission constraints (or carbon taxes). The monetary value of coal subsidies is estimated at $6.7 billion in 1990, equivalent to DM94,000–145,000 per job per year. The study finds that subsidies to coal production become increasingly expensive as carbon constraints become tighter. Removing these subsidies without any additional controls on emissions would increase national income by almost 1%. The effects on emissions are not reported (see Böhringer 1996).

3.3 Conclusions

All OECD countries subsidise to some extent, in various ways and for differing reasons the production, supply and use of energy. However, few countries systematically attempt to quantify the value of those subsidies and their overall economic and environmental impact. This is largely because of the complexity of the task, including difficulties in compiling data and applying appropriate methodologies. Various studies and analyses have nonetheless sought to shed some light on the issue. The main findings of this work are as follows:

- Significant energy subsidies, mostly to producers, remain in place in OECD countries. They are nonetheless much smaller generally than in non-OECD countries.
- Most OECD countries have reduced direct subsidies to energy in recent years. Coal subsidies, in particular, have been reduced considerably. Regulations supporting the supply or use of particular energy sources, discriminatory taxation and R&D may also have been reduced overall, though the empirical evidence to support this hypothesis is incomplete.
- Most of the subsidies that remain are intended to promote the production and use of indigenous fossil fuel resources (for regional economic, employment and energy security reasons) and renewable energy sources and energy-efficient technologies (for environmental and industrial policy reasons), and to lower the cost of energy for poor people (for social reasons).
- Many subsidies that encourage the production and consumption of fossil fuels by lowering the price are offset by taxes, such that net subsidies are small or negative. This is especially true for oil products. Nonetheless, market distortions are caused by differential taxation of energy sources.
- The scope for CO_2 emission reductions through the removal of remaining subsidies to fossil fuels is probably significant in some countries but may be modest for the OECD as a whole. There is more scope for reducing emissions by increasing subsidies to low carbon-intensive or carbon-free fuels: for example, by taxing fossil fuels or carbon emissions more heavily or increasing direct subsidies to renewables, nuclear power or energy-efficiency and conservation programmes.
- Coal is still heavily subsidised in a small number of OECD countries for protectionist reasons. Despite the fact that they raise the price of coal in some cases, they probably lead in general to slightly higher consumption of fossil fuels than would otherwise be the case, such that their elimination would most likely reduce CO_2 emissions. The impact of coal subsidy removal in any given country depends critically on the form of subsidy and national circumstances, which affect the extent to which production would be replaced with imports.

- Subsidies to support the development and use of renewables, nuclear power and energy-efficient technologies may help reduce emissions of greenhouse gases and other pollutants depending on how the subsidies are structured and market conditions. However, subsidies may not be the most efficient way of achieving this.
- It is not clear whether reduced spending on fossil fuel R&D would lead to lower emissions, since much of this effort is aimed at improving combustion efficiency and therefore reducing fuel requirements.
- While subsidy reform, involving a reduction in certain types of subsidy to fossil fuels, may yield positive environmental effects, it can also have major social implications. Dealing with distributional effects is often a major element in overcoming political obstacles to subsidy reform. In some cases, energy security may be affected. This explains the difficulties some OECD governments face in trying to reform remaining environmentally harmful energy subsidies.

The complexities and trade-offs associated with subsidies suggest that a pragmatic, targeted approach to reforming them may be appropriate. This would involve identifying and suppressing those subsidies that are most obviously harmful from an environmental perspective while bringing the least-obvious economic, energy security or social benefits. Such an approach would require better information and analysis of the impact of subsidies in each country and sector that currently exists in most cases.

4

Energy subsidies in the Czech and Slovak Republics

Energy subsidies, mainly benefiting fossil fuels, were very large in the Czech Republic and the Slovak Republic in the 1990s, leading to serious economic and environmental problems. By holding back the restructuring of the economy and hindering innovation, energy subsidies are a primary cause of the high energy intensity that persists in both countries. They have also exacerbated the harmful environmental effects of energy production, supply and consumption, mainly through local and regional air pollution, including urban smog and acid rain. Land degradation due to mining activities is also a problem. Greenhouse gas emissions are also high relative to GDP, as a result of energy-intensive heavy industry and low energy efficiency compared to Western European countries. While substantial progress has been made in removing these subsidies in recent years, some direct and indirect subsidies, such as large-scale support for the mining industry, remain. Further effort is needed to reform these subsidies within the framework of ongoing market-based economic restructuring.

4.1 Economic and political overview

The Czech and Slovak Republics belong to the group of countries that for 40 years were part of the communist bloc. Their transition from a centrally planned economy to one based on market principles and private property is the most profound economic event in the recent history of both countries. One of the immediate effects of the transition, which began in earnest at the beginning of the 1990s, was a severe drop in GDP and household incomes (for details, see Svejnar 1995).

Heavy industry played a dominant role in the economy of the former Czechoslovakia, which split into the Czech and Slovak Republics in 1993. In meeting its large energy needs, industry relied mainly on domestic coal and lignite. It used these fuels very inefficiently. While structural changes have been made over the last decade or so, heavy industry remains important to both economies and energy is still being used less efficiently than in Western industrialised countries.

The economic development of the two countries has differed in some respects since their separation (see IMF 2002a, 2000b). In the Czech Republic, GDP per capita, measured using the purchasing power parity (PPP) approach in 2001, was €14,732. Economic growth is slowing down due to weaker foreign demand and household spending, the unemployment rate is set to rise to 10% and the fiscal position is gradually deteriorating. The central government's budget deficit has increased over the past five years, reaching 9% of GDP in 2000. The problem is largely structural, resulting from a gradual increase in government expenditure. This trend is partly explained by high and steadily increasing mandatory and quasi-mandatory public spending commitments. Until now, the government has done little to address this problem. The economic costs of delaying deficit reduction are significant. Increased government spending is generating inflationary pressure, while rising borrowing requirements could crowd out bank lending to enterprises, especially to small and medium-sized companies, which need credit for restructuring and export-oriented investment.

In the Slovak Republic, per capita GDP (using PPP) is only €9,150, despite rapid economic growth in recent years. Growth in industrial output has been particularly strong. Domestic demand is expected to slow considerably in the near term as tough measures to stabilise the economy take effect. Unemployment, which was 16.4% in October 2002, is declining. The government is committed to fiscal reform. The 2003 budget proposal targets a public finance deficit below 5% of GDP and the government has declared it will reach the EU target of 3% by 2006.

4.2 Energy market overview

4.2.1 Czech Republic

Indigenously produced coal meets almost half of the Czech Republic's primary energy needs (Table 4.1). Oil and gas, most of which have to be imported, account for most of the rest. Total net imports of crude oil, natural gas, petroleum products and nuclear fuel account for around a quarter of total primary energy supply. The Czech Republic exports coal and small amounts of electricity. The percentage of fossil fuels in the primary energy mix, at 88%, is very high.

Electricity generation and consumption have risen steadily in recent years. Generation increased by over 9% per year from 1993 to 1999, reaching 61 TWh. Over the same period, consumption increased by 7%. Electricity exports have become increasingly important for the Czech Republic over the past few years, peaking in the first six months of 2001 at 6.7 TWh. Most of these exports went to Germany. Exports to Germany have fallen by over 30% since May, 2001 when the German company, E.ON, cancelled its contract with CEZ, the dominant Czech electricity company.

	Coal	*Crude oil*	*Oil products*	*Gas*	*Nuclear*	*Hydro*	*CRW**	*Other*	*Total*
Domestic production	966	16		7	146	6	29		1,170
Net imports	–225	247	81	311				–12	404
Stock changes	36	–3	5	5					41
TPES	777	260	86	324	146	6	29	–12	1,615

* Combustible renewables and waste TPES = total primary energy supply

Table 4.1 **Primary energy supply in the Czech Republic, 1999 (PJ)**

Source: IEA 2001c

The share of industry in total final energy consumption has been declining. As in the Slovak Republic, consumption in the transport, services and household sectors has been increasing (UNCTAD 2002).

Power generation is based primarily on coal, providing 69% of total output. About 20% is produced by a single nuclear station. A second nuclear plant, Temelin, with two reactors, is in the process of being brought into service. This will raise the total amount of electricity supplied by nuclear plants to almost 40% and aims to reduce air pollution. In the 1990s, the Czech power system sought to drastically reduce air pollution from coal-fired power plants. A number of obsolete plants were closed and fluid-bed boilers and flue-gas desulphurisation equipment was installed in the plants that were kept open.

District heating has a long tradition and is an important part of the energy system in the Czech Republic. Almost a third of households are connected to a local district heat network, providing 20% of the sector's final energy needs. There is still a large, unexploited potential for combined heat and power-based district heating in smaller towns and large villages. The introduction of district heating there would support regional development, increase efficiency and reduce pollution.

4.2.2 Slovak Republic

The Slovak Republic is a net energy importer. In 1999, energy imports in the form of crude oil, oil products, natural gas and coal amounted to approximately 69% of the Slovak Republic's primary energy supply not including nuclear fuel imports. Domestic production of hydropower provided 2% of supply, lignite 6% and oil and gas 2%. The share of fossil fuels in total primary energy consumption is about 78%.

Industry, especially heavy manufacturing, has traditionally been the largest consumer of energy in the Slovak Republic. In 1999, it accounted for 55% of total final energy consumption. The three largest industries—steel, aluminium and oil refining—account for 22% of total energy consumption in industry and the 30 largest companies for over 50%. Nevertheless, the importance of industry is falling. The

	Coal	Crude oil	Oil products	Gas	Nuclear	Hydro	CRW*	Total
Domestic production	43	3		7	143	16	3	216
Net imports	167	221	−92	222				518
Stock changes	6	2	−1	14				21
TPES	216	226	−93	243	143	16	3	754

* Combustible renewables and waste TPES = total primary energy supply

Table 4.2 **Primary energy supply in the Slovak Republic, 1999 (PJ)**

Source: IEA 2001c

shares of transport, which accounts for 10% of final demand, trade and services, with 15%, and households, with 17%, are increasing. Approximately half of the Slovak Republic's 5.4 million inhabitants live in apartment buildings. Of these, 40% are supplied with heat and hot water from district heat systems.

Just under half of power generation comes from nuclear plants and about 23% from coal. Two new reactors came online in 1998 and 2000, reducing the country's reliance on coal and heavy fuel oil. There is substantial unused hydropower potential.

4.2.3 Energy intensity

In both countries, total primary energy use and greenhouse gas emissions fell considerably between 1990 and 1999. Nonetheless, both economies remain very energy-intensive. Figure 4.1 compares primary energy intensity, measured as energy consumption per unit of GDP (using market exchange rates and PPP) in the Czech and Slovak Republics with neighbouring countries, the European Union and the OECD. Intensity in the two countries has fallen significantly since the early 1990s, but remains well above other countries and regions—even when calculated on the basis of PPP. Emissions per unit of GDP and per capita are also high, largely because energy intensity is high and because coal is still the main source of power generation (see Jilkova *et al.* 2001; MOE-CR 2001).

The relatively high proportion of coal and natural gas in the primary energy supply is a legacy of the communist era, when those fuels could be procured at relatively low cost. In contrast to most countries in Western Europe, oil use was relatively small. Oil use is now increasing, mainly due to the growing importance of transport. Coal is being replaced mostly by nuclear in power generation, natural gas in industry and electricity in households.

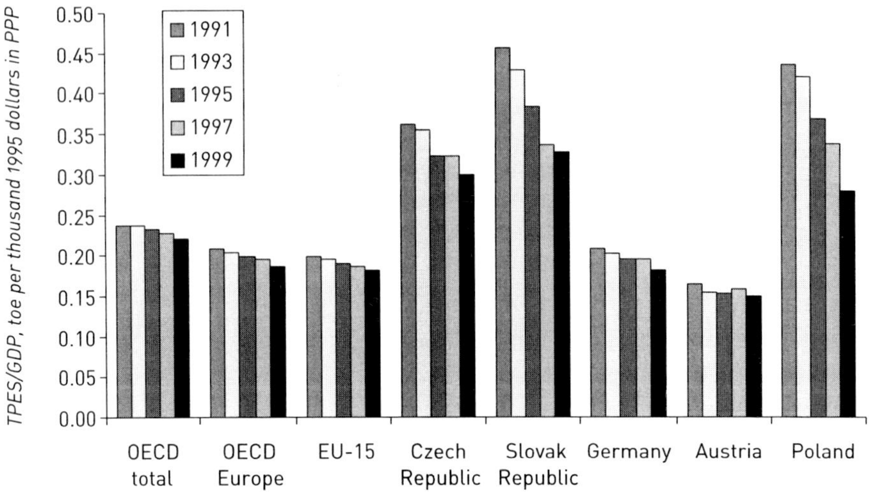

Figure 4.1 **Primary energy intensity**

Source: IEA 2001c

4.3 Energy policy developments in Central and Eastern Europe

Under central planning, priority was given to meeting production targets and little account was taken of the environmental effects. Economic development was highly focused on heavy industry, mining and energy production, which resulted in serious pollution. In the absence of private ownership and proper markets, there were no economic incentives to use natural resources, including energy, efficiently. While politicians publicly advocated energy conservation and improved energy efficiency, no funds were provided to achieve these aims. The technologies used were often obsolete, and hardly any measures to deal with pollution were adopted. The adverse environmental effects in the region were compounded by the consumption of very-low-quality domestic coal. The main energy source, lignite, has the lowest energy content of any quality of coal and is the most polluting type of fossil fuel.

With the transition to a market economy, a pressing need to improve energy efficiency in the region has emerged in support of the following goals:

- Increasing competitiveness on the EU and world markets
- Improving the foreign trade balance by reducing energy import costs
- Complying with the requirements for entry into the European Union

- Fulfilling international commitments such as the Protocol to the Energy Charter on Energy Conservation, the Kyoto Protocol and other international protocols, mostly concerned with air-pollution control
- Reducing the adverse environmental effects of energy use

Since the early 1990s, significant progress has been made in addressing the negative environmental effects of energy production and use. New environmental laws, including the introduction of emission limits, have been implemented and large investments have been made in environmental protection. The substitution of domestic lignite with natural gas and oil has significantly lowered energy intensity. The slump in economic activity and industrial production in the early 1990s also helped to lower energy consumption.

4.3.1 Energy pricing

Energy subsidies represent one of the most significant obstacles to the successful transformation of the energy economies of the central European region at the beginning of the process. Direct subsidies, in the form of direct cash payments to suppliers and consumers, have been reduced significantly due to financial pressures on the government. But dealing with cross-subsidies and distortions in energy prices has been harder, because of ignorance about the size of these subsidies and because of the political consequences of unpopular energy price increases. In general, energy prices remained under government control for longer than most other commodity prices.

Energy price reforms have nevertheless been implemented in Central and Eastern European countries. In many cases, the prices of gasoline and other oil products have been completely deregulated. But the prices of electricity and gas to households are often still below the economic cost of supply, even though subsidies have been reduced in most cases. Harmonisation with EU law, which restricts opportunities for subsidising industry, is a major driving force behind moves to eliminate remaining subsidies.

Energy price liberalisation has been gradual. Progress has been slowest in the case of energy supplied through networks: that is, electricity, gas and district heat. Recently, price reform has accelerated in the EU accession countries, as full price liberalisation is a requirement for joining the Union. The main features of this process are as follows:

- Oil and oil product prices were raised gradually to market levels reflecting full economic costs in most Central and Eastern European countries by 1991/92. In most cases, they were adjusted to reflect import prices. For countries that import Russian gas paid for in kind for transit, prices were increased more slowly.
- By 1992, electricity and gas prices for industry in Poland, Hungary and the Czech Republic were close to levels in Western Europe.
- The prices of electricity and heat for households have increased least and, in many cases, remained perversely below industrial prices. This cross-

subsidy emerged as the biggest problem of price liberalisation in the transition economies.

- The approach to setting the price of network energy was often based on historic average costs. Governments have tried to balance different interests by reflecting the cost of energy supply in wholesale prices but keeping a cap on end-user prices. The main reasons for subsidising prices are to enhance energy supply security, increase industrial competitiveness and protect jobs by favouring domestic resources, and to support household incomes.

Efficient pricing requires raising all energy prices to full cost levels, i.e. the long-term marginal cost for electricity and international market prices allowing for transport costs for oil products and other traded fuels. Doing so would improve incentives to use energy efficiently and reduce environmental effects. Many Central and Eastern European countries have started to implement energy efficiency programmes without first adjusting energy prices. The results have been disappointing, because incentives for consumers to change their behaviour or to invest in energy-efficient equipment and technology are weak.

Politicians have been particularly reluctant to raise prices to households for social reasons and because of public opposition and fear over the impact of energy price rises on the general inflation rate. The impact on the living standards of the poorest households was the main reason for the initial slow progress in raising household prices. Delaying price increases hindered efforts to improve energy efficiency in this sector. The adverse social effects would have been dealt with more effectively by direct welfare support to poor households that were most vulnerable to increases in energy bills. Such a system was introduced in the Czech Republic in the second half of the 1990s.

4.3.2 Energy market liberalisation

The liberalisation of the electricity and gas markets in the European Union has accelerated deregulation of energy prices in the EU accession countries in Central and Eastern Europe. The EU directives on common rules for the creation of an internal energy market require electricity and gas markets to be opened gradually to competition. At present, roughly one-third of these markets in EU countries must be open by 2003. The accession countries have negotiated longer transitional periods, but all must liberalise their markets fully by 2007. This will involve removing controls over prices to eligible customers.

4.4 Measuring energy subsidies

4.4.1 Methodological considerations

The following overview of energy subsidies in the Czech and Slovak Republics is based on studies undertaken by SEVEn, the Energy Efficiency Centre based in

Prague (Florian 1999; Krivosik 2001). These studies review direct payments from the public budget that benefit the supply or use of energy, as well as other indirect policies that favour the production and consumption of energy. The problem of external costs and benefits was not considered. Determining the subsidy for uncovered external costs would require a full assessment of these costs. This approach is in line with that adopted in other studies of this kind (see Oosterhuis 2001).

The term 'direct subsidy' was used for public expenditures supporting the production and consumption of energy, including direct payments and other public expenditures. An indirect subsidy refers to any accompanying policy such as regulatory measures and cross-subsidies. Funds from international programmes were also included in direct subsidies on the grounds that this support is channelled through the public authorities and either reduces energy prices paid by consumers, raises prices received by producers or lowers the cost of production. However, these sources of subsidy are small in comparison with subsidies from the national budget.

Only limited empirical analyses are available. The original data for the Czech and Slovak Republics was taken from the State Final Account, which is broken down by ministry and other government institutions. The collection and presentation of data does not follow a strict and unified methodology, which makes comparisons difficult. The only available sources of information about energy subsidies in the Czech and Slovak Republics are the studies undertaken by SEVEn. In these documents, data for different fuels and subsidy categories is included. However, differences in methodology and presentation limit the extent to which the findings in the two countries can be compared and trends discerned. The studies cover the period between 1994 and 1998 for the Czech Republic and 1993 to 1999 for the Slovak Republic.

4.4.2 Czech Republic

During the period 1994–98, energy subsidies amounted to $7 billion, one-third of which were direct (Table 4.3). Of the more than $2 billion of direct fossil fuel subsidies, district heat subsidies were the largest component—$899 million. The government financed directly the difference between the regulated price of heat and the real costs of supply. This subsidy was eliminated at the end of 1998. On the other hand, the size of the second-biggest category, environmental clean-up and restoration as a consequence of coal mining, is expected to rise in the future. A major source of direct subsidy not included in Table 4.3 is support for the increased use of natural gas as a heating fuel. Local and national governments financed the construction of natural gas pipeline networks to rural areas, which the gas distributors considered uneconomic. The exact amount of these subsidies is estimated at around $160 million, though the accuracy of this figure is questionable since those subsidies were not specified clearly in council budgets.

Tax exemptions and cross-subsidies accounted for the bulk of indirect subsidies. A value-added tax (VAT) on electricity and natural gas was set at a special rate of 5% rate compared to the usual rate of 22% until the end of 1997. Residential electricity and gas prices were held below production costs. The difference was partly offset

	Fossil fuels	*Nuclear power*	*Renewables & conservation*	*International*	*Total*
Coal-mining limitation and environmental consequences	747.4	–	–	9.4	756.8
Uranium-mining limitation	–	321.5	–	–	321.5
Heat prices	899.0	–	–	–	899.0
Rural gas distribution	159.0	–	–	–	159.0
Total direct subsidies	1,936.9	346.5	9.4	9.4	2,302.2
Lower VAT tariff	834.5	150.3	22.8	–	1,007.6
Cross-subsidies	2,878.0	670.1	101.8	–	3,649.9
Electricity	2,513.0	670.1	–	–	3,183.1
Natural gas	365.0	–	–	–	365.0
Total indirect subsidies	874.2	160.9	23.1	21.2	1,0794
Total	2,811.1	507.4	32.5	30.6	3,381.6

Note: Cross-subsidies are not included in the total, as it is not clear by which ratio these have been paid by customers and by the state-owned energy utilities. Direct and indirect subsidies, on the other hand, are a form of state expenditure. The table does not include all sub-categories of the major subsidy categories.

Table 4.3 **Subsidies by fuel and type in the Czech Republic, 1994–98 ($ million)**

Source: Florian 1999

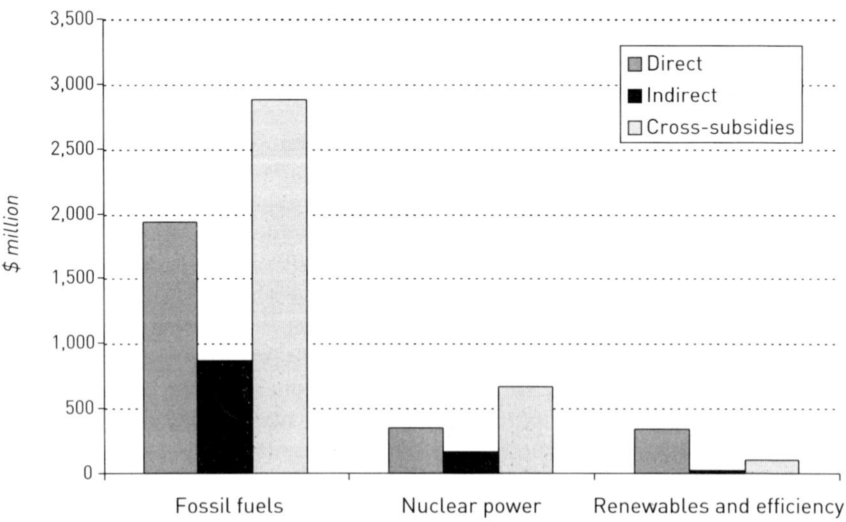

Figure 4.2 **Energy subsidies in the Czech Republic by fuel and category, 1994–98**

Source: Florian 1999

by commercial end users. These cross-subsidies, which amounted to a total of $3.65 billion from 1994 to 1998, were eventually removed in 2002. Renewable energy sources and energy conservation have received only a small fraction of total energy subsidies, mostly in the form of lower VAT rates and under-pricing of electricity produced from hydropower plants.

International support programmes were mainly devoted to promoting efficient energy use (53%), cleaning up the environmental damage caused by fossil fuel production (26%) and enhancing the use of renewables (6%).

More than 80% of the total amount of subsidies was given to fossil fuels, 16% to nuclear energy and some 3% to renewable energy sources and energy conservation. This was broadly in line with the breakdown of primary energy supply (Table 4.3).

	Share of energy subsidies (%)	*Share of energy supply (%)*
Fossil fuels	80.3	89.3
Nuclear energy	16.6	10.2
Renewables	3.1*	0.45*

* Includes energy conservation and efficiency

Table 4.4 Share of fuels in energy subsidies in the Czech Republic, 1994–98

Source: Florian 1999

4.4.3 Slovak Republic

Between 1993 and 1999, total energy subsidies in the Slovak Republic amounted to $3.231 billion, of which cross-subsidies accounted for $1.622 billion (Table 4.5 and Fig. 4.3). Almost three-quarters of all subsidies went to fossil fuels. The nuclear energy sector received $690 million (11%) while renewable energy sources and energy savings received $450 million (15%), of which $191 million was in the form of state guarantees for bank loans to large hydropower plants.

As in the Czech Republic, heat subsidies represent the single-largest category of energy subsidies. Since practically all of the district heat systems in the Slovak Republic are supplied by fossil fuels, the entire estimate of $808 million is classified as a subsidy in favour of fossil fuels. Heat subsidies grew between the years 1993 and 1999, but were almost entirely removed in 2000.

Cross-subsidies are a major source of indirect subsidies. Electricity cross-subsidies grew between 1993 and 1999, but were largely removed in 2000 when electricity prices for households were increased sharply. Cross-subsidies in the natural gas sector also grew steadily in the 1990s. The other main source of indirect subsidies is lower taxation. VAT for electricity and gas sales was subject to a special rate of 6% compared to the standard rate of 22% for most other goods and services. The purpose of this subsidy was to keep prices down for household customers. VAT rates were raised to 10% for electricity and 23% for gas in 1999.

	Fossil fuels	*Nuclear power*	*Renewables & conservation*	*Other and international*	*Total*
Direct subsidies	907.9	29.4	24.3	–	961.7
Heat prices	808.3	–	–	–	808.3
Indirect subsidies	1,183.0	660.8	425.7	110.0	2,269.5
Lower VAT tariff	189.8	75.7	29.7	–	295.3
Rural gas distribution	94.6	–	–	–	94.6
Nuclear liabilities insurance	–	14.6	–	–	14.6
State guarantees to bank loans	–	28.3	191.1	–	219.3
Cross-subsidies	896.4	520.9	204.8	–	1,622.2
Total	2,090.9	690.2	450.0	110.0	3,231.2

Table 4.5 **Energy subsidies by fuel and type in the Slovak Republic, 1993–99 ($ million)**

Source: Krivosik 2001

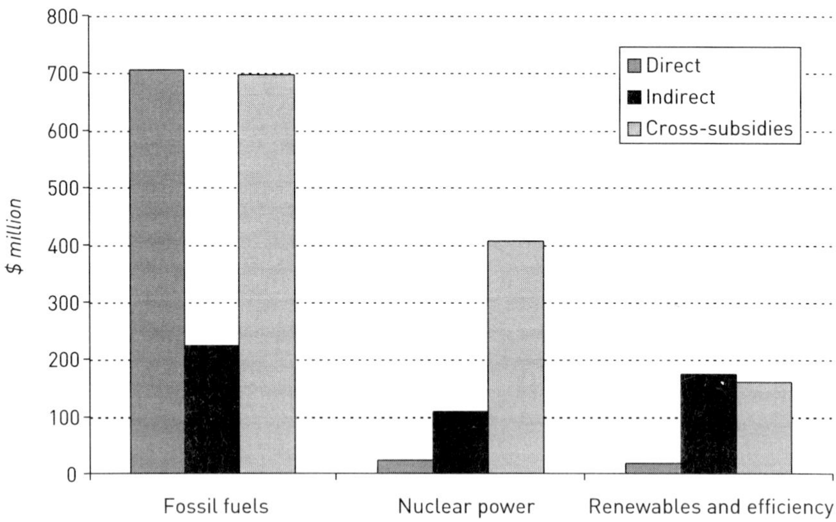

Figure 4.3 **Energy Subsidies in the Slovak Republic by Fuel and Category, 1993–99 ($ million)**

Source: Krivosik 2001

The value of nuclear liabilities insurance and state guarantees for bank loans to nuclear power plants construction were small, although they were important to the development of the nuclear industry. Construction of the second Slovak nuclear power plant would not have taken place without these subsidies. State guarantees for bank loans have also been used to support the building of large hydropower plants.

Table 4.6 indicates the size and value of average annual energy subsidies in the Slovak Republic during the period 1993–99. They were equivalent on average to almost half of the central government budget deficit.

	Amount (billion US$)	*Energy subsidies as a percentage of state budget and GDP*
Energy subsidies*	0.23	–
State budget: income	4.88	4.7
State budget: deficit	0.52	44.4
State healthcare expenditures	0.48	47.7
GDP: current prices	17.77	1.3

* Excluding cross-subsidies

Table 4.6 **Comparison of annual energy subsidies, state budget and GDP in the Slovak Republic, 1993–99**

Source: Krivosik 2001

4.5 Effects of energy subsidies

Despite the importance of energy subsidies in both countries, no detailed study has been carried out with the aim of identifying their effects and proposing reforms. However, there is plenty of evidence that energy subsidies have led to major social, economic and environmental problems.

4.5.1 Economic effects

Past energy subsidies are a primary cause of the high energy intensity in the Czech and Slovak Republics. They have held back the restructuring of the economy and hindered innovation. In addition, energy subsidies have had other harmful economic effects, including the following:

- As there are negligible resources of fossil fuels in the Czech and Slovak Republics, a large proportion of the countries' energy needs have to be imported. Subsidies, by lowering prices and increasing consumption, have raised the two countries' dependence on imports and undermined the foreign trade balance. Both countries currently have trade deficits.

- Subsidies, in the form of tax rebates and exemptions—notably the lower rate of VAT applied to electricity and gas—have reduced tax revenues and contributed to chronic budget deficits in both countries.

4.5.2 Environmental effects

Energy subsidies have accentuated the harmful environmental effects of energy production, supply and consumption, mainly through increased local and regional air pollution, including urban smog and acid rain. Land degradation due to mining activities has also become a major problem.

Emissions of some specific pollutants, notably SO_2, NO_X and particulates, have been reduced in recent years. This resulted mainly from a combination of regulatory and economic instruments, as well as a decline in energy use in heavy industry. But greenhouse gas emissions remain high relative to GDP, mainly due to the continued importance of energy-intensive industry to the economy and low energy efficiency.

4.5.3 Social effects

Social reasons are one of the main arguments for subsidising energy, yet the public authorities have still to carry out a detailed study of the social effects of price reform. Politicians have been reluctant to increase energy prices, mainly because of concerns about the social impact, despite claims by energy companies that price increases would have little impact on household budgets.

4.6 Case study of electric heating subsidies

The widespread use of electricity for space and water heating purposes illustrates how energy subsidies can distort energy-use patterns. Electricity prices in both the Czech and Slovak Republics were heavily cross-subsidised in the 1990s. Households generally paid less for a unit of electricity than industry and services, even though the costs of supplying households are much higher. Electricity is supplied to households at lower voltages, which reduces economies of scale. Unit billing and metering costs are also higher. Furthermore, household consumers have steeper load profiles than industry, raising capacity costs. For much of the decade, household tariffs failed to keep pace with increases in tariffs for industry and services (Figs. 4.4 and 4.5). The size of cross-subsidies increased up to 1996 in the Czech Republic and up to 1999 in the Slovak Republic (Fig. 4.6).

Because of these cross-subsidies, household electricity consumption in both countries increased steadily in the 1990s, driven largely by heating demand (Figs. 4.7 and 4.8). Direct electric heating represented only 1.5% of total household electricity consumption in the Slovak Republic in 1993. By 1996, this share had soared to almost one-quarter. Household electric heating accounted for over one-third of the total growth of electricity consumption between 1992 and 2000. A

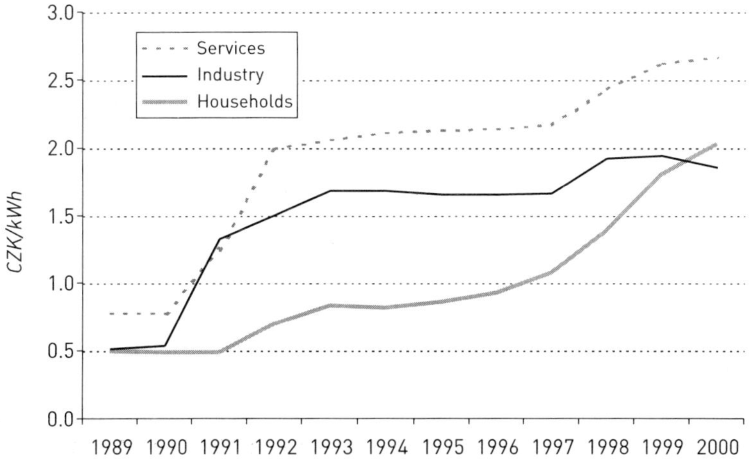

Figure 4.4 **Average electricity prices by sector in the Czech Republic, 1989–2000**

Source: Koneko 2001

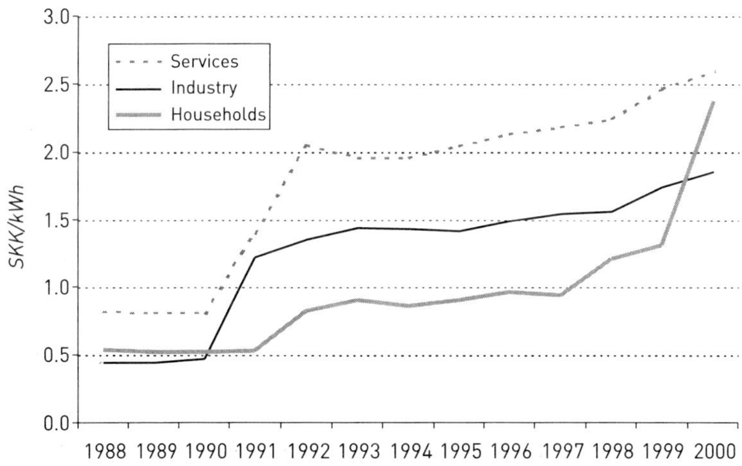

Figure 4.5 **Average electricity prices by sector in the Slovak Republic, 1988–2000**

Source: Krivosik 2001

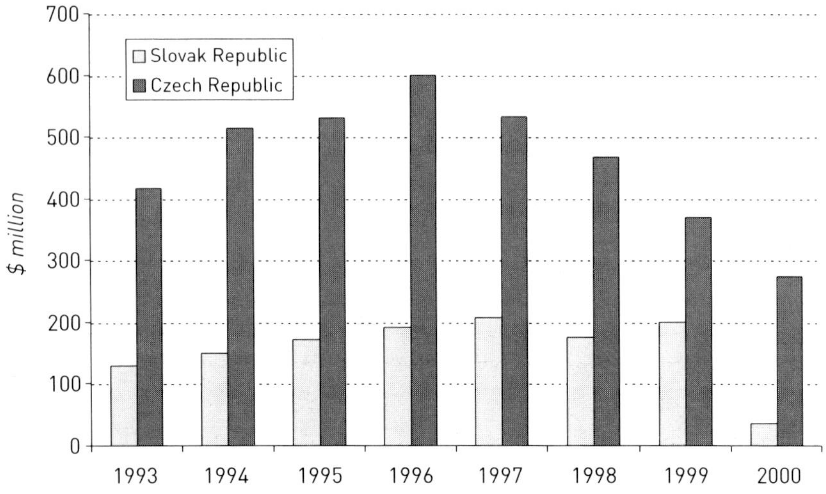

Figure 4.6 **Electricity cross-subsidies in the Czech and Slovak Republics, 1993–2000**

Source: Krivosik 2001; Koneko 2001

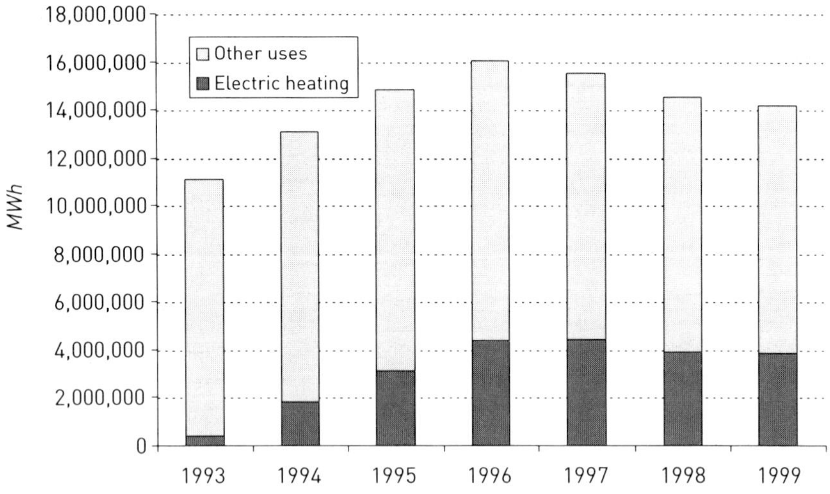

Figure 4.7 **Household electricity consumption in the Czech Republic, 1993–99**

Source: Krivosik 2001

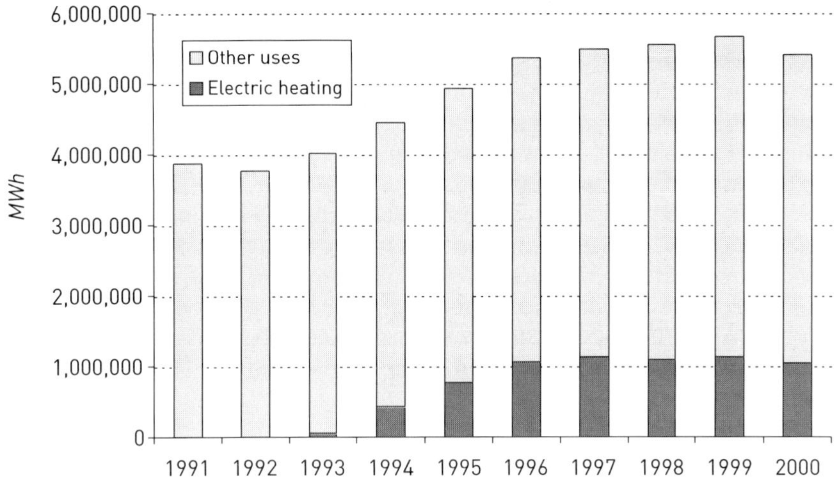

Figure 4.8 **Household electricity consumption in the Slovak Republic, 1991–2000**

Source: Krivosik 2001

similar development occurred in the Czech Republic (Fig. 4.7). In addition to the low price of electricity for heating, the low cost of electric heaters compared to other heating systems contributed to the rapid growth in electric heating demand. Increases in electricity prices for heating halted the growth in demand in the late 1990s in both countries.

A major disadvantage of direct electric heating is that the generating, transmission and distribution capacity required to supply power is used only in the winter months. This capacity is mostly idle in the summer. The regional electricity distribution companies have struggled to finance the investments needed to reinforce their networks to meet peak winter demand. Households also had to invest in electric heaters and in replacement heating systems as cross-subsidies were phased out.

The boom in direct electric heating also caused distribution companies to incur major financial losses, because they were forced to sell electricity used for direct heating in households at tariffs below those at which they were buying it from generators. The aim of both governments to privatise these regional distributors at the highest possible prices was the main reason why these cross-subsidies were removed.

4.7 Policy implications

In both countries, fossil and nuclear fuels have been subsidised much more than renewables and energy conservation and efficiency. Substantial progress has been made in removing these subsidies over the last decade, but some direct and indirect subsidies, such as large-scale support for the mining industry, remain. Moreover, prices do not reflect external negative environmental effects.

While the environmental and economic effects of subsidies are fairly well understood, their impact on social welfare and employment is not as obvious due to measurement difficulties. The links between all of these effects are even more difficult to assess. Policy reform is hindered by this lack of understanding.

There is strong evidence that market-based reforms, such as increased competition and enterprise restructuring and privatisation, have made industry more energy-efficient and less polluting in the transition economies as a whole. These reforms have reinforced the effect of raising prices to economic levels, inducing greater allocative efficiency and reducing harmful environmental effects.

A number of lessons can be drawn from these developments:

- Energy price reform has had the greatest impact in raising overall energy efficiency and promoting cleaner energy use. The biggest reductions in greenhouse gas emissions have been achieved in the privatised industries and in the energy sector.
- Energy price reform reinforced other policy measures to increase energy efficiency.
- Price reform was delayed and is still being hindered by concerns about the adverse effects on poor households. However, there is a growing recognition that this problem is better addressed through welfare programmes aimed at specific sections of the population rather than through energy pricing.
- Timetables for the transition to full-cost pricing should have been established to allow energy users to plan their investment decisions. In many cases, price distortions led to investments that proved to be inefficient later on as price reforms were implemented.
- More attention should have also have been paid to indirect energy subsidies, such as financial support for the mining industry.

The experience of the Czech and Slovak Republics in the last decade shows that piecemeal efforts to reduce and remove energy subsidies are less effective than a comprehensive strategy of subsidy reform. The need to reduce state aid and liberalise the energy market under the terms of accession to the European Union has given impetus to subsidy reform.[14] A fundamental restructuring of the whole system of public financing, including taxes, together with subsidies to energy efficiency and renewables is currently under discussion in both countries. However, reaching a political consensus is proving difficult. In addition, the co-ordination of energy and environmental policies is not perfect. The preparation of coherent policies must involve consultation with major stakeholders.

14 Nonetheless, many European governments and the Union itself continue to subsidise various energy sources. See Chapter 3 and Oosterhuis 2001.

The Czech Republic has been considering a 'Green Budget Reform' based on a proposal by the European Commission (EC 1997). This involves increasing excise taxes on selected fossil fuels and electricity generated from them, while at the same time reducing labour taxes. Under this reform, energy taxes should meet the following criteria:

- Respond flexibly to changing economic conditions
- Promote a stable and predictable economic climate
- Be implemented gradually to reduce adjustment costs
- Be transparent and politically acceptable
- Have a favourable effect on the economy as a whole

Discussions on realising this type of reform have raised a number of issues that require further analysis and discussion among political leaders. As the overall tax burden in the Czech Republic is already very high, budget neutrality remains one of the basic requirements for such a reform. But it is clear that this approach would penalise the most energy-intensive industries. Such a reform must, therefore, include some mechanism to cushion the impact on these industries without reducing incentives for using energy more efficiently and cleanly.

Discussions about the tax reform stalled in 2001. The new Czech government, which came to power in 2002, has adopted the goal of budget-neutral environmental tax reform. Progress in drawing up and implementing reforms is expected soon. The new government has entered into discussions with stakeholders from Germany on how to introduce and design an Ecological Tax Reform (ETR) and how to move towards a broader Environmental Fiscal Reform (EFR) or Green Budget Reform (GBR).

5

Energy subsidies in Russia

The case of district heating*

Energy subsidies to household consumers of gas, electricity and district heat remain a serious economic problem in Russia. District heat, which plays a large role in the Russian energy sector, is heavily subsidised. Direct subsidies to heat suppliers and benefits and welfare allowances to low-income families amount to roughly $2 billion per year and the government also offers interest-free loans to supply fuel to district heating companies in remote locations.

District heat is generally used very inefficiently in Russia, but only partly because it is under-priced. In the residential sector, end-users are often not billed for the actual amount of heat they use because supplies to individual dwellings are not metered. As a result, when heat is adequately supplied, households have little incentive to use heat efficiently or conserve it. In addition, in large housing blocks it is often not possible to adjust the amount of heat supplied to each apartment. Raising prices would not reduce subsidies if end-users respond by refusing to pay. This has been a major problem in recent years. For technical and social reasons, it is often difficult to cut supplies to households that do not pay their bills. Reducing costs through energy-efficiency improvements in supply and use may be a more effective approach to eliminating heat subsidies. But achieving these improvements will require a major restructuring of the district heat sector.

5.1 Energy subsidies in Russia

Energy subsidies remain a serious economic problem in the Russian Federation, despite progress in reducing them within the framework of the country's transition to a market economy. The bulk of energy subsidies go to household consumers

* This chapter is based on two presentations made by Igor Bashmakov at meetings at the International Energy Agency in 2002. It also draws on Bashmakov 2000a.

of natural gas, electricity and district heat. The government is currently pursuing policies to reform pricing and subsidies. They involve:

- Imposing more government control over energy monopolies' investment plans so as to ensure that only justified investments are reflected in regulated tariffs
- Increasing domestic natural gas prices to economic levels
- Eliminating subsidies to electricity in the context of power-sector reforms
- Reforming the system of district heat subsidies so that the overall level of subsidy is reduced and remaining subsidies go only to low-income households

Subsidies to natural gas and electricity are described briefly below. A more detailed discussion of district heat subsidies follows in Section 5.2.

5.1.1 Natural gas

A recent IEA study (IEA 1999) estimates how much natural gas is subsidised in Russia by comparing the average price of domestically consumed gas with the economic or market price based on the opportunity cost of that gas. The latter is calculated as the current export price minus estimated transportation costs. Using 1997 data, prices to households were estimated to cover only 9% of the economic price, industrial prices just under half and prices to power stations around 64%. According to the study, eliminating these subsidies would reduce domestic consumption by about 150 billion cubic metres.

The IEA study did not, however, take account of the impact that the increase in the volume of gas available for export would have on the price of exports to Western Europe. Such a large increase in export potential would probably depress export prices significantly in the long run. Gas subsidies may, therefore, be much less than that suggested by the IEA study. Gas subsidies have also declined in the last five years. Export prices fell by 23% in 2002, while domestic prices increased by 25%. The government has authorised Gazprom, the monopoly gas supplier in Russia, to raise prices by a further 20% in 2003, although the company had requested a 40% price increase. The gap between domestic and export prices is, therefore, shrinking.

The Russian government's domestic gas pricing policy is not aimed solely at bringing prices into line with international market levels. The government is also seeking to promote competition among suppliers and between fuel types and to restructure Gazprom in order to reduce supply costs. This would have the effect of softening the impact of subsidy removal on final prices and on households' purchasing power.

The government is reducing gas subsidies in a phased manner to smooth the increase in end-user prices and to give consumers time to adjust. Domestic prices in 2004–2005 are planned to reach on average $32–35 per thousand cubic metres, which is considered even by Gazprom to be an economic price.

5.1.2 Electricity

There is considerable debate in Russia about electricity tariffs and the extent to which electricity is still under-priced. RAO UES, the largest electricity firm, the Ministry of Economic Development, the Federal Energy Commission, large industrial consumers such as aluminium plants, regional authorities and experts have been unable to agree on what the correct economic level of electricity prices should be. They also disagree on how to implement the transition to economic prices and how to regulate tariffs.

The power companies argue that the regional regulatory authorities keep end-user prices artificially low for political reasons (Russian Ministry of Energy 2001). They point to much higher prices in Western Europe as evidence of under-pricing and subsidisation. This assertion is supported by the 1999 IEA study, which estimates that electricity prices were on average subsidised by 42% in 1997 based on estimates of long-run marginal costs. Under-pricing undermines the profitability of the industry and its ability to invest.

Some Russian experts disagree, arguing that the economic price of power supply should reflect the over-capacity that has characterised the industry for many years. Raising prices immediately to long-run marginal cost levels would be inappropriate, as it would over-remunerate the owners of generation assets and leave the generation companies with large retained earnings and cash surpluses. Nevertheless, efficient prices would be expected to rise over time towards long-run marginal costs as demand picks up and the need for large-scale investments grows. They also argue that, under current arrangements, generation capacity is not dispatched in least-cost merit order, resulting in an economically irrational use of generation assets and higher wholesale power costs. The plants with the lowest marginal operating costs—hydro and nuclear facilities—are usually dispatched only after centralised fossil fuel and local co-generation plants. Operating and capital costs are also thought to be much lower in Russia than in industrialised countries because the cost of labour and materials is a lot lower.

Cross-subsidies in the electricity sector remain a major problem. Residential electricity prices have recently increased significantly relative to industrial prices in many Russian regions, implying that cross-subsidies have been reduced. In most cases, however, industrial prices remain higher even though supply costs are much lower.

Planned regulatory reforms to make the wholesale market work more efficiently and the introduction of competition in electricity supply to encourage improvements in productivity could contribute to lower costs and, therefore, help to reduce subsidies. In the context of industry restructuring, the Ministry of Economic Development initially planned to raise electricity tariffs on average by 15–18% per year from 2002 to 2004. In fact, prices were increased by 27% in 2002 and are due to rise by a further 30% in 2003. These increases are nonetheless much lower than those sought by RAO UES.

5.2 District heat subsidies

District heat plays an exceptionally large role in the energy sector in Russia. It meets over a third of final energy needs of industry and close to half those of the commercial and household sectors. The value of heat sales was about $20 billion in 2002, compared to around $27 billion for both domestic and export sales of natural gas. Close to 50% of primary energy consumption in Russia is used directly and indirectly for heat generation, transmission and distribution.

District heat supplies are heavily subsidised. Total budget allocations for heat currently amount to an estimated $3.5–4.0 billion per year, of which about $2 billion are subsidies in the form of payments to heat suppliers and low-income families, and the government also offers interest-free loans to supply fuel to district heating companies in remote locations. Prices vary across the country, ranging from $6 to $75 per Gcal.

The government decided in 2001 to raise heat prices quickly to 100% of costs for most residential customers and retain subsidies only for poor households whose housing and associated costs exceed 22% of income. At the beginning of 2002, a smoother transition to full-cost pricing was agreed in the face of public resistance and political opposition.

The district heat industry is characterised by poor metering of supplies and consumption, and inadequate monitoring of fuel inputs to heat-generation plants. There is enormous uncertainty about the efficiency of boilers in heat plants, technical losses in heat production and distribution and the extent to which the debts of the suppliers are caused by under-billing rather than under-pricing. This complicates the task of establishing a rational pricing structure. Table 5.1 provides broad-brush estimates for selected indicators for the Russian district heat sector. Table 5.2 provides examples of estimates of subsidies to heat supply from the federal government and selected regional governments and public institutions.

District heat is generally used very inefficiently in Russia. In the residential sector, end-users are often not billed for the actual amount of heat they use because supplies to individual dwellings are not metered. Households are often underheated. But, when they are adequately heated, they have little incentive to use heat efficiently or conserve it. In addition, in large housing blocks, it is often not possible to adjust the amount of heat supplied to each apartment. As a result, many household consumers of district heat effectively have a zero price elasticity of demand: they cannot meter, adjust or even refuse heat consumption. This has led many households to refuse to pay for heat supplies that they claim they did not request. Installing metering and heat-control systems and implementing billing systems based on individual households' consumption is expensive and complex.[15]

There are several major, interrelated problems with regard to setting heat tariffs:

15 For example, in the city of Moscow, 200,000 water meters have been installed in individual apartments, but residents of these flats are still billed for water based on the number of household members.

Indicator	*Units*	*Amount*
Numbers of:		
combined heat and power plants	Units	485
large boilers	Units	190,000
individual heat generators and boilers	Units	>600,000
Heat generation	Million Gcal	2, 120
Own use	Million Gcal	50
Network losses	Million Gcal	450
Heat consumption	Million Gcal	1,600
Fuel efficiency	%	71.5
Total energy inputs to heat generation	Million Gcal	3,500
Heat tariffs, average	$/Gcal	12
Heat tariffs, range	$/Gcal	6-75
Heat sales	$ billion	20.0
Heat sales, of which:	$ billion	5.2
paid by households	$ billion	2.6
covered by subsidies	$ billion	1.6
shortfall	$ billion	1.1
Potential savings from efficiency improvements	$ billion	8.0

Table 5.1 **Russian district heat indicators**

- Standard cost-plus tariff methodologies used by most municipalities do not motivate suppliers to reduce their costs.
- The lack of metering makes it difficult to set tariffs on the basis of cost.
- Under current regulatory rules, most combined heat and power production costs are allocated to heat supplies, giving an economic advantage to electricity. As a result, the production of co-generated heat is declining, even though it is a more economically efficient source of heat than boilers.
- There is a lack of co-ordination in regulating prices between the Federal Energy Commission, which sets gas prices and wholesale electricity prices, the Regional Energy Commissions, which set co-generated electricity and heat prices, and municipalities, which set prices for heat transmission and heat generation by boilers.

	Year	*Amount*
Federal government		
Consolidated federal budget (with public buildings)	2002	3,500
Heat supply subsidies	2002	1,690
Heat supply benefits for separate groups of residents	2003	265
Heat supply welfare allowances	2003	63
Winter preparation	2002	1,000
Interest-free loans for fuel supply to regions with limited fuel shipment period	1999	160
Regional governments		
Interest-free loans for fuel supply to regions with limited fuel shipment period (Sakhalin oblast—650,000 residents)	1998	20
Financial transfers to support housing and utility costs of municipal budgets (Sakhalin)	1998	83
Winter preparation (Sakhalin)	2000	8
Assistance in preventing system failures and handling emergencies (Sakhalin)	1998	0.7
Regional investment programmes (Sakhalin)	2001	4
Public institutions		
Heat bills of public institutions	2002	1,050
Heat bills of the Ministry of Education (Russian Federation—more than 1,000 institutions)	2002	125
Heat bills of public institutions (Rostov oblast—more than 7,000 public institutions)	2002	16
Capital repairs of public buildings (Rostov-on-Don—educational institutions)	2002	0.5
Meter installation (Rostov oblast—900 meters)	2002	1.7
Heat-metering service (Rostov—900 meters)	2003	0.3
Energy efficiency improvements (Ministry of Education, Russian Federation)	2001	9.0
Subsidies to heat suppliers		
Heat supply subsidies (City of Norilsk—216,000 residents)	2002	22.5
Heat supply welfare allowances (Norilsk)	2003	8.5
Subsidies to residents		
Subsidies for coal purchases (Sakhalin)	1998	4.0

Table 5.2 Examples of subsidies to district heat supply ($ million)

- Heat prices do not vary according to the time of year, even though production costs are much lower in the summer. Consequently, boilers cannot supply heat competitively in the summer, further reducing the market share of co-generated heat.
- Tariff-setting procedures are not transparent and are driven by political considerations.

Rising heat prices and the inability of growing numbers of customers to pay for their supplies has resulted in deteriorating payment discipline and rising debts of end-users with heat suppliers. In practice, when prices are raised by 1%, the collection rate for heating bills goes down by around 0.2%. For technical and social reasons, it is often difficult to cut supplies to households that do not pay their bills. Those debts reached $3 billion at the beginning of 2002, of which public-sector organisations owed $1.5 billion and households $0.15 billion. But they are more than offset by the heat suppliers' own debts, which now stand at $4.2 billion.

These payment problems, together with tariffs that fail to cover full costs, have reduced funds for maintenance and repair. This has harmed the physical reliability of the heat supply system and raised the cost of handling emergencies. Rising losses and emergency costs have further increased heat supply costs and made the financial health of the heat suppliers even worse. Their poor financial shape discourages financial institutions from lending them money and investors from buying their equity.

The transition to full-cost pricing to residential customers has already been accomplished in a number of cities, such as Cherepovetz. Part of the savings in subsidy payments by the municipal authorities has been used to finance welfare payments to poor households. The federal government has recommended that those households whose combined housing costs and utility charges exceed 22% of their income should be eligible for welfare payments. Some Russian regions have opted for lower thresholds of between 10% and 14%, arguing that such levels are more in line with the purchasing power of poor households.[16] Experience has shown that, unless welfare payments are introduced for poor households, eliminating heat subsidies often leads to a decline in collection rates and a deterioration in the heat suppliers' financial health.

The removal of heat subsidies also has to go hand in hand with the installation of meters and billing systems. This will ensure that households are billed for the amount of heat they actually consume. However, residents would still pay for inefficiencies in heat production and distribution, which they are not responsible for and cannot control. For example, in the city of Dmitrov, local district heat supply system efficiencies range from 14% to 73% and average 38%. One possible solution is to bill customers for the notional costs of an efficient system taking account of the normal thermal losses in heat generation and distribution. Those costs would equate to around 70% of actual costs today. The municipality would pay the rest. This mechanism would give the municipality a strong incentive to improve system efficiency.

16 For example, Moscow has applied a threshold of 13% and Cherepovetz 14%. The UK government defines 'energy poverty' as a situation where a household's energy costs exceed 10% of its disposable income.

Reducing costs through energy-efficiency improvements in supply and use may be a more effective approach to eliminating heat subsidies. Efficiency improvements could generate estimated savings in total heat subsidies of between $2.5 billion and $3 billion per year. But achieving these improvements will require a major restructuring of the district heat sector, involving the following key measures:

- Elimination or rescheduling of the debts of the heat suppliers.
- The reorganisation of heat markets. This should involve, *inter alia*, the introduction of competition in supply and the awarding of distribution concessions, unbundling of heat generation and distribution and a clarification of the contractual obligations of both heat suppliers and consumers (Bashmakov 2002b).
- Improved metering and billing practices, including the introduction of inexpensive apartment-level billing systems in multi-dwelling buildings.[17]
- The development of comprehensive municipal energy plans.
- The development and implementation of energy-efficiency policies and strategies aimed at reducing costs, stabilising the finances of municipal district heat companies and improving system reliability (see Bashmakov *et al.* 2000; Bashmakov 2002b).
- The development of credible institutions and mechanisms for promoting energy conservation, efficient energy use in the public and residential sectors. Small energy service companies, which could take on the task of running the heating systems of residential, commercial and small and medium-sized industrial buildings, should be established. Associations of communal service customers should also be set up in the residential sector.

Inefficiencies in the production, distribution and use of district heat contribute significantly to airborne emissions of pollutant gases in and around Russian towns and cities. They are also responsible for about half of the country's greenhouse gas emissions. Policies to address these inefficiencies could play a major role in addressing local pollution problems and the risk of global climate change.

Policy-makers will need to take account of several factors, including the sensitivity of demand to price changes, the technical ability of end-users to respond flexibly to price signals and household incomes and purchasing power in reforming heat-subsidy and pricing policies. This will require a better understanding of consumer behaviour and the barriers to efficiency improvements. Without this understanding, policies that involve raising prices could simply aggravate problems of non-payment.

17 CENEf is currently helping to set up such a system in the city of Cherepovets.

6
Electricity subsidies in India

Electricity subsidies in India are very large and give rise to major economic, environmental and social costs. They encourage waste and over-consumption, exacerbate the country's worsening pollution problems, increase CO_2 emissions and hold back rural electrification. They cause the electricity companies to make huge commercial losses and so undermine their ability to improve the quality of service and to invest in new capacity. Cross-subsidies, which raise prices to industry, impede economic development. Reform of electricity subsidies is one of the most pressing issues in India today.

Retaining a degree of subsidy to improve access to electricity services for the poor is justified, in part because of the lack of social welfare infrastructure for distributing income support to the poor. A lifeline-rate system limiting subsidies to low consumption levels would be far cheaper than the current system of cross-subsidies. Whatever the chosen mechanism, subsidies need to be made transparent and must be properly accounted for. Subsidies should be transparent and funded directly rather than, as at present, through a system of cross-subsidies.

6.1 Energy market and policy overview

India's primary energy demand has grown spectacularly over the last three decades in line with rising population, industrial output and household incomes. India now accounts for over 5% of world energy demand in total and around 3% of commercial energy use. Coal and oil represent just under half of India's total energy consumption, with most of the rest made up by combustible renewables and waste—essentially biomass and animal waste used mostly by poor households (Table 6.1). The share of gas is small but growing quickly (from 2.8% in 1990 to over 4% in 2000). Around 29% of primary energy supply is used in power generation, and more than 80% of generation is based on coal.

	Coal	Oil	Gas	Electricity	CRW*	Other	Total
Indigenous production	154.3	32.9	21.9	0.0	201.6	10.9	421.6
TPES	165.1	102.3	21.9	0.1	201.6	10.9	501.9
TFC	32.4	91.6	10.3	31.0	201.6	0.0	366.9
Of which:							
Industry	25.2	22.3	9.6	13.3	23.0	0.0	93.4
Transport	0.0	43.6	0.0	0.7	0.0	0.0	44.3
Other†	7.2	20.7	0.7	17.0	178.6	0.0	224.2
Non-energy	0.0	5.0	0.0	0.0	0.0	0.0	5.0

* Combustible renewables and waste † Residential, commercial, public sector and agriculture
TFC = total final consumption (of energy) TPES = total primary energy supply

Table 6.1 **Indian energy balance, 2000 (Mtoe)**

Source: IEA 2002e

The Indian government has traditionally intervened heavily in the energy sector, both through state ownership and through regulation, including price controls and subsidies. As part of its economic reform programme, the government has sought in recent years to modify its role in the energy sector. Measures that have been introduced recently or are planned include:

- Opening up the energy sector to private and foreign investment, including, in some cases, privatisation
- Setting-up of independent regulatory commissions in the electricity and gas sectors
- Removing trade restrictions
- Dismantling the system of oil price controls, known as the Administered Pricing Mechanism (APM)

Progress in implementing these reforms has been slow, due to entrenched interests and political resistance.

Reforming the system and structure of energy subsidies has been a central issue. A *Discussion Paper on Energy Subsidies*, presented to parliament in 1997, called for a phased overall reduction in subsidies through higher, more cost-reflective prices. It also recommended that subsidies be limited to 'merit' goods and services, with well-established positive externalities (external benefits). The impetus to reform subsidies has been boosted by their rising financial cost and growing evidence of their detrimental impact on investment and market development.

6.2 Electricity sector policies

6.2.1 Market structure

India had 101.6 GW of installed generating capacity on 31 March 2001, an increase of 3.8% over the previous year. Power generation, which totalled 500 TWh in 2000/2001,[18] has increased rapidly over the last decade, at an average annual rate of growth of 6.5%. Transmission and distribution losses amounted to 133 TWh, or 27% of gross generation—a very high level compared to most other countries. Industry accounts for 43% of total final consumption, agriculture[19] 25% and the household sector 20%.

Power shortages, resulting in brownouts and blackouts, are a major problem. According to official data, the overall demand–supply gap decreased from an estimated 11.5% in 1996/97 to 5.9% in 1998/99, but rebounded to 7.8% in 2000/2001. Peak power shortages were 13% in 2000/2001.

More than 60% of generating capacity is owned and operated by State Electricity Boards (SEBs). The rest is owned mainly by central public companies, such as the National Thermal Power Corporation. Independent private producers account for a small share. The central government, through its ownership of the Power Grid Corporation, has exclusive responsibility for high-voltage inter-state transmission, which represents a small but growing share of total transmission. Transmission within states and most local distribution is in the hands of the SEBs.

6.2.2 Structural and regulatory reform

India launched a programme of power-sector reforms in 1991 aimed at restructuring the industry, reforming pricing and introducing more market-based mechanisms. Initial steps involved decentralising supply and encouraging new private investments in generation. States were given responsibility for attracting investment in independent power production (IPP) to boost capacity and output. These reforms produced disappointing results. Despite considerable initial interest from private investors, few IPP projects have been developed. This is partly due to a slow project approval process, restrictions on foreign direct investment, doubts about the SEBs' ability to guarantee payment for electricity that they would buy from IPPs and regulatory uncertainties.

More recently, the Indian government has undertaken a number of steps to modernise the regulatory regime. The 1998 Electricity Regulatory Commissions Act established the Central Electricity Regulatory Commission (CERC) with a mandate to set tariffs for inter-state trade, supplies from multi-state generation compa-

18 Financial year, which runs from 1 April to 31 March. The source of all electricity market data is TERI 2002.

19 It is thought that a significant proportion of consumption reported as being in the farming sector is in reality for commercial, industrial or household uses. This is because agricultural consumers enjoy much lower prices. In addition, reported agricultural consumption may include losses (including theft) incurred in other sectors, since agricultural consumption in the country is largely unmetered and estimated on a residual basis.

nies and central government-owned power corporations. The Act also allowed for the setting-up of state electricity commissions (SERCs) to regulate retail tariffs. The central government has set up the Power Trading Company to buy the power from large IPPs or public plants and sell it to the SEBs or to large consumers. This is intended to reduce the financial risk for private investors, who have been reluctant to invest because of the poor financial situation of the SEBs.

The government has also taken steps to restructure the SEBs. An amendment to the 1948 Electricity (Supply) Act in 1998 decreed the separation of generation from transmission functions and gave Power Grid responsibility for inter-state transmission and centralised dispatch. In December 2000, the CERC decreed a change in the way prices for power supplied to the SEBs by government-owned power corporations were set. The ultimate aim of these actions is to create a competitive wholesale power market.

The states of Orissa, Andhra Pradesh, Rajashtan, Haryana, Karnataka and Uttar Pradesh have made most progress in implementing reforms. Orissa, Andhra Pradesh and Haryana have already unbundled the generation, transmission and distribution activities of their respective SEBs by setting up separate corporate entities. All these states have set up a SERC. The main objectives of the SERCs are to:

- Promote the development of the power sector by ensuring economically efficient investment (in generation, transmission and distribution) through competition in electricity generation and supply
- Provide more reliable and better-quality service to end-users
- Ensure the financial viability of the SEBs and thereby attract private investment by basing tariffs on costs

Improving the financial health and operational performance of the SEBs is crucial to the development of the Indian electricity sector. Under the Electricity (Supply) Act 1948, confirmed by a 1996 government power-sector plan, SEBs are required to achieve a rate of return of not less than 3% on their fixed assets in service after interest and depreciation charges. In 1999/2000, only two were showing a positive return. Under-pricing of electricity is the main cause of the SEBs' financial losses, although theft, poor management, non-metering and corruption have contributed. The SEBs' dire financial state is, in turn, undermining their capacity to invest in new generation capacity and grid expansion.

Further reforms are planned. A new bill, drawn up by the government in 2000, is still under discussion. Key measures include:

- Easing licensing restrictions for new power projects (other than hydropower projects)
- Open access in transmission
- An obligation on states to establish regulatory commissions, which would set retail tariffs on the basis of full costs and promote competition
- A requirement that any subsidies on electricity retail sales be paid out of state budgets rather than through cross-subsidisation

6.2.3 Rural electrification

Rural electrification is a major policy objective in India. By the end of 1999/2000, almost 507,000 villages had been electrified, covering an estimated 88% of the total rural population. However, village electrification rates vary greatly across the country from as little as a third in some states in the east and north-east to 100% in some northern states. In addition, many households in electrified villages do not have access to electricity because of the high cost of connection. The IEA estimates that, in total, 579 million people, mostly in rural areas, do not have access to electricity (IEA 2002c). These people represent 57% of the population.

The primary use of electricity in villages is powering pump-sets, mainly for irrigation. The number of electrified pump-sets has risen steadily in recent years, from 8.9 million in March 1991 to 12.5 million in March 2000. This increase has exceeded the rate of growth of electricity consumption in the farming sector. The Rural Electrification Corporation (REC), which the government set up in 1969, helps provide financial assistance for rural electrification. Projects include electrification of villages, energisation of pump-sets, provision of power for small, agro-based and rural industries, lighting of rural households and street lighting.

In 1998, the government launched the Kutir Jyothi (literally 'household lighting') programme, aimed at accelerating electricity connections to households. Under this programme, it is compulsory for SEBs to connect households under the poverty line. The government and the SEBs provide grants up to a maximum limit of 1,000 rupees per connection with the installation of a meter or 800 rupees per connection without a meter to rural households. The full cost of connection with a meter is typically around 3,000 rupees. The implementation of the programme has been hindered by difficulties in identifying eligible households and the SEBs' severe financial problems.

6.3 Electricity pricing and subsidies

The SEBs' end-use electricity tariffs vary widely according to customer category. The major categories are households, agriculture, commercial activities, industry and railways. Electricity subsidies stem largely from under-pricing of power: in most cases a deliberate move for social policy reasons. Subsidies also occur because of under-recovery of revenues, largely due to inadequate metering, poor credit control and theft.

There are large cross-subsidies between customer categories: tariffs for households and agriculture are generally well below actual supply costs, while tariffs to other customer categories are usually above the utilities' reported average cost of supply. In 2000/2001, the average price of electricity sold amounted to 212 paise (around 5 US cents) per kWh—30% below the average cost of supply (see Fig. 6.1).

According to official data (Government of India Planning Commission 2001), the total under-recovery of costs—the difference between total costs and total revenues—amounted to 260 billion rupees in 2000/2001. Cost recovery rates vary markedly across the country: rates are lowest at under 60% in Andhra Pradesh,

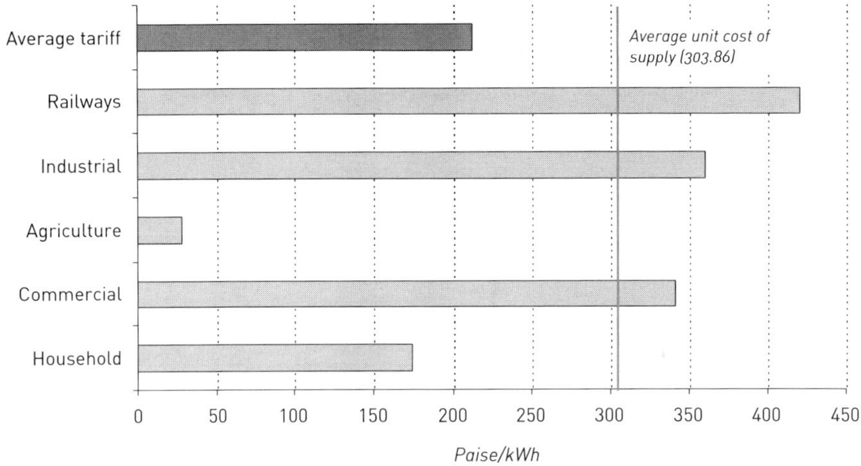

Figure 6.1 **Average tariffs and unit cost of supply, 1999/2000**

Source: TERI 2002

Bihar, Haryana, Jammu, Kashmir and Rajashtan, while the highest rates, at over 80%, are in Himachal Predesh, Kerala, Maharashtra, Orissa and Tamil Nadu.

The degree of subsidisation is by far the greatest for the agriculture and household sectors, which are cross-subsidised by above-cost tariffs for commercial and industrial customers and railways. A cost-reflective tariff structure would normally result in the lowest tariffs for industrial customers with the highest consumption and load factor, and the highest tariffs for household customers.[20] In 2000/2001, the average price paid by consumers registered as being in the agricultural sector was only 28 paise/kWh. The average household price was 174 paise/kWh. Official data shows that the nominal value of total subsidies to the household customers more than quadrupled to 95 billion rupees over the period 1992/93–2000/2001; subsidies to agriculture almost quadrupled to 271 billion rupees over the same period.

Under-pricing and poor collection rates have worsened progressively over the past decade. By 2000/2001, average revenues covered only 70% of average costs—down from 82% in 1992/93 (Fig. 6.2). In some states, notably Andhra Pradesh, the cost recovery rate is much lower. The deterioration in cost recovery is mainly due to a decline in real tariffs to agriculture. This has happened in spite of the introduction in Haryana, Himachal Pradesh, Orissa, Uttar Pradesh and Meghalaya of a minimum rate of 50 paise/kWh, as called for in a 1996 government plan.[21] That plan also calls for all end-use sectors to be ultimately charged no less than 50% of

20 In most industrial countries, the cost of supplying electricity to household consumers is on average around 50% higher than to industrial consumers. Electricity is supplied to industry at higher voltages, which give rise to economies of scale. Furthermore, industrial consumers have flatter load profiles than households, so that capacity costs are lower. Unit billing and metering costs are also lower for industry.

21 *Common Minimum National Action Plan for Power.*

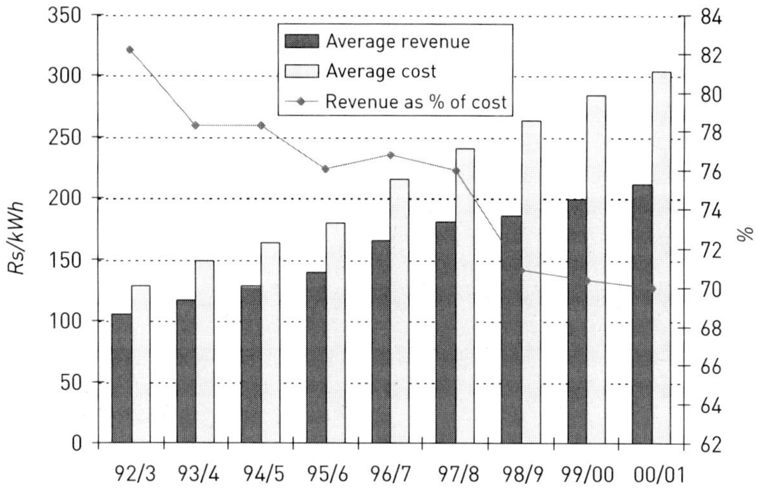

Figure 6.2 **Average electricity supply cost, revenues and cost recovery rate**

Source: TERI 2002

the average cost of supply (across all sectors), and within three years for agriculture. In no state has this goal been achieved.

Revenue arrears have also worsened. The share of arrears in total revenues has increased on average from 30% in 1996/97 to 34% in 1997/98, the latest year for which data is available. In that year, four states had arrears in excess of one year of sales revenue. Arrears are worst for agricultural consumers. Collection rates among this consumer category are thought to be as low as 50% (IEA 2002c).

The true size of the subsidy problem is even larger than that suggested by the data presented here, mainly because of network losses. Up to half of all transmission and distribution losses, which are very large by international standards, are caused by inadequate metering and billing systems, and theft. Many customers, especially in rural areas, do not pay while continuing to receive service. These customers effectively enjoy a 100% subsidy. Total losses amounted to 27% in 1999/2000. In Jammu and Kashmir, losses were a staggering 47%.

6.4 The impact of electricity subsidies

6.4.1 Economic effects

The primary effect of the subsidies described above is to distort the overall energy market in favour of electricity. Households, farmers and others who benefit from under-priced or free electricity maximise their consumption. As a result, they account for the bulk of demand.[22] Consumption of electricity by agriculture multiplied by a factor of 20 from 1971 to 2000, whereas overall consumption multiplied by only 7. As a result, India has a higher electricity intensity of GDP than most other countries in Asia at a similar stage of economic development (Fig. 6.3).

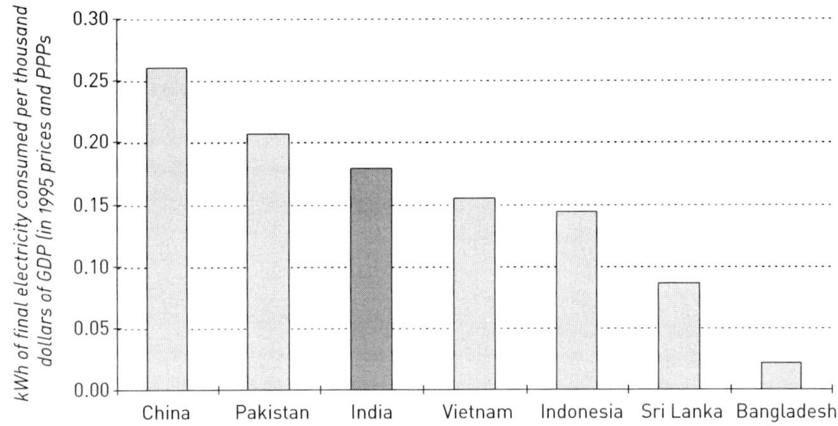

Figure 6.3 **Electricity intensity of GDP in India and other Asian countries**

Source: IEA 2002f

Electricity subsidies are a major cause of the financial problems faced by SEBs in India. Virtually every SEB has made a financial loss each year since 1992/93. Total losses amounted to over 200 billion rupees in 2000/2001 and would have been 260 billion rupees had the central government not provided subsidies in the form of grants. The return on capital was minus 27%. As a result, the SEBs are unable to finance investment in new power stations and in transmission and distribution networks to improve the reliability and quality of service. The government is therefore required to directly finance almost all the required investment in public supply, although this is supplemented by some private investment in IPPs.

The economy as a whole suffers from these problems. The high price paid by industrial consumers is not compensated by good-quality supply. Industry is subject to planned load-shedding,[23] power cuts, voltage collapse and frequency variations. The poor quality of electricity service contributes to substantial industrial output losses. It has also encouraged industry and commercial businesses to build and operate their own generating facilities, even though this solution is rarely as economic as obtaining bulk supply from the grid. The 1996 *Common Minimum*

22 In the rest of Asia, the domestic and commercial sectors account for well under half of electricity consumption and agriculture for only 2%.

23 The process of deliberately disconnecting preselected loads from the power system in response to a loss of power input to the system, in order to maintain the nominal value of the frequency.

National Action Plan for Power sought to promote investment in auto-generation and to increase its efficiency by calling on SEBs to provide access to their grids to transmit power that is surplus to a company's own on-site needs to other end-users.

The 1999 IEA study described in Chapter 2 attempts to quantify the size of electricity subsidies in India using a price-gap approach. It also assesses the potential impact subsidy removal would have on electricity consumption, as well as related CO_2 emissions (see below). That analysis has been updated with more recent price data (for 1999) and has been extended to cover agriculture. Table 6.2 summarises the results.

	Average price (rupees/kWh)	***Reference price (rupees/kWh)***	***Rate of subsidy (%)****	***Potential primary energy saving from subsidy removal (%)***†
Households	1.50	3.56	57.9	48
Industry	3.50	3.42	–	–
Agriculture	0.25	3.56	93.0	86
Average	–	–	38.0	34

* Difference between actual price and reference price as percentage of reference price
† TPES saved/TPES for the sectors covered by the study

Table 6.2 **Size and impact of electricity subsidies in India**

Source: IEA 2001d

Using 1999/2000 price and cost data, the rate of subsidy expressed as a proportion of the full cost-of-supply reference price amounted to 93% for agriculture and 58% for households. Electricity sales to industry are not subsidised. Using a –0.1 direct price elasticity of demand for the household, industry and agricultural sectors, electricity subsidy removal would lead to significant reductions in electricity consumption, particularly in the agricultural sector. In total, electricity use would be 34% lower in the absence of any subsidies. Assuming that the removal of electricity subsidies reduces the demand for fuel inputs to power generation in equal proportion and that average thermal efficiency is constant at lower production levels, the use of coal and oil in thermal power plants would also drop by around a third.

It is important to bear in mind the limitations of the price-gap approach, which identifies only static effects. It compares the actual situation with a hypothetical situation in which there are no subsidies, keeping all other factors constant. In reality, this would never be the case. The dynamic effects of removing subsidies are likely to be important. It could bring benefits in the form of greater price and cost transparency, gains in economic efficiency through increased competition and accountability, and, consequently, accelerated technology deployment. These changes would offset, at least to some degree, the long-run static effects of subsidy removal on energy demand and related CO_2 emissions. This would be especially true for the electricity industry.

Subsidy reform, to the extent that it increases the SEBs' financial viability, would boost their capacity to invest and, therefore, increase sales to customers who are currently denied access to electricity. In the long run, a reduction in subsidies would be expected to lead to an increase in electricity consumption by end-users not currently served or whose supply is severely curtailed by blackouts, brownouts or time-limited service. Indeed, this is the implicit goal of electricity-sector reforms, including subsidy reduction.

Whether this dynamic effect would be large enough to completely offset the static effect of higher prices on consumption by end-users that already have unrestricted access to electricity supply is unclear. The speed with which subsidy removal would lead to increased investment is also uncertain. Any attempt to quantify the impact of electricity subsidy reform on investment in power generation would also need to take into account the economics of auto-generation.

6.4.2 Environmental and social effects

The rapid increase in electricity production has contributed substantially to India's severe air pollution and rising CO_2 emissions. Urban air pollution, caused by the burning of fossil fuels, contributes to millions of premature deaths each year (Goldemberg 2000). Concentrations of sulphur dioxide and airborne particulates in most Indian cities greatly exceed international standards. Coal burned in power stations is a major source of pollution. India's coal is of poor quality, with high ash content and low calorific value, which means more coal needs to be burned for each kWh of electricity generated. In addition, the thermal efficiency of India's power stations is low compared to other countries, which raises the ratio of toxic emissions to output.

The high share of coal, the most carbon-intensive fossil fuel, in inputs to power generation also increases CO_2 emissions. In 2000, coal use in power stations contributed just over half of India's total emissions. This share is expected to increase further in the next three decades if the authorities do not take drastic action to mitigate these emissions (Fig. 6.4).

Under-pricing of electricity, by boosting consumption, exacerbates the problems of urban pollution of and rising CO_2 emissions. The removal of all energy subsidies would lead to an estimated 105 million tonne reduction in power-sector CO_2 emissions, equivalent to about a third of current emissions. Most of this reduction—99 million tonnes—would come from lower coal use brought about by lower demand for electricity resulting from the removal of electricity subsidies.

Electricity subsidies may also indirectly hold back rural development, even though subsidies to farmers are intended to boost rural incomes. By undermining the ability of the SEBs to invest in extending distribution networks to villages, they have restricted rural access to electricity services. Today, less than a third of rural households in India have access to electricity (IEA 2002c).[24] Lack of electricity keeps communities in poverty and contributes to its perpetuation, as it precludes

24 Chapter 13 includes a detailed discussion of the link between energy use and poverty.

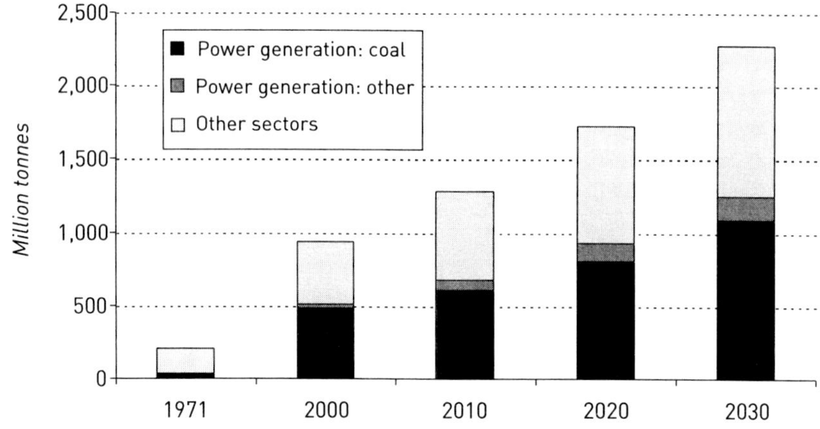

Figure 6.4 **CO_2 emissions in India, 1971–2030**

Source: IEA 2002c

most industrial activities and the jobs they create. Access to electricity and other modern energy sources is a necessary precondition for economic and social development.

6.5 Reforming electricity subsidies

There is unsurprisingly considerable resistance to reforming electricity subsidies from those current consumers of electricity that enjoy prices below full supply cost—especially farmers and landowners, and urban middle-class households. Nonetheless, there is a growing consensus that subsidy reform within the framework of the restructuring of the electricity industry more generally is needed. There is widespread agreement, supported by international organisations such as the World Bank (World Bank 2000a), that reform should aim to limit rather than totally eliminate electricity subsidies.

The main rationale for subsidising electricity at all is to assist poor people in gaining access to electricity-based energy services. Electricity service is needed for effective lighting and refrigeration; alternative energy sources are either more expensive, less effective in providing the service or carry health risks such as pollution from indoor burning of biomass. Access to electricity is recognised as being an essential element in economic development, by reducing manual labour, improving health, enhancing productivity and educational attainment and improving the quality of life of poor people. In reality, these benefits may well exceed the long-run costs involved in providing electricity service. But the high costs of connection[25] or non-availability of service may prevent poor people from gaining access to electricity. In this case, a degree of subsidy would, in principle, be justified.

The challenge for the Indian authorities is to ensure that electricity subsidies achieve the objective of promoting access to electricity for the poor in a cost-effective manner while ensuring the financial viability of the electricity supply industry. The key issues that need to be addressed are as follows:

- **Which consumers to subsidise.** At a minimum, subsidies could be provided to households and farmers that are not already connected to the distribution network. Subsidies to the poorest existing customers may also be justified.
- **Type of service to subsidise.** For customers without service, it would be reasonable to subsidise access to the service. For example, grants could be made available for the capital cost of connection. The electricity supplier could also roll part of the cost of connection into monthly charges. Local circumstances will determine whether it is more economic to extend the existing grid or to develop decentralised production and distribution networks, possibly based on locally sourced renewables, such as biomass or hydropower. For both new and existing customers, there may be a case for subsidising service through special, low tariffs—often called lifeline rates—for poor households, defined by income or consumption.
- **Subsidy mechanism.** Experience has shown that demand-side subsidies tend to work better than producer subsidies in ensuring that subsidies go to targeted customer groups and provide incentives for efficient service delivery, although the management of programmes such as distribution of connection grants can be expensive. There is evidence that a programme introduced by the Indian government that subsidises the production of photovoltaic system has tended to encourage manufacturers to gear production to maximising revenues from the subsidy rather than meeting the needs of the market (World Bank 2000a).[26]
- **Amount of subsidy.** In principle, subsidies should be large enough to provide an incentive to distributors to extend service to poor households that would otherwise not receive it, while not undermining incentives to provide service on an sustainable, profitable basis nor creating unnecessary market distortions. Lifeline rates, if used, should be limited to modest levels of consumption such that subsidies are targeted effectively and not appropriated by richer households.[27]

25 Connection charges can run as high as several hundred dollars per household. In practice, charges depend on the distance from the existing grid and the total number of households in a village to be connected.

26 Several states, including Karnataka, Himachal Pradesh, Andhra Pradesh, and Orissa, have recently introduced lifeline rates in an attempt to better target subsidies.

27 This can be achieved by applying the lifeline rate to households that subscribe to the lowest capacity or by applying the rate only to the first tranche of consumption, with full cost-based rates applied to higher levels of consumption. In the latter case, richer

The following calculation is designed to give an indication of how much a sensibly sized electricity subsidy programme to facilitate access for only the poor would cost in India. It assumes that the government decides to facilitate the access of poor households to electricity by providing them with a financial support covering the initial connection to the grid and a fixed monthly quantity of power. It is assumed that the monthly consumption per household for which financial support is provided is 50 kWh/year per household. This roughly corresponds to the consumption of low-income groups in Indian cities.[28] The total expenditure—which should be borne in a transparent fashion either by the central or state governments—required to give the targeted population minimum electricity service has two components:

- The cost of connection, either to the central grid or to local grids based on decentralised electricity production (C)
- The cost of poor households' daily consumption of power (E)[29]

The first component is a non-recurrent expenditure, while the second is recurrent. The first component is significant in developing countries where the need to connect household customers is great and where the cost of connection may be large compared to the economic value of the electricity supplied.

The financial transfers involved in providing such a subsidy could take various forms. The mechanism that involves the lowest administrative costs is likely to be most appropriate. For example, money could be provided directly to the service provider, or to the final consumer, through a fixed amount deducted from the electricity bill.

For a given number of households connected, the total cost of the subsidy would be C + E where:

$$C = (C \times p) / H; \text{ and}$$

$$E = (S \times P) / [H \times (K \times \{1 - B\})]$$

households benefit to the same extent in absolute terms as poor households, but less in proportionate terms.

28 Poor households consume small quantities of electricity. A field survey made in a large city of south India in 1994 (Alam *et al.* 1998) showed that electricity represents one-quarter of the total energy consumed in the household sector (the rest is firewood, kerosene and LPG). In that survey, the lowest income groups consumed an average of 7 kWh per capita and per month (57 kWh per household). The figure for the richest income group was 41 kWh per capita (180 kWh per household), while the average was 15 kWh (90 kWh per household). The choice of 50 kWh as a threshold is debatable and is probably on the high side. Similar progressive tariffs in other developing countries have sometimes been applied at lower consumption levels: for example, up to 20 kWh per household per month.

29 Note that the category of 'poor households' here belongs to a part of the population that would benefit from subsidised access to power and does not necessarily reflect the whole population with income below the poverty line. In practice, this target population can be defined according to income or to electricity consumption levels, with or without a reference to a poverty line.

where:

C is the average connection cost (per household).

P is the number of poor urban population to be connected.

H is the number of persons per household.

S is the marginal supply cost of power for residential consumption (production plus transmission and distribution).

P is the estimated poor population.

K is the lifeline consumption level.

B is the fixed percentage of electricity billed and paid for.

In this case, the calculation of E is based on a simplified lifeline rate system. All consumers are assumed to be billed for their electricity at marginal cost, except for consumers with consumption below the chosen lifeline level. The latter are charged a fixed proportion of the actual marginal supply cost of the electricity service. This provision facilitates management of the financial transfer to households as it can be handled directly by the electricity provider. At the same time, it avoids supplying a totally free service, which would encourage waste.

The supply cost for households is estimated to be 3.56 rupees per kWh (see Table 6.2 on page 84). It is assumed that one-third of the existing customers and half of the additional households to be connected each year benefit from this lifeline rate. It is also assumed that the price charged to this category of the population is one rupee per kWh, and that 4 million households are connected each year.[30] Other assumptions and primary data used in this calculation are shown in Table 6.3.

On these assumptions, the maximum annual direct expenditure to be borne by the government would be 46.9 billion rupees (roughly $1.1 billion): 11 billion rupees for the connection of new customers and 36 billion rupees for the consumption of poor households. This is likely to be a maximum, as the amount of subsidy is calculated on the assumption that subsidised households consume their entire 50 kWh per month. Actual consumption would probably be much lower. Special attention would have to be paid to the regular increase over time of the total direct expenditure as a result of additional consumers being brought in (assuming the share of poor customers remains constant), if the support mechanism is maintained.

The direct expenditure or cost of this targeted support mechanism would be much less than the current cost of subsidies to electricity consumption. Subsidies to households and agriculture currently amount to over 365 billion rupees.

30 The current annual rate of connection is slightly above 3 million.

Primary data (1997)	
Population (millions)	980
Number of households (millions)	163
Households living in electrified zone (millions)	90
Existing household customers (millions)	70
Total household consumption (TWh)	59
Average annual household consumption (kWh)	846
Distribution lines of 500 kV and under (km)	3,108,830
Cost of purchase and installation of meter (rupees)	583
Cost of connection to grid per household (rupees)	2,783
Assumptions	
Number of persons per household	6
Length of cable to be installed for each new household (metres)	20

Table 6.3 **Data and assumptions to calculate the hypothetical cost of a targeted household electricity subsidy scheme in India**

Source: IEA analysis; CEA 1998; IEA 1999; RSEB 1999; CMIE

7
Oil subsidies in Indonesia

The Indonesian government directly subsidises oil prices as a way of supporting the incomes of poor households. Consequently, oil-product prices in Indonesia are among the lowest in South-East Asia. These subsidies, which currently absorb more than 10% of the state budget, incur large economic, environmental and social costs. A recent government review of the subsidy policy concludes that eliminating subsidies would reduce government expenditure, increase foreign exchange earnings and reduce environmental damage, particularly from airborne emissions of particulate matter and lead. The net economic cost of the subsidies applied to kerosene, automotive diesel, industrial diesel, motor gasoline and heavy fuel oil amounted to almost $4 billion in 2002. It is projected that between 2000 and 2005 a total of $36 billion would be spent on oil subsidies if they are left unchanged. In addition, the value of lost foreign exchange earnings caused by lower exports would reach $16 billion. Subsidy reform would allow financial resources to be redirected towards supporting the poor in more effective ways, such as through a voucher scheme. Such an alternative approach, however, would need to overcome practical problems. In addition, the removal or elimination of subsidies would reduce pollution exacerbated by over-consumption of oil products.

7.1 Energy market and policy developments

Energy plays an important role in the Indonesian economy. In 2000, Indonesia was ranked 17th among world oil producers, accounting for just under 2% of world production. Indonesia's oil reserves are approximately 9.6 billion barrels. Indonesia's production of crude oil and condensates declined gradually from 1.56 million barrels of oil per day in 1998 to 1.23 mb/d in 2002.

With a large population of 225 million, Indonesia is a big consumer of oil products. According to the national oil company, Pertamina, domestic fuel consumption for 2002 exceeded 52.7 million kilolitres (about 0.9 mb/d)—down from 54.6 mkl in 2001. Automotive diesel oil accounts for the largest share of total oil consumption, at 43%, followed by motor gasoline (21%), kerosene (20%), fuel oil (10%) and industrial diesel oil (3%). Consumption of automotive diesel totalled 20.0 million kilolitres in 2001, motor gasoline 13.0 mkl, kerosene 10.7 mkl, fuel oil 6.8 mkl and industrial diesel 1.7 mkl (World Bank 2002b).

	Power	*Industry*	*Transportation*	*Households*	*Total*
Kerosene	–	0.63	–	99.37	100.00
Automotive diesel	15.13	30.83	54.04	–	100.00
Motor gasoline	–	–	100.00	–	100.00
Industrial diesel	1.31	91.70	6.99	–	100.00
Heavy fuel oil	23.02	73.01	3.97	–	100.00

Table 7.1 **Oil consumption in Indonesia by fuel and sector in 2001 (%)**

Source: Directorate General of Oil and Gas, cited in *KOMPAS*, 14 April 2001

The government is pursuing policy reforms and implementing legislation aimed at rationalising the use of energy resources. A key aim is to prolong Indonesia's status as a net oil exporter. In October 2001, a law removing Pertamina's exclusive rights over upstream oil development within two years was adopted. Pertamina's monopoly over the distribution of oil products will also be lifted within four years. The Ministry of Mines and Energy will take over the function, currently carried out by Pertamina, of awarding and supervising production-sharing contracts with foreign oil companies. The government also plans to reduce oil-product subsidies as part of its policy to cut the country's budget deficit and restrain the increase in domestic oil consumption. The government plans to use part of the saving in oil subsidies to finance education and poverty alleviation policies.

7.2 Oil product pricing and subsidies

Since the 1970s, the Indonesian government has applied subsidies to various oil products. At present, subsidies are applied to five regulated oil products: motor gasoline, automotive diesel oil, industrial diesel oil, kerosene and heavy fuel oil. These products account for 97% of total oil consumption.

Since January 2002, Pertamina sets the domestic prices of these products each month based on changes in the prices of oil on the international market (Table 7.2). If international oil prices increase, Pertamina can raise domestic prices as long as they remain below ceilings determined by the government. For example, the ceiling price of premium gasoline is currently 1,750 rupiahs ($0.175) per litre. The prices of at least three products—kerosene, automotive diesel and industrial diesel—do not cover production costs. If actual consumption turns out to be

Effective date	*Unleaded gasoline*	*Regular gasoline*	*Kerosene*	*Automotive diesel*	*Industrial diesel*	*Heavy fuel oil*
1 January	–	1,450	820	900	740	616
17 January	2,200	1,550	1,230	1,150	1,110	925
1 March	2,200	1,550	1,270	1,150	1,120	950
1 April	2,300	1,600	1,310	1,250	1,240	1,030
3 May	2,400	1,750	1,410	1,400	1,390	1,120
1 June	2,400	1,750	1,410	1,400	1,390	1,150
1 July	2,400	1,750	1,320	1,350	1,320	1,110
1 August	2,400	1,735	1,290	1,325	1,300	1,090
1 September	2,400	1,690	1,390	1,360	1,340	1,150
1 October	2,500	1,750	1,520	1,440	1,420	1,150
1 November	2,500	1,750	1,650	1,550	1,520	1,150

Table 7.2 **Evolution of regulated oil product prices during 2002 (rupiahs per litre)**

Source: www.pertamina.com/indonesia/head_office/hupmas/news/news-awal-english.htm

higher than budgeted for, the government must either increase subsidies or allow Pertamina to increase its prices if the company is to avoid making financial losses. However, raising prices would add to inflation and might trigger social unrest.

A 10% VAT is currently applied to all products. A 5% motor tax is also levied on sales of gasoline and automotive diesel. These taxes only partly offset the effect of subsidies.

7.3 Cost of oil subsidies

The financial cost of the subsidies for the five regulated oil products in 1999—measured as the difference between their true market value and actual selling prices—was about $4.9 billion. This was equal to over a quarter of the government's operating expenditures. The government's own estimates, which are derived from a financial or accounting-based calculation, show the total amount of subsidy to be about 27 trillion rupiahs or $ 3.4 billion in 1998. Spending on oil subsidies increased from around 53 trillion rupiahs in 2000 to 63 trillion rupiahs in 2001, despite an across-the-board increase in oil prices in October 2000. The price of gasoline, which accounts for the largest share of total oil subsidies, has increased dramatically in recent years as a result of higher international prices (Fig. 7.1). The fall in the rupiah against the dollar since the 1997 financial crisis has boosted the market value of oil products consumed domestically and has, therefore, increased the size of subsidies.

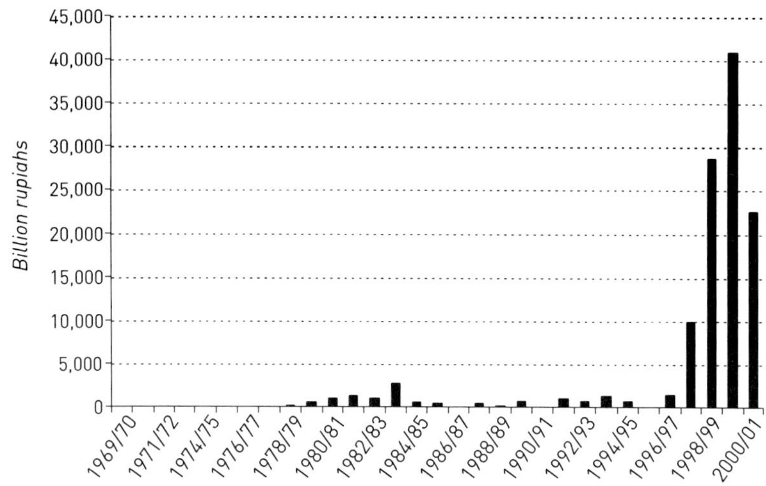

Figure 7.1 **Gasoline subsidies in Indonesia, 1970–2001**

The government plans to reduce subsidies rapidly in line with its International Monetary Fund commitments. The 2002 state budget allocated 32.3 trillion rupiahs (about $3.8 billion) to oil subsidies, while the revised 2003 budget allocates only 14.5 trillion rupiahs. To achieve this reduction, oil prices were increased in January and September 2002. Subsidies are due to be phased out completely in 2004. If the subsidies had been left unchanged, the financial costs between 2000 and the end of 2005, based on current international prices, would have amounted to about $36 billion.

The loss in economic efficiency in terms of the fall in the aggregate welfare of consumers and producers resulting from these subsidies has been large.[31] The net economic cost in 1999 is estimated at about $1 billion. The losses for kerosene alone were about $700 million. On current trends losses would reach almost $2 billion per year by 2005.

These costs are manifested in various ways. Cheap oil has encouraged excessive consumption and undermined incentives to conserve it. Over-consumption has also reduced the country's export potential, reducing foreign exchange earnings. Indeed, if subsidies are not reduced, Indonesia will become a net oil-importing country by 2010. Furthermore, subsidies have led to smuggling of oil as neighbouring country prices are at least 80% higher than domestic prices. Oil subsidies have also undermined the development of the domestic gas industry.

This study has not quantified the costs resulting from relative price distortions. However, such costs are thought to be substantial, as a result of distorted consumption patterns and the subsequent misallocation of resources. Such distortions are particularly costly in the refining sector. For example, major investments in refiner-

31 See Chapter 2, Section 2.2 for a discussion of welfare losses caused by subsidies.

ies have had to be made to boost production of automotive diesel to meet surging demand.

Oil products are subsidised primarily for social reasons. They are intended to make energy more affordable for low-income groups. In practice, however, high-income groups and large manufacturers have been the principal beneficiaries of these subsidies. The biggest subsidy goes to kerosene, the main consumers of which are households.

7.4 Economic and fiscal benefits of subsidy reform

Removing oil subsidies would enhance Indonesia's growth prospects through greater allocative efficiency and fiscal benefits, although there would be significant adjustment costs in the short term. Higher energy prices would raise the cost of living and producer costs. The cost of living would rise directly and indirectly, through the effect of increased fuel-input costs on the price of consumer goods. The net increase may be slightly higher for producer costs. However, the increase in prices is not expected to have a major impact on the inflation rate, which has been high in the past few years.

Eliminating oil and other energy subsidies would improve the national budget balance substantially. In addition, removing subsidies would provide Indonesia with a hedge against exchange-rate fluctuations. This is crucial, since about two-thirds of the recent rise in the external debt was due to the fall in the value of the rupiah. If the subsidies were not reduced, the government would need to spend about $36 billion between 2000 and 2005. The value of lost foreign exchange earnings due to over-consumption of fuels would be about $16 billion.

7.5 Environmental benefits of reform

Eliminating subsidies would also bring significant environmental benefits. Measures to combat pollution and the harmful effects of energy use adopted over the years in Indonesia have been overwhelmed by rising energy use encouraged by subsidies. Subsidies have led to over-consumption of oil products, particularly transport and industrial fuels, resulting in serious environmental consequences. Chief among these are increases in emissions of particulate matter, lead and nitrogen oxides, which are responsible for respiratory illnesses—the sixth leading cause of death in Indonesia. Pollution is especially bad in Jakarta. Emissions of climate-destabilising carbon dioxide have also increased.

These environmental problems provide grounds not just for eliminating subsidies but for levying taxes on oil products—especially automotive fuels. Fuel taxes would need to be applied nationally to avoid arbitraging of products among regions. A comprehensive study of fuel taxation is needed.

7.6 Social benefits of subsidy reform

Only a small amount of the subsidies to oil products currently reaches the poor in Indonesia. The poor, defined as those people living on less than $2 per day, represent almost 20% of the population; and the near-poor, those living on between $2 and $3 per day, another 10–12%, according to 1998 data. But they consume only about 10 million barrels of kerosene out of about 65 million consumed each year. This is because the poor use kerosene mostly used for lighting. Only half of the urban poor use kerosene for cooking; the rest use fuelwood. About 20 million barrels were used in the non-household sector in 1998, and the remaining 35 million were consumed by middle- and high-income households. In 1999, only about $260 million, or roughly 15% of the total kerosene subsidy of about $1.75 billion, reached the poorest 30% of the population.

Thus, removing subsidies would, at the aggregate level, affect high-income households more than the poor. However, experience in other countries has shown that the poor suffer more in relative terms since a greater proportion of their budget is spent on fuel. Therefore, some sort of safety net is essential. But the cost of such a safety net would be significantly less than the current cost of oil subsidies.

7.7 Implementing reforms

The government recognises the need to reduce subsidies, but in a way that does not harm the welfare of the poorest households. The implementation of a scheme that targets subsidies at the poor is one possible approach. In addition, the government could allocate at least part of the savings from the removal of oil as well as power subsidies to programmes for alleviating poverty, expanding access to education, improving public transportation and health services and other social programmes. Direct income support would be much more effective than indirect support such as oil subsidies. Direct payments to the poor should be clearly identified in the national budget.

Both the government and the House of Representatives have agreed to implement a two-tiered pricing policy for oil products. This plan ensures that the prices of kerosene for low-income groups and fuel for public transportation are not increased. The government has also proposed a coupon system, whereby coupons would be allocated to eligible holders giving them the right to buy kerosene at a subsidised price. However, this proposal is unlikely to work well in practice. The administration costs would be excessive as it involves too many institutions. And abuses of the system, including the production of fake coupons, the distribution of coupons to unintended recipients and the resale of coupons for profit, would undoubtedly be a major problem.

8
Energy subsidies in Korea

The current system of energy subsidies in Korea distorts energy markets and runs counter to the country's energy policy goals of enhancing energy security, promoting economic development and protecting the environment. Fundamental reform of energy subsidies, as well as of the system of energy taxation, is needed urgently. Coal mining and new and renewable technologies are the main recipients of direct subsidies. Subsidies to coal mining amount to around $500 million per year. There are major cross-subsidies in the electricity and gas industries, too. Differential tax rates on oil products, which are much more highly taxed than other energy sources, also distort the energy market.

Energy subsidy and tax reforms will need to minimise potential adverse social and economic effects. The benefits of reform are expected to outweigh the costs. The question is how to implement reforms in a socially equitable way. Reforms that benefit mainly the rich would be difficult to justify, no matter how great the resulting gains in economic and energy efficiency.

8.1 Introduction

There are major subsidies in the Republic of Korea's energy sector. Coal mining and new and renewable technologies are the main recipients of direct subsidies. There are major cross-subsidies in the electricity and gas industries, too. These subsidies distort inter-fuel competition. Differential tax rates on oil products, which are much more highly taxed than other energy sources, also distort the energy market. Taxation, rather than direct subsidies or price controls, is the primary form of government intervention in the Korean energy market. Tax revenue is used to secure stable supplies of energy as well as to enhance economic development.

Korea has limited energy resources, so it relies heavily, and increasingly, on imported energy.[32] Securing a stable supply of low-priced energy to support eco-

32 Imports as a share of total primary energy supply grew steadily from 47.5% in 1970 to 97.1% in 1998.

nomic growth has, therefore, been a key objective of Korea's energy policy since the 1960s. The government uses a diverse array of subsidies and differential tax rates to help achieve this goal.

The 1997 financial crisis, which drove the Korean economy into a recession unparalleled since the 1960s, caused a dramatic slump in primary energy use. In 1998, consumption fell by 8.1%—even more than GDP, which fell by 5.8%. This was a sharp turnaround compared to the growth of 5.9% in energy use and 5.0% in GDP in 1997. In 1999, however, the Korean economy bounced back from this recession with energy consumption picking up by 9.3% and GDP by 10.7%. Despite this economic recovery, the government has recognised the need to deal with structural problems in the energy sector. It has launched a programme of restructuring of the energy sector, including privatisation of the state-owned monopoly electricity company, Korea Electric Power Corporation (KEPCO), and is proceeding with a major overhaul of the system of energy subsidies and taxation.

8.2 Energy subsidies

8.2.1 Oil products

The Korean government began to reduce its intervention in the petroleum market in 1983, culminating in the complete deregulation of the prices of oil products, except for LPG, by January 1997. Today, there are no direct subsidies to oil. Oil products remain subject to several taxes, the primary purpose of which is to raise revenue. In 1996, the government replaced the *ad valorem* value-added tax system with fixed-rate duties on final sales of all oil products, except transport fuels. As in most other countries, gasoline is the most heavily taxed product, giving diesel and LPG used by vans and taxis a relative price advantage.

8.2.2 Electricity

Under the Electricity Enterprises Act, the government regulates the prices that KEPCO is allowed to charge for electricity on the basis of the cost of providing service. Prices are meant to reflect the cost of supply plus a fair return on investment. But KEPCO provides a number of public services, such as campaigns to promote electricity savings and extensions to the grid to supply remote areas, which cannot be served profitably. The cost of these public services ranges from $500 million to $670 million per year, and has been rising in recent years. Not all these costs are recovered in KEPCO's tariffs. The government plans to take on these costs directly once KEPCO is privatised.

There are important cross-subsidies in the electricity sector. Prices to residential and commercial customers and schools on average exceed the total cost of supply. Commercial customers are estimated to pay on average 34% more than the economic price. On the other hand, prices to industry cover only 96% of costs, while those to agriculture, including fishing, cover only 48%. The annual subsidy to agriculture and to remote areas amounts to an estimated $113 million (IEA 2002g).

8.2.3 Renewable energy sources

Renewable energy sources and emerging technologies accounted for just over 1% of total primary energy supply (TPES) in 1999. Around 93% of renewables supply comes from waste incineration. The share of renewables in Korea's energy mix is low compared to an average of 1.4% in other OECD countries. Increasing the share would have significant overall positive economic and environmental implications. Lower dependence on conventional fossil fuels would reduce the country's vulnerability to external supply shocks, such as disruption in oil supplies from the Middle East. It could also cut urban air pollution and greenhouse gas emissions.

The Korean government is trying to boost the role of renewables. It subsidises them by providing low-interest loans for new projects, on condition that the loans are paid back within five years.[33] Borrowers also benefit from a three-year grace period. To date, most loans have been used to build facilities or install equipment. Research and development has accounted for only 2.6% of all the money lent. The government is also developing various renewables pilot projects aimed at enhancing public awareness and stimulating the development of a market for them. They are also intended to stimulate private investment.

8.2.4 Coal

While most coal used in Korea is imported, it is also the only fossil fuel found in significant quantities in that country. However, the demand for coal has been falling in recent years as consumers have switched to cleaner and more convenient fuels. Costs are too high to make exports profitable, so production has declined. Nonetheless, the government continues to subsidise the coal industry for social, political and regional economic reasons. Coal mining remains important to employment and to economic activity in the main producing regions.

Direct financial subsidies to the coal industry fell between 1997 and 1999, mainly due to the devaluation of the Korean won. Subsidies have since more or less stabilised at around $500 million per year. The government plans to phase out subsidies gradually by promoting the economic diversification of mining regions through support for other industries such as tourism.

8.2.5 Natural gas[34]

In Korea, natural gas is imported exclusively by KOGAS (Korea Gas Corporation) in the form of liquefied natural gas (LNG). KOGAS operates the country's high-pressure transmission system and sells gas wholesale to local distributors and to large industrial customers and power stations.

33 Until recently, this rate was very attractive compared to the prime rate of 11.1% in 1996, 15.3% in 1997, 11.1% in 1998 and 8.5% in 1999.

34 This subsection draws heavily on SRI Consulting and Korean Energy Economics Institute 1998.

It appears that the prices charged by KOGAS incorporate cross-subsidies between different customer classes. An internal KOGAS report[35] on costs and prices suggests that prices charged to industrial consumers cover only about 30% of total supply costs. Prices for most other customer categories cover more then 80% of costs, while prices for general business consumers and households cover over 100%. The cost–price ratio for power generators is around 80%. The 1998 study by SRI Consulting and Korean Energy Economics Institute also provides evidence of cross-subsidies from households to industry.

8.3 Energy tax reform plan

The Korean government recognises the problems arising from the current system of energy subsidies and cross-subsidies and is taking action to address them. Gradual reform of the energy-tax system, launched in 2001, is intended to complement energy subsidy reform and establish a more rational pricing structure. Tax reform is intended to improve transparency and fairness, promote technological innovation and ultimately strengthen industrial competitiveness, encourage energy conservation and more efficient energy use, and, thereby, improve environmental performance and enhance energy security.

Tax reforms are being gradually implemented over the period from July 2001 to July 2006. In general, the reform plan has so far been implemented on schedule, although a subsidy to taxis and public buses equivalent to the size of the tax increase in 2001 has not been removed as planned. This is because of concerns about the effect of higher LPG and diesel taxes on the taxi and bus businesses.

8.4 Concluding remarks

The current system of energy subsidies in Korea distorts energy markets and runs counter to the country's energy policy goals of promoting economic development and protecting the environment. Fundamental reform of energy subsidies, as well as of the system of energy taxation, is needed.

These reforms will need to minimise the potential adverse social and economic effects. The benefits of energy subsidy reform are expected to outweigh the costs. The question is how to implement the reform in a socially equitable way. Reforms that benefit mainly the rich would be difficult to justify, no matter how great the resulting gains in economic and energy efficiency.

35 Cited in SRI Consulting and Korean Energy Economics Institute 1998.

9
Energy subsidy reform in Iran

Iran spends enormous sums on subsidising energy each year. Those subsidies fail to achieve their objectives. They mainly benefit higher income groups because they consume larger amounts of subsidised energy. Poor households gain little benefit since their energy consumption is generally modest. However, eliminating subsidies would have a dramatic impact on households as well as businesses. This chapter reviews the current system of energy pricing and subsidy policies in Iran and recommends a pragmatic approach to subsidy reform. This would involve gradually raising energy prices to economic levels and developing welfare systems for addressing social objectives in a more direct and efficient way than energy subsidies.

9.1 Economic situation

The Islamic Republic of Iran is the largest economy in the Middle East. Its population of nearly 64 million exceeds the combined total of all the countries in the Persian Gulf. Population has grown on average by more than 2.4% per year during the last two decades, but has recently slowed to 1.5%. After two years of economic stagnation in 1997–99, the Iranian economy recovered following the rebound in world oil prices and the adoption of economic reforms. Higher oil prices have boosted government revenues and facilitated government investment in all sectors. This factor, together with stricter monetary and fiscal policies aimed at controlling credit, curbing inflation and strengthening the foreign exchange market, paved the way for the implementation of economic reforms in the first two years of the Third Five Year Development Plan covering the period between March 2000 and March 2005.

According to preliminary estimates, GDP grew by 5.9% in 2000, due to increases in export-driven oil and manufacturing output and construction. Consumer price inflation fell to an average of under 13% from an average of 20% in 1999. Unemployment in 2000 was about 14%.

9.2 Energy market overview

9.2.1 Energy reserves

Iran has vast oil resources. Proven oil reserves amount to about 79 billion barrels, equal to 9% of the world total. In addition, it has the world's second-largest gas reserves, estimated at 939 trillion cubic feet—about 15% of world reserves. Coal reserves, at 3.6 billion tonnes, are also large, although coal production and use are modest (Table 9.1).

Energy source	*Reserves (billion barrels of oil equivalent)*	*Share of total domestic reserves (%)*
Oil and condensate	100	35.7
Natural gas	162	57.9
Coal	18	6.4
Total	280	100

Table 9.1 **Proven energy reserves in Iran, 2000**

Source: Iranian Ministry of Energy 2000, 2001a

9.2.2 Energy consumption

Total primary energy consumption in 2000 was roughly 886 million barrels of oil equivalent or 13.9 boe per capita. Primary energy use has increased on average by 5.8% annually since 1990. Total final energy consumption in 2000 was about 673 million boe, or 10.6 boe per capita, having increased at an average annual rate of 5.4% over the previous ten years.

Over the last decade, the share of oil in final energy demand has fallen from 72% to 57% while that of natural gas has increased from 19% to 33% (Table 9.2). The residential/commercial sector remains the largest consuming sector, accounting for more than a third of total final consumption. Transport's share of final demand has risen to more than a quarter. Energy intensity, measured as primary energy use per unit of GDP has increased progressively over the last few decades (Fig. 9.1), mainly due to low energy prices and rapid and urbanisation.

	Amount (Mboe)		Share (%)		Annual growth rate 1990–2000 (%)
	1990	2000	1990	2000	
Total	397.0	673.3	100	100	5.4
By sector					
Industry	114.9	168.5	28.9	25.0	3.9
Residential and commercial	122.1	250.3	30.8	37.2	7.4
Transportation	96.2	183.5	24.2	27.3	6.7
Agriculture	29.7	30.9	7.5	4.6	0.4
Non-energy uses	34.0	40.1	8.6	5.9	1.7
By energy type					
Oil	284.6	382.9	71.7	56.9	3.0
Natural gas	74.9	220.5	18.8	32.7	11.4
Electricity	29.6	56.5	7.5	8.4	6.7
Solid fuels	7.9	13.3	2.0	2.0	5.3

Table 9.2 **Final energy consumption in Iran**

Source: Iranian Ministry of Energy 2000, 2001a

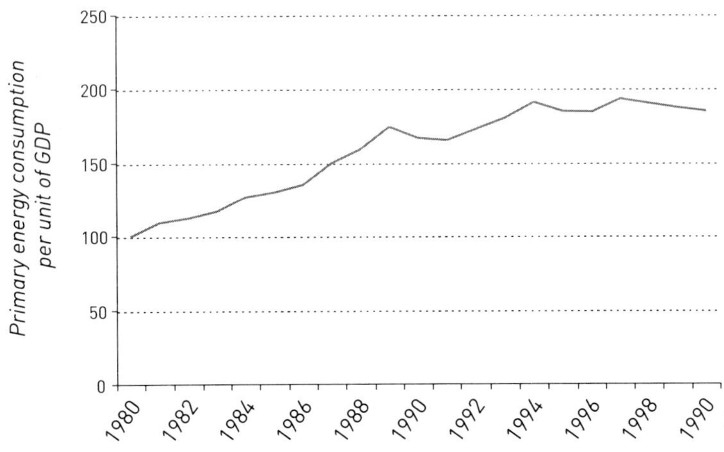

Figure 9.1 **Primary energy intensity in Iran, 1980–2000**

Source: Iranian Ministry of Energy 2000, 2001a

9.2.3 Energy prices and pricing

The prices of all forms of energy, which are set by parliament, are low compared to the underlying costs of supply. The prices of household fuels are kept particularly low to make those fuels more affordable.

Energy prices differ according to the consuming sector. There is a two-tiered pricing structure for oil products for power plants and for other consumers. The retail prices of natural gas and electricity prices are different across the household, industry, commercial and agricultural sectors and for different types of consumer within each sector. Commercial consumers generally pay the highest energy prices, while the agricultural sector pays the lowest. Prices for households and industries are between these two extremes, with household prices below those for industry.

In the face of rapidly increasing energy demand, the government has tried to raise energy prices in recent years. During the Second Development Plan over the period 1995–99, prices increased on average by 20% per year for natural gas and electricity, 37% for gasoline and 50% for gas oil, kerosene and heavy fuel oil. But, since inflation averaged about 20%, only oil prices have increased in real terms. Since the start of the Third Development Plan, energy prices have risen on average by only 10% per year, which is below the inflation rate. Despite resistance from consumers, the government recognises that pricing reform is a key element for improving the efficiency of energy use and supply.

9.3 Energy subsidies

End-user energy prices are well below the full economic cost of supply—border prices for petroleum products and natural gas, and marginal or average cost for electricity. Tables 9.3 and 9.4 provide estimates of the total value of energy subsidies according to consuming sectors and types of energy. The total value of energy subsidies in 2000 was roughly $15.6 billion. The transport sector accounts for the largest share: about a third. Households account for just over a quarter. Gas, oil and electricity are the most heavily subsidised energy types, each receiving more than a quarter of total energy subsidies. Energy subsidies amount to $245 per capita and $1,126 per household.

9.4 Distribution of energy subsidies

One of the main objectives of energy subsidies is to make energy more affordable for poor households who would otherwise be unable to pay the full economic cost. It is therefore necessary to assess the distribution of subsidies among households according to income to determine if subsidies are achieving their intended objective. For this purpose, households have been divided into ten equal groups

	Household	*Industry*	*Agriculture*	*Transport*	*Commercial*	*Others*	*Total*
Gasoline	–	10.1	3.4	2,740.5	0.3	18.2	2,772.4
Kerosene	1,175.3	7.3	33.0	–	22.1	33.9	1,271.6
Gas oil	205.1	599.3	649.8	2,334.8	97.5	211.6	4,098.2
Heavy fuel oil	–	1,547.2	14.5	85.9	184.0	25.7	1,857.3
LPG	400.6	4.3	–	58.0	24.0	–	487.0
Electricity	1,554.4	1,241.1	513.1	–	164.8	535.0	4,008.4
Natural gas	624.8	389.9	–	–	73.4	–	1,088.1
Total	3,960.2	3,799.2	1,213.8	5,219.2	566.2	824.3	15,582.9

Notes: Subsidies are the difference between domestic sales prices and export prices for oil products, actual import prices for natural gas (in 2001, 4.5 million m^3 was imported from Turkmenistan) and average supply costs for electricity. The exchange rate used for these calculations is 8,190 rials per $—the approximate average exchange rate in the free market in 2000.

Table 9.3 **Energy subsidies in Iran, 2000 ($ million)**

Source: Iranian Ministry of Energy 2001a

	Household	*Industry*	*Agriculture*	*Transport*	*Commercial*	*Others*	*Total*
Gasoline	–	0.1	0.0	17.6	0.0	0.1	17.8
Kerosene	7.5	0.0	0.2	–	0.1	0.2	8.2
Gas oil	1.3	3.8	4.2	15.0	0.6	1.4	26.3
Heavy fuel oil	–	9.9	0.1	0.6	1.2	0.2	11.9
LPG	2.6	0.0	–	0.4	0.2	–	3.1
Electricity	10.0	8.0	3.3	–	1.1	3.4	25.7
Natural gas	4.0	2.5	–	–	0.5	–	7.0
Total	25.4	24.4	7.8	33.5	3.6	5.3	100.0

Table 9.4 **Breakdown of energy subsidies by sector and energy type, 2000 (%)**

Source: Iranian Ministry of Energy 2001a

based on their annual expenditure or income. Households within the first group represent the poorest social group. Households in the tenth group correspond to the richest members of society.

Although the poor benefit from energy subsidies, their financial value will usually be small since their energy consumption is generally modest. Richer households tend to benefit much more since they consume a larger share of subsidised energy. This is most evident with oil products, because their prices do not vary in line with consumption.

The distribution of energy subsidies among urban household income groups is highly inequitable. This is especially true for gasoline and gas oil (Figs. 9.2 and 9.3). For example, in 1996, the amount of gasoline subsidy that went to the highest income group was 57 times greater than the amount received by the lowest income group. By 2000, the ratio had increased to 78. In the case of gas oil, while the 10% of urban households with the lowest incomes receive only 0.1% of the subsidy, the highest income group received 42% of the total. The distribution of gasoline and gas oil subsidies among rural households is just as unequal. Rural households with the lowest income receive 0.2% of gasoline subsidies and 0.4% of gas oil subsidies; the wealthiest households receive 39% and 39% respectively (Iranian Ministry of Energy 2001b).

Subsidies for some energy types such as kerosene (Fig. 9.4) of LPG are more evenly distributed. For example, the wealthiest urban households receive only 12% of kerosene subsidies and 11% of LPG subsidies. The poorest 10% of households receive 6% of kerosene subsidies and 7% of LPG subsidies.

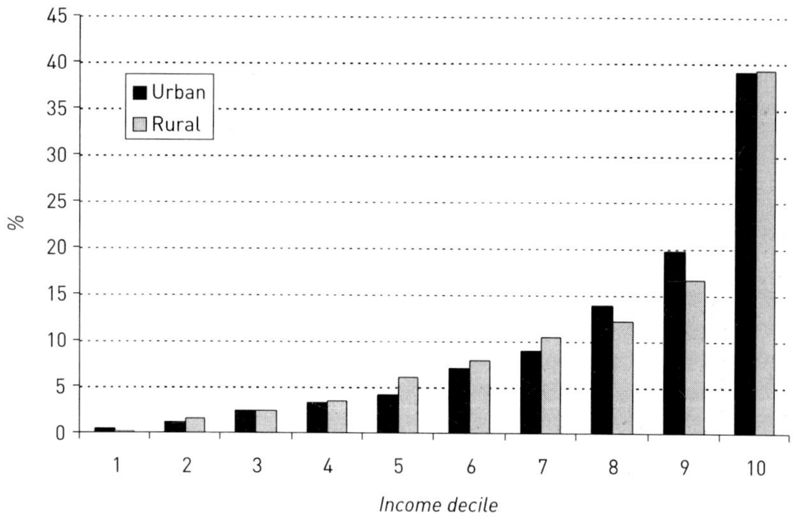

Figure 9.2 Distribution of gasoline subsidies among households by income decile, 2000

Source: Iranian Ministry of Energy 2001a

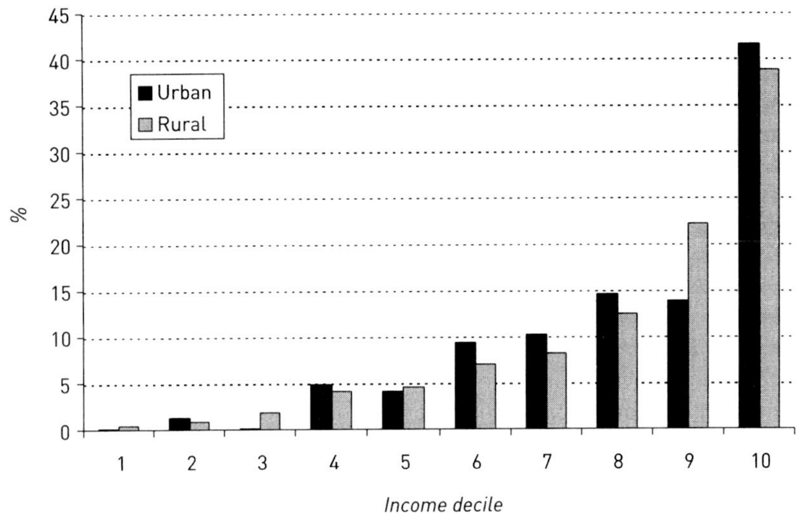

Figure 9.3 **Distribution of gas oil subsidies among households by income decile, 2000**

Source: Iranian Ministry of Energy 2001a

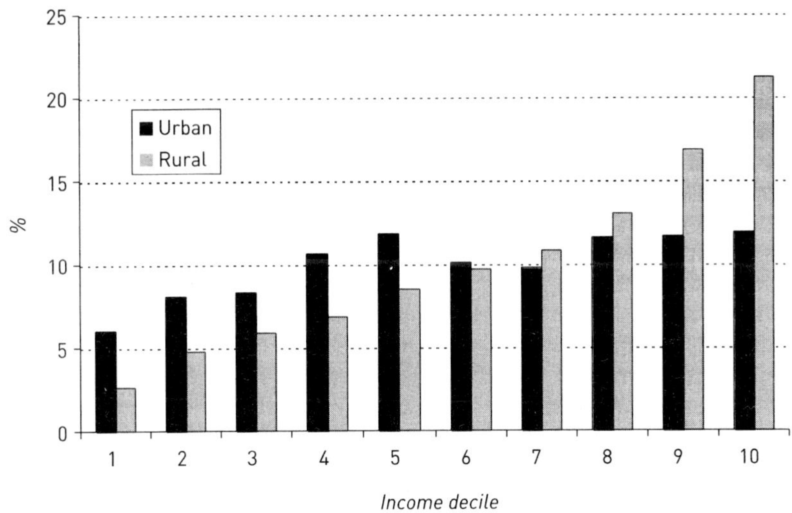

Figure 9.4 **Distribution of kerosene subsidies among households by income decile, 2000**

Source: Iranian Ministry of Energy 2001a

9.5 Inflationary impact of increasing energy prices

Increasing energy prices to eliminate subsidies has two kinds of inflationary effect on the economy. First, it increases the direct energy expenditures of households. Second, by raising the input prices of energy, it increases the production cost of other goods and services. This also indirectly affects household spending.

The direct and indirect effects of higher energy prices on general price levels in the economy as a whole have been calculated using the findings from an energy input–output table. The results of the analysis show that increasing energy prices by 10% (14% for natural gas) in 2000 contributed 1.1% to the increase in the consumer price index (Table 9.5). Increasing gas oil price had the greatest effect on inflation, causing a 0.4% increase. The 10% increase in the gasoline price alone increased the inflation rate by 0.3%. Increasing the prices of natural gas, fuel oil and kerosene had a relatively small impact on inflation.

		Sales prices (rials/unit)			
	Unit	**1999**	**2000**	**Change 1999–2000 (%)**	***Inflationary effects (%)***
Kerosene	litre	100	110	10.0	0.14
Fuel oil	litre	50	55	10.0	0.07
Gasoline	litre	350	385	10.0	0.29
Gas oil	litre	100	110	10.0	0.43
Electricity	kWh	80.3	88.5	10.2	0.18
Natural gas	cubic metre	47.2	53.8	14.0	0.05
Total	–	–	–	–	1.15

Table 9.5 **The inflationary effects of raising energy prices, 2000**

Source: Iranian Ministry of Energy 2001a

Increasing energy prices in 2000 has raised overall spending by urban households by an estimated 1.1% and by rural households by 1.3% (Table 9.6). The impact was greater for rural households because of the larger share of energy in their total spending and because of the larger share of kerosene and gas oil in their energy mix. But the increase in prices and spending was far below the general inflation rate of 20% (see Section 9.2.3). It is estimated that removing subsidies totally would have increased urban household spending on energy by 80% and rural household spending by 100% in nominal terms.

Households	*Kerosene*	*Fuel oil*	*Gasoline*	*Gas oil*	*Electricity*	*Natural gas*	*Total*
Urban	0.11	0.07	0.29	0.41	0.19	0.04	1.10
Rural	0.21	0.07	0.30	0.49	0.16	0.06	1.29

Table 9.6 **Impact of energy price increases on total household spending, 2000 (%)**

Source: Iranian Ministry of Energy 2001a

9.6 Problems caused by energy subsidies

Iran is currently in the midst of a major programme of economic reorientation and social and institutional reform. In March 2000, the parliament approved the Third Development Plan, which sets out the framework for economic reforms and social priorities over the five years to 2005. Substantial progress has been made in the implementation of these reforms. In preparing the Third Development Plan, the Iranian authorities consulted with a wide range of stakeholders on the objectives of the country's energy policy and how they could be achieved. Energy subsidies were identified as a major cause of inefficiency in the energy sector. Ways in which these inefficiencies are manifested include the following:

- Insufficient cash flow to finance investment needs
- Cross-border smuggling of oil products to neighbouring countries
- Rapid growth in energy demand and related problems, such as pollution, lower energy exports and increasing imports
- Distortions in demand across different types of energy caused by large, arbitrary differences in prices. The current price of gasoline, for example, is approximately four times that of gas oil and kerosene.
- Weak incentives for consumers to use energy efficiently and minimise environmental damage

These problems have worsened in recent years as subsidies have grown larger. In addition, energy subsidies are failing to achieve stated social policy objectives.

Iran's overall economic reform strategy is based on a two-pronged approach. First, the government intends to promote a more competitive economy by liberalising the pricing system, including that for energy, and moving towards market-based pricing to achieve a more efficient allocation of resources. Second, the strategy involves legal and institutional reforms to promote the development of private-sector participation, restructuring and privatisation of public enterprises and reform of the financial sector.

The reform of the pricing system includes:

- Unification of the multiple exchange-rate system and a move towards market determination of exchange rates
- Trade liberalisation, including lowering high non-tariff barriers and streamlining tariffs
- Moving away from the system of administratively determined credit allocation and negative real interest rates, toward competitive allocation of credit
- Reform of energy subsidies

Energy price adjustments have, however, proven to be a highly sensitive topic politically, because of their importance to the population, the difficulty in developing comprehensive criteria to identify target groups and fears about the shock to the economy that raising energy prices to economic levels would cause. As a result, proposals for raising energy prices presented to parliament since 2000 have been rejected. Many public and private organisations, however, are continuing to evaluate and examine the effects of alternative price adjustment strategies, while developing compensation strategies that would cushion the effects of energy price reform.

9.7 The environmental effects of energy subsidies

This section briefly considers the impact of energy subsidies on airborne emissions.[36] Gasoline and gas oil, which are mainly used in the transport sector, produce most air pollutants in Iran. It has been calculated that roughly 98% of carbon monoxide (CO) and 74% of unburned hydrocarbons released into the air come from gasoline use. Gas oil accounts for 48% of NO_x, 81% of suspended particulate matter (SPM) and 35% of SO_2 emissions. Figure 9.5 shows the estimated airborne emissions of these pollutants from the use of energy by end-use sector.

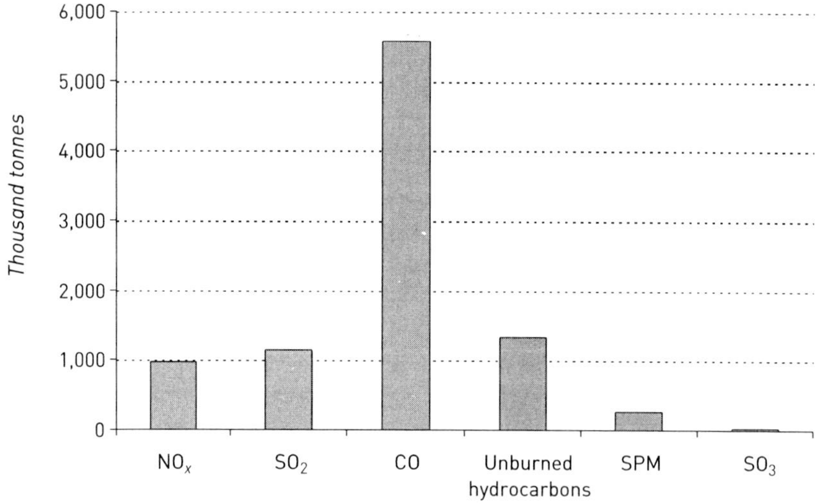

Figure 9.5 **Energy-related airborne emissions in Iran, 2000**

36 It should be noted that energy subsidies sometimes have a positive effect on other aspects of the environment. For example, low prices of fossil fuels encourage rural households to consume these fuels instead of fuelwood, thereby discouraging deforestation.

The estimated social costs of the main air pollutants—NO_X, SO_2 and CO_2—from the use of energy are shown in Table 9.7. Total costs amounted to over $14 billion in 2000. CO_2 contributes to about half of this amount. More than 40% of these costs come from the transport sector.

	NO_x	SO_2	CO_2	*Total*	*Share (%)*
Household	287.9	41.9	1,424.6	1,754.4	12.3
Commercial	205.5	94.6	377.3	677.4	4.8
Industry	850.3	270.4	1,490.4	2,611.0	18.3
Agriculture	398.6	59.8	259.4	717.8	5.1
Transportation	3,738.6	249.5	1,766.1	5,754.3	40.4
Power plants	712.4	287.0	1,717.5	2,716.9	19.1
Total	6,193.3	1,003.1	7,035.3	14,231.6	100.0
Share	43.5	7.0	49.5	100.0	–

Table 9.7 **Social costs of the main air pollutants by sector in Iran, 2000 ($ million)**

Source: Iranian Ministry of Energy 2000, 2001a

9.8 Implementation of subsidy reforms

Currently, experts and policy-makers are faced with many difficult issues in reforming energy subsidies in Iran. These include the following:

- What is the *correct* level of energy prices and how can they be estimated?
- How are subsidies distributed, by energy type and by consumer sector?
- What are the short- and long-run effects of reforming or removing subsidies on the economy, including the inflation rate, household spending and government revenues?
- Should prices be raised to economic levels gradually or suddenly? If the latter, should reform be undertaken in all sectors simultaneously or on a sector-by-sector basis?
- Which social groups should be compensated for the loss of income that reducing or removing subsidies would involve?
- What would be an appropriate amount of compensation and what would be the best method of payment?

Reform is needed urgently. If subsidies are not reduced soon, Iran's exports of crude oil will decline rapidly as production will be unable to keep pace with soaring domestic consumption. Additionally, in view of the detrimental economic and environmental effects of energy subsidies and the impact their removal would have on income distribution and social welfare, subsidy reform needs to be implemented. The aim should be to increase energy prices progressively to economic levels while compensating consumers that stand to lose out most through more direct and efficient welfare payments.

This approach differs fundamentally from that so far considered by the government, which has never seriously considered the total elimination of energy subsidies. The policy at present is to seek ways of channelling subsidies more effectively to targeted groups.

10
LPG subsidies in Senegal

The objective of the Liquefied Petroleum Gas Programme in Senegal, launched in the early 1970s, was to substitute part of the charcoal consumed in urban areas with LPG. Government support initially involved exemptions from customs duties on equipment connected with butane. In 1987, fuel subsidies were introduced on the fuel itself. As the programme developed, cooking equipment was also subsidised. The programme led to a remarkable boom in LPG consumption, which grew from less than 3,000 tonnes in 1974, to 15,000 tonnes in 1987 and nearly 100,000 tonnes today. Nearly 85% of households in the capital city, Dakar, and 66% of those in the other main urban areas now own LPG stoves. Although the programme has not succeeded in fully replacing other fuels, it has at least encouraged some diversification of cooking fuels and brought significant environmental benefits. However, subsidies are now being phased out gradually because of their high financial cost.

10.1 Country profile

With a surface area of 196,722 km², Senegal is a flat, low-lying country situated in the extreme western part of Africa. The country has a semi-arid tropical Sudano-Sahelian climate, with a relatively narrow temperature span. The rainy season is limited to a single summer monsoon. Rainfall has declined significantly in the last three decades. It fluctuates widely from year to year and from one region to another, ranging from just over 1,000 mm/year in the southern part of the country to less than 250 mm/year in the northern part. As a consequence, vegetation varies from bushy steppes in the north to forest stands in the south and south-east. The central part of the country consists of Sudano-Sahelian and Sudano-Savannah terrain. Senegal's soils are dry and sandy in the north, ferrous in the central regions and lateritic in the south. In general, soil fertility is very poor and the soil is extremely vulnerable to wind and other forms of erosion.

In 1998, the population of Senegal was estimated at around 9 million. It is growing at an annual rate of 2.9%. At this rate, the population will double every 25 years. Some 65% of the population is concentrated on 14% of the national territory. The national average population density is 44 inhabitants per km^2. The largest urban centre is the Dakar area, with 23% of the total population and an average density of 3,659 inhabitants/km^2. Urbanisation in that area continues to increase steadily, causing many social problems such as unemployment and poor sanitation. Social services are saturated and urban poverty is growing.

Over the last ten years, the Senegalese economy has experienced a two-phased evolution:

- The period from 1990 to 1993 was characterised by poor macroeconomic performance, despite the implementation of IMF structural adjustment policies.
- The period since 1994 has been marked by a clear economic recovery. GDP growth has stabilised at between 5% and 6%. Most sectors have performed well. Inflation fell to 1.9% in 2000 and the government has tightened control over the public finances.

Senegal has a modest but relatively diversified energy resource base. However, exploitation of those resources is associated with major environmental problems in the case of forest-based wood and charcoal. It also requires substantial investment in the case of fossil fuels and renewables, especially hydroelectricity, solar and wind power.

Senegal is largely dependent on imported oil products for its energy needs. Modest amounts of oil (just under 70,000 barrels between 1996 and 2000) and natural gas (235 million m^3 over the same period) are produced from Diam-niadio Kabor near Dakar. All the gas is used for power generation. There is no residential gas distribution network in Senegal. The country's hydropower potential, based on the Senegal and Gambia rivers, is estimated at about 1,000 MW, capable of producing 280 GWh in an average year. The Organisation pour la Mise en Valeur du Fleuve Senegal (OMVS) is building a dam on the Senegal River in Mali.

The potential supply of wood energy is not well known. In 1980, woodland was estimated at 12 million hectares, covering 60% of the country. Closed and open forests represent 20% of the woodlands and Savannah, while steppes represent 80%. Depending on the source and assumptions used, total productivity was estimated for that same year to be between 8.6 and 13.4 million m^3 per year. Availability was estimated in 1980 at 7.3 million m^3 per year. According to the Plan RENES 2000, some 80,000 hectares of forest disappear each year due to land clearing for agriculture, bush fires, production of charcoal and fuelwood, overgrazing, and lack of rainfall (Direction de l'Energie 1991). Annual deforestation for charcoal production alone is estimated at more than 30,000 hectares/year.

According to International Energy Agency data, total final energy consumption in Senegal in 2000 was 2.4 Mtoe (IEA 2002e). Per capita energy consumption of 240 kg of oil equivalent is relatively high compared with most West African countries. Forest-based traditional fuels, such as fuelwood and charcoal, and agricultural residues used mainly by households for cooking represented 54% of final energy consumption. Oil products account for 41% and electricity a mere 4%. Up-to-date information on charcoal use is not available. In 1992, charcoal consumption was estimated at 330,000 tonnes, equivalent to 1.8 million tonnes of fuelwood. Around three-quarters of this was consumed in the principal urban areas. The conurbation of Dakar alone consumed an estimated 150,000 tonnes.

10.2 Objectives of the LPG Programme

As in other Sahelian countries, discussions about the environment in Senegal since the 1970s have been dominated by concern about declining forest cover, soil erosion and local climate changes. Human activity, including the over-use of grazing and pasture land, the expansion of farming into marginal and ecologically fragile land, bush fires associated with various rural activities and charcoal production, is thought to have contributed to the process of land degradation and changes in the climate in the region.

Against a background of a constantly increasing population, fuelwood consumption towards the end of the 1970s amounted to more than 60% of the country's total energy consumption. This type of consumption, which at that time accounted for about 90% of household energy needs, was extremely detrimental to the country's natural forest cover. The use of fuelwood and charcoal for domestic purposes was increasing most rapidly in urban areas, where population growth was fastest. Deforestation is thought to have accentuated the problem of desertification and drought that ravaged Senegal and other Sahelian countries in the early 1970s.

Charcoal production has other harmful environmental and social effects. A survey of village women carried out in the early 1990s found that about half of them blamed charcoal producers for wood scarcity (Amous 1992). The disappearance of game species, destruction of fodder, conflicts over water rights and social problems were other reasons why more than half the women would prefer local charcoal production to cease. While stopping charcoal production in Senegal would certainly not halt land clearing, and the precise nature of damage to rural environments by this industry is not fully understood, a pervasive impression is that charcoal production is one of the key causes of environmental degradation in Senegal (see World Bank 1989; Cavard and Sokona 1992).

In response to these problems, the government devised strategies aimed at reducing the impact of biomass energy use through inter-fuel substitution, improved efficiency of wood stoves and charcoal kilns, and improved woodland management. The authorities devoted particular attention and priority to measures favouring the intensification of domestic consumption of modern energy sources, particularly of LPG, in urban areas. The promotion of modern fuels to substitute for traditional fuels in household end-uses such as cooking has been a common strategy among many developing countries. Such a strategy has commonly involved fuel and/or equipment subsidies. These subsidies have been justified both by the environmental benefit, including reduced deforestation and indoor pollution, and the support they provide for the incomes of poor households. The LPG (butanisation[37]) programme in Senegal, launched in 1974, aimed to eventually replace 50% of charcoal consumption with LPG in major urban areas through subsidies and promotional campaigns.

10.3 Implementation of the LPG Programme

The Société Africaine de Raffinage (SAR) handles the supply of LPG. It has a legal monopoly on the production and importation of oil products in Senegal. Throughout the 1970s, the SAR refinery at Dakar produced enough to meet local demand, which remained modest. In the 1980s, especially after 1987, LPG consumption surged, outstripping production at the refinery. As a result, it became necessary to import increasing volumes of LPG. Today, three main firms—TotalFinaElf, Shell and Mobil—largely control inland distribution (World Bank/WLPGA 2001).

The growth of LPG use in Senegal has gone through several stages, characterised by shifts on government measures affecting both supply and demand:

- In July 1974, a so-called 'popular adapted gas' cook-stove model, the Blip Banekh, for use with a 2.75 kg capacity gas bottle was launched on the market. All import duties were removed on the bottle and cooker. The gas, which was not subsidised, was also sold in larger 12.5 kg and 38 kg cylinders, and in bulk.
- From 1976, the government decided to subsidise the 2.75 kg gas cylinders but withdrew the tax exemption on imported equipment. There were, nonetheless, several price increases in the late 1970s and early 1980s due to the increase in world oil prices, exchange-rate fluctuations and domestic inflation.
- From 1983, in response to the needs of large families, a new cooker model, the Nopalé, adapted to fit a 6 kg capacity cylinder, was launched on the market.
- During the period 1985–86, as part of the Structural Adjustment Plan, the government decided to cushion the global drop in oil prices for consumers, resulting in the effective removal of subsidies on LPG sold in smaller bottles.
- In July 1987, the government, while introducing a new price structure for gas, decided to revive LPG subsidies.
- In March 1998, a new law setting the framework for the reform of oil product pricing was adopted. This law provides for the complete liberalisation of the oil sector and the removal of monopolies, the stimulation of competition and the elimination of oil price regulation. The gradual

37 LPG used in Senegal is primarily made up of butane.

elimination of LPG subsidies, due to their rising financial cost, forms part of this new policy. LPG subsidies were gradually reduced in 20% steps beginning in 1998 (Table 10.1). However, the government did not complete the process of phasing out subsidies in mid-2002 as planned, because of negotiations within the West African Economic Union over harmonisation of economic policies. One objective of the new policy is to promote kerosene as a household fuel, particularly for cooking purposes.

Stage	Date change in subsidy takes effect	Subsidy to 6 kg cylinders (fcfa/tonne)	Subsidy to 2.75 kg cylinders (fcfa/tonne)
1	1 July 1998	168,652	159,603
2	1 July 1999	126,489	119,702
3	1 July 2000	84,326	79,802
4	1 July 2001	42,163	39,901
5*	1 July 2002	0	0

* Suspended

Table 10.1 **LPG subsidy removal plan in Senegal, 1998–2002**

Source: Iranian Ministry of Energy 2000, 2001a

10.4 Impact of the LPG Programme

National consumption of LPG has risen steadily since the LPG Programme was launched in 1974. Sales reached around 100,000 tonnes in 2000 compared to less than 3,000 tons at the start of the programme. By 1979, the amount of gas sold in 2.75 kg cylinders was almost twice as much as that sold in all other cylinder sizes. Consumption shifted to the 6 kg cylinder after its introduction in 1983: this size today represents the overwhelming bulk of total sales, while the other smaller 'popular' cylinders account for most of the rest (Fig. 10.1). Annual consumption of gas in larger, 'traditional' cylinders (12.5 kg and above) is flat at around 4,000 tonnes.

Demand has nonetheless slowed since 1999 in response to price increases caused by the devaluation of the CFA franc (fcfa) in 1998, the phase-out of subsidies and higher international oil prices. The annual growth rate of sales in the 'popular' 2.7 kg cylinder exceeded 12% in 1974–98, peaking at 57% in 1988. The price of that cylinder size rose from 121 fcfa/kg to 158 fcfa/kg in 1998, an increase of 31%. However, this was not accompanied by any significant reduction in the rate of growth in sales, which remained at 13%. A 20% cut in subsidies in 1999 had the effect of increasing the price again, to 173 fcfa/kg in July, 202 fcfa in September and 209 fcfa/kg in November. Two further subsidy reductions in 2000 resulted in an increase in the price to 249 fcfa/kg. Demand growth slowed to 10.5% in 1999, 4.5%

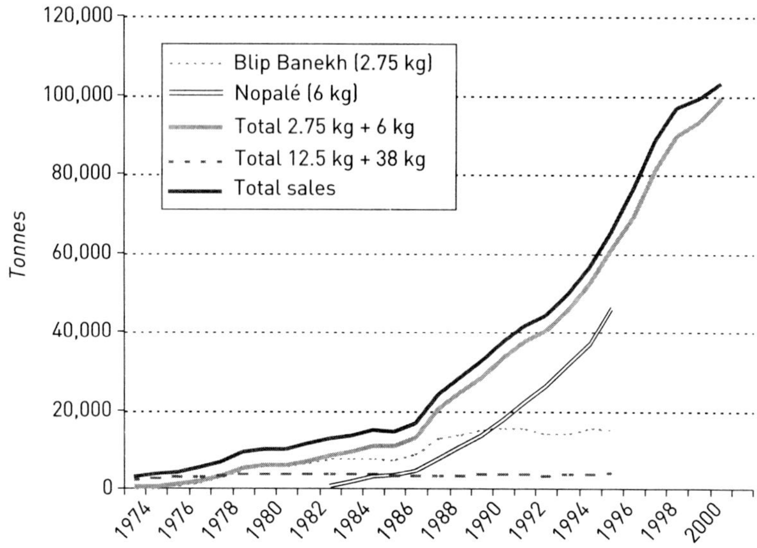

Figure 10.1 **LPG consumption in Senegal by bottle size, 1974–2000**

Source: Groupement des Professionnels du Pétrole

in 2000 and 6.2% in 2001, compared to annual increases of between 13% and 17% between 1994 and 1997.

It is very difficult to estimate how much the growth in LPG use has affected the consumption of traditional fuels, particularly charcoal. Statistics on charcoal production, supply and consumption are not reliable. However, deliveries of fuelwood in Dakar have visibly declined as LPG deliveries have risen. Over the years, the LPG programme has clearly modified household energy use patterns in urban areas.

As in most African countries, a comprehensive model of energy consumption does not exist in Senegal. Extreme disparities in income and lifestyles, particularly between cities and rural areas, mean that energy consumption patterns, particularly the role of modern fuels, vary enormously. Fuelwood use in Dakar, for example, is now very small. However, the city, with 25% of the country's population, accounts for over 80% of all charcoal use. This is because most of the Senegal's industrial and commercial activities are concentrated there and because charcoal has a higher energy content than fuelwood by weight making it more efficient to transport into the city.

According to estimates provided by the Ministry of Energy (Direction de l'Energie 1991; Ministère de l'Energie et de l'Hydraulique du Sénégal 2000), the growth in LPG use has resulted in annual savings of about 70,000 tonnes of fuelwood and 90,000 tonnes of charcoal. This is equivalent to 700,000 m^3 of wood a year, or 15% of the amount now being collected.

Initially, LPG use was concentrated among rich households in Dakar and its vicinity. Over the years, use of the fuel has spread to poorer households all over Dakar and its distribution is extending slowly into other regions. However, 80% of all LPG sold in Senegal is still consumed in Dakar. On average, more than 50% of urban households now use cookers with gas bottles. In the major western towns, Dakar, Thiès and Mbour, where the price of LPG bottles is lowest because of low transport costs, LPG has become the main cooking fuel. LPG consumed in this zone is transported over short distances, while charcoal is often brought in from as far as 600 km away. In other towns, LPG remains a backup fuel for charcoal and wood. It is estimated that there are over 1.5 million gas cookers (Ministère de l'Energie et de l'Hydraulique du Sénégal 2000; Sow and Sagna 1999: 102).

10.5 Key policy issues

In implementing the LPG Programme, the government encountered a number of problems, notably the following:

- Gas stoves had to be found that were suited to the needs of Senegalese households. The standard gas stove model that was originally available had to be attached to a 12 kg or 38 kg cylinder by a flexible tube and a metal exhaust valve. This was not only too costly for most households but also ill suited to their cooking habits. At an early stage, a gas cooker was designed with the burner screwed directly onto a 2.75 kg gas cylinder. Later, a more robust model was added with a 6 kg cylinder that was better adapted to the cooking habits of average-sized families. For both models, the burner is the only element that has to be imported. The metal cooking pot support, which has been adapted to standard Senegalese cooking utensils and practices, is manufactured locally.
- The removal of duties on imported equipment was not a sufficiently strong incentive to generate any significant consumer interest in switching to LPG. For this reason, the government introduced subsidies on the fuel itself to make using LPG more affordable to low- to middle-income households. Later, unlike other oil products, the government switched between subsidising and taxing LPG, depending largely on the world oil price, to keep end-user prices constant.

In order to achieve the target rate for expanding LPG use, three different price structures were set up, with price revisions every three months: one for 2.75 kg bottles, one for 6 kg bottles and one for large 12.5 kg cylinders. Only the first two sizes were subsidised. The price structure is set by presidential decree on the joint recommendation of the Ministries of Energy and Trade. The general aim was to tax more heavily than other oil products, particularly fuel oil, to make LPG sold in smaller bottles cheaper. The price structure is made up of the ex-refinery price, port dues, a price-stabilisation component (part of the subsidy), a distribution margin and value-added tax.

Effective management of the pricing structure, which provided incentives for distributors to expand sales, made it possible to quickly develop the market in

Senegal. The SAR refinery handles all LPG production and imports. It has a crude oil throughput capacity of 1.2 million tonnes per year. LPG production capacity is limited to around 9,000 tonnes per year. Price liberalisation, which has boosted the profitability of the refinery, should pave the way for modernisation of the refinery in order to produce more LPG. The three main oil companies handle most LPG storage, bottling, distribution and retailing. These companies have invested heavily both in distribution infrastructure and end-use equipment. The construction of new refilling centres in some regions well away from Dakar have helped encourage the development of LPG sales in more remote areas.

The government supplemented its policy of encouraging LPG consumption with measures to rationalise wood resource management. These included regulations concerning the exploitation and use of forest products such as an increase in wood-cutting licence fees, tighter production quotas, the creation of a land-allocation system for charcoal production and a progressive increase in the official sales price of charcoal.

It is not unclear what the long-term effect of the termination of LPG subsidies will have on consumer habits. Consumer associations, non-governmental organisations and the media argued strongly against this move, stressing the damage that an increase in LPG prices could have on the incomes of poor families and, if they go back to using charcoal, the environment. At present, there is no information on the elasticity of demand for LPG in Senegal. Still, it is likely that most housewives will choose to continue using more expensive LPG given the fuel's greater convenience and cleanliness—especially if they have invested heavily in the gas stove and bottle. In this case, higher LPG prices might result in people reducing their consumption of other goods and services.

10.6 Conclusions

Despite the successful introduction of LPG in urban areas in Senegal, particularly in Dakar, fuelwood consumption is still very high. This is largely because LPG consumption remains concentrated in urban areas. Nevertheless, urban LPG use certainly relieves deforestation pressures and fuelwood scarcity in rural areas. A key feature of fuelwood consumption in rural areas is that the villagers themselves collect the wood lying around their villages. As a result, commercial vendors supply only small quantities of charcoal, which is considered a luxury product in rural areas. Charcoal producers that pass through villages collecting deadwood and cutting down trees are largely responsible for deforestation. Village dwellers suffer the consequences, since they are forced to forage for fuelwood further away. Sometimes, they have to cut down trees to meet their immediate cooking energy needs. By reducing urban charcoal demand, LPG has had the beneficial effect of enabling better access to fuelwood in the rural areas. Improving rural access to LPG would bring further environmental and social benefits.

The LPG Programme in Senegal inspired the launch in the late 1980s of a similar programme in the Sahel region, financed by the European Economic Community

(EEC) and implemented by the Interstate Committee for Drought Control in the Sahel (CILSS). The objective of the programme was to contribute to the efforts being deployed to combat desertification by encouraging the substitution of LPG for fuelwood. The money provided by the EEC was used to provide subsidies for the type of equipment used in Senegal to the firms distributing LPG and to fund an awareness-raising campaign. LPG consumption in the nine countries was targeted to rise from 27,000 tonnes in 1987 to 66,000 tonnes in 1992 and to 92,000 tonnes by 1996. It was reckoned that meeting these targets would displace 673,000 tonnes of wood, assuming 7.5 tonnes of wood per tonne of LPG consumed. This initiative, which lasted only a short time, yielded very poor results. Although consumption almost reached the target in 1992, the EEC decided to discontinue the programme based on the findings of an external evaluation mission. That evaluation concluded that household fuel substitution in general and LPG in particular was not a priority option in most countries and that the programme had had little impact on the penetration of LPG where distributors were already expanding their activities.

The remarkably rapid development of the LPG market in Senegal resulted both from structural changes in demand for energy and from government policy. Energy use would have shifted to modern fuels in response to urbanisation, rising incomes and increasing scarcity of traditional fuels. But the LPG Programme, in addition to other policy initiatives, accelerated this development. In addition to subsidising LPG prices, the government has also at times implicitly manipulated charcoal prices relative to LPG prices, often by allowing charcoal retail prices to rise well above regulated levels.

LPG has become the principal cooking fuel for most urban households, especially in the Dakar region. However, charcoal will remain an important fuel. Many households still prefer to use charcoal for certain purposes, such as ironing. And poor households still struggle to afford the initial cost of purchasing an LPG cylinder and cooker and the recurring cost of refilling the cylinder. Charcoal is cheaper and can be purchased on a daily basis in smaller quantities than gas.

The Senegalese experience with subsidising LPG demonstrates that rapid switching away from traditional fuels to modern forms of energy does not occur automatically. It requires effective government policies applied over a reasonably long period. Subsidies must also be supported by a number of other measures, including:

- The establishment of a reliable and effective supply system
- The adoption of technology that is appropriate to local needs
- The introduction and enforcement of regulations to discourage deforestation
- Appropriate pricing and taxation policies
- Attractive incentives for distributors and consumers
- An effective information and awareness-raising campaign

11
The impact of removing energy subsidies in Chile

This chapter analyses the economic, environmental and social effects of removing oil product and coal subsidies in Chile applying the computable general equilibrium model, ECOGEM-Chile. Two policies are analysed: the actual removal of a coal subsidy in 1995 in Chile and the hypothetical removal of an implicit subsidy to oil prices between 1999 and 2000. The results show that the removal of oil subsidies would have had negative short-term economic and distributional effects. The elimination of the coal subsidy was broadly beneficial both economically and socially in the short term. Sectoral and distributional effects in each case differ, depending on how each policy is implemented. The environment clearly benefits in both cases since considerable emission reductions of CO, particulate matter and CO_2 are achieved. The results provide empirical evidence of the type and magnitude of the trade-offs faced by policy-makers in Chile when deciding on the desirability of eliminating an energy subsidy.

11.1 Introduction

In Latin America, energy subsidies have been in place for many years for various reasons and in various forms. They are particularly pervasive in the oil-exporting countries, notably Venezuela, Mexico and Ecuador, where petroleum product prices are by far the lowest compared to world market prices (Rogat and Sterner 1998). Consumer subsidies have encouraged the use of fossil fuels—the main cause of CO_2 emissions in Latin America in recent years. The effects of eliminating energy subsidies would vary from country to country depending on several factors, such as natural resource endowments, factor prices and the degree of dependence on oil products.

In this chapter, the economic and environmental effects of removing oil product and coal subsidies are evaluated for Chile using a general equilibrium framework. The removal of oil subsidies is simulated by evaluating the economic and environmental effects that would have occurred had a stabilisation fund for oil prices that reduced the impact of a price increase been eliminated (CNE 2000). The fund effectively subsidised oil product prices by an average 12% over the period August 1999 to June 2000.[38] In the case of coal, the effects of the actual elimination of a subsidy in 1995 are modelled. These effects are then compared to what actually happened after 1995, in order to validate the model.

The computable general equilibrium model, ECOGEM-Chile, is used for this analysis.[39] The model is a static neoclassical type. Its main features are sector multiplicity, labour differentiation, five quintiles of income and 18 production sectors. It includes the three main economic agents—firms, households and government—flows of goods and services, factor payments, international trade and relationships with the environment. Each agent is modelled according to behavioural assumptions such as optimising behaviour among producers and consumers. In addition, each market is modelled based on actual characteristics. For instance, the degree of competition and the rate of unemployment are taken into account. The model reaches equilibrium according to Walrus's law, which equates demand and supply in all markets simultaneously, determining prices and quantities in each market.

11.2 Economic, social and energy issues in Chile

During the 1990s, Chile undertook extensive trade liberalisation reforms and extensive privatisation programmes, promoting exports and open, competitive markets as the main drivers of economic growth. The government deregulated prices, with the exception of public transport and some public utilities and port charges. The government focused its efforts during this period on maintaining macroeconomic stability, improving infrastructure and tackling social problems. The policies applied were very successful. Economic performance in that decade was the strongest of the 20th century. The country grew at an impressive average rate of 8% per year between 1989 and 1998.

Historically, Chile's economy has been based on its natural resources, both renewable and non-renewable. Chile is the world's leading copper and iodine producer and is a growing source of gold, lithium and other non-metallic minerals. Copper is by far the biggest export product, accounting for almost 40% of the country's total exports. This share has fallen, however, from a high of 80% in the 1980s, as a result of export diversification. Exports of agricultural products, fish and forestry products, cellulose and fishmeal have grown very rapidly in the last

38 This subsidy effectively resulted from the sharp increases in oil prices over the period analysed.

39 The model is an adaptation of a model developed earlier by the OECD. See Beghin *et al.* 1996.

decade and are now important export industries. Capital goods and energy make up most of the country's imports.

Poverty declined significantly during the 1990s. The share of households living below the poverty line fell from 45% in 1987 to 22% in 1998 and 21% in 2000. This is a very large reduction for such a short period of time. However, income distribution remains highly uneven. Although the minimum wage has increased faster than the average wage, it was still only $160 per month in 2002—barely twice the poverty line. The richest 20% of households received more than 15 times the income of the poorest 20% in 2000. The Gini coefficient was close to 0.48. The uneven distribution of income has hardly changed in recent decades despite policies to reduce income differentials.

In the 1990s, the government increased spending on social programmes significantly to reduce high levels of poverty. Between 1990 and 1998, public social expenditure grew by 88% (66% in per capita terms), or 8.2% per year. This increase was much higher than the average of 5.5% in Latin America over the same period (UN ECLAC 1999). As a result, social expenditure rose from 61% of total expenditure in 1990 to 70% in 2000. It also grew faster than GDP. Following the basic principles of equal opportunities and an acceptable standard of living for all of the population, social policies have been geared to improving the quality and coverage of health, education and housing programmes. Efforts to promote development in poor rural areas have also been stepped up.

Energy use in Chile has changed in the past few years. The consumption of natural gas has increased sharply since 1997 with the building of four gas pipelines from Argentina and now accounts for almost a quarter of the country's primary energy needs. Gas has replaced coal to a large extent. The competitiveness of coal declined with the elimination of subsidies in 1995. Oil products are still the most important energy source (Table 11.1).

Fuel	**Indigenous production**	**Imports**	**Changes in stocks**	**Consumption**	
				Teracalories	**%**
Oil	2,970	105,054	2,736	105,288	41.0
Natural gas	22,755	40,832	3,277	60,310	23.5
Coal	2,562	30,813	1,248	32,127	12.5
Hydropower	17,289	0	879	16,410	6.4
Wood and solid biomass	42,544	0	0	42,544	16.6
Biogas	51	0	0	51	Negligible
Total	88,171	176,699	8,140	256,730	100.0

Table 11.1 **Primary energy production and consumption for 2000 (teracalories)**

Source: CNE 2002

Electrical generation in Chile is still largely based on hydropower, but thermal plants are growing in importance. In 2000, a drought year, thermal plants accounted for 71% of total generation, compared to only a quarter in 1992. Natural gas-fired combined-cycle gas turbine plants have become a major source of thermal generation, reaching 54% in 2000. The share of coal-based plants in thermal generation has dropped from 92% in 1996 to 38% in 2000.

11.3 Petroleum and coal sectors in Chile

Prior to the launch of reforms in the 1970s, Chile's oil industry was controlled by the state. From 1920 and until 1942, the government was directly responsible for the exploration, production and refining of crude oil and the distribution of oil products. Between 1943 and 1950, these activities were carried out by the state company Corporación de Fomento (CORFO). In 1950, the state company Empresa Nacional del Petróleo (ENAP) was created. Until the middle of the 1970s, ENAP was responsible for operating most of the country's oil industry, either directly or through its subsidiaries. The prices of most oil products, including kerosene and diesel, were kept low.

In the mid-1970s, Chile began major political, social and economic reforms, with major implications for the energy sector. These reforms included a reduced role of the state and increased private participation in productive activities. Energy-sector reform was implemented in two phases. In the first phase, from 1974 to 1977, a process to prepare the necessary economic and financial conditions for the reform in the energy sector was begun. Energy prices were also adjusted to narrow the gap between domestic and international prices. The second phase, from 1978 to 1989, emphasised institutional reforms including the regulatory framework, legal aspects and ownership. In 1978, the National Energy Commission (CNE) was created and given responsibility for developing and implementing radical new energy policies. The distribution of oil products was privatised, and is now carried out by domestic and foreign firms. ENAP is still responsible for exploration and production, importing and refining. According to the UN Economic Commission for Latin America and the Caribbean (ECLAC), the energy reforms have yielded a number of benefits including greater competition, private investment, decentralisation, improved economic efficiency and deregulation of the commercial sales of energy products (see UN ECLAC 1995).

Oil product prices are semi-regulated. Ex-refinery prices are set freely but have to be consistent with the prices of imported products plus a 10% import tax. Estimated transportation, storage and marketing costs are added to ex-refinery prices to yield final retail prices, to which VAT of 18% is then added. Overall taxes are relatively low by international standards. A special duty is levied on this price for diesel and gasoline. In 2002, the tax applied to diesel fuels was 1.5 UTM per 1,000 litres for diesel ($0.23/gallon) and 6.0 UTM per 1,000 litres for gasoline ($0.93/gallon). This duty increases the final price by approximately 22% for diesel and 75% for gasoline.

Coal is not traded openly to the same degree as oil products, so data on prices is more difficult to obtain. This complicates a detailed analysis of the coal market and international comparisons. Indigenous production by four local firms covers only 16% of national demand. Two companies import coal. Total coal consumption in Chile reached 3.6 million tonnes in 2001. Almost two-thirds was used for generating electricity. As with petroleum products, state-owned companies dominate the coal industry. Coal prices in Chile are relatively high. For example, in 1997, the average coal price was $95 per tonne, compared to $54 in Brazil, $52 in the United States and $57 in France.[40]

Until 1995, coal production was subsidised. ENACAR, the state-owned enterprise, paid relatively high wages to coal workers and sold coal at below market prices. The state covered the resulting losses. Subsidies were eliminated in 1995 when the government decided to allow ENACAR to go bankrupt. As a result, domestic coal production fell from 1.7 million tonnes in 1994 to 0.4 tonnes in 1998.

11.4 The petroleum price stabilisation fund

In 1991, the Chilean government created the petroleum price stabilisation fund, FEPP.[41] The purpose of this fund is to cushion domestic oil product prices from international price fluctuations. The government supports the fund by granting loans or by levying taxes, depending on the difference between a predetermined parity price and a reference price for each product. The parity price is calculated every week based on the import price from the previous week and the expected import price for the coming week. The reference price is an average of the international oil price for the last two years, and of projected prices in the medium and long term. An upper and lower limit for the difference between parity and reference price of 12.5% is allowed. If the difference between the parity and reference price is more than 12.5%, the government provides a loan to the fund covering all of the difference. If the difference is less than 12.5%, the government levies a 60% tax on it.

Because international oil prices tended to increase after the creation of the fund, the government was obliged to lend increasing amounts. In 2000, the government injected $62 million. The total amount required to cover the difference between the parity and reference price reached approximately $250 million in the year to June 2000, equivalent to an average subsidy of around 12% on end-user oil-product prices (UN ECLAC 2000).[42] Because of the growing burden on public finances, the government decided in 2000 to reform the fund rules. The new fund was capped and new rules require it to act only as a stabilisation fund and no longer as a subsidy.

40 Database of World Energy Data SA, Grenoble, France.
41 The initial government contribution to the fund was $200 million.
42 This rate of subsidy is net of taxes.

11.5 The ECOGEM-Chile model and data[43]

The static, multiple-sector ECOGEM-Chile model was developed to analyse the impact of policies affecting the whole economy in Chile. It is a neoclassical model, driven by savings. Substitution is allowed between the three main production factors—labour, capital and energy. Substitution is also possible between different forms of energy. The model distinguishes between different categories of labour. Households are divided by income, in this study by quintiles of income. The model also differentiates between trading partners, covering 27 countries and world regions.

Households divide their income between savings and consumption through an extended linear expenditure system (ELES) utility function. Once intermediate demands and household demands are set, remaining final demands—investment, government spending and trade margins—are determined as fixed shares of total final demand.

For this analysis of subsidy reform, the energy-input substitution is very important. It allows emission reductions in each sector to be modelled by changing inputs as well as by reducing output. The mix of inputs as well as outputs determines emissions.[44] There are, therefore, two types of emission coefficient: those related to the use of inputs and those related to the total output of each sector. Total emissions of pollutant p, E_p in the model, are defined as:

$$E_p = \sum_i \upsilon_i^p \cdot XP_i + \sum_i \pi_i^p \left(\sum_j XAp_{ij} + \sum_h XAc_{ih} + \sum_j XFd_{if}\right)$$

where:

XP_i is the total output of sector i.

XAp_{ij} is the intermediate consumption of good i by sector j.

Xac_{ih} is the consumption of commodity i by household h.

XFd_{if} is the consumption of the other final demands f (investment, government expenditure, margins) of commodity.

υ_{ip} is the emission coefficients associated with the output of sector i of pollutant p.

π_{ip} is the emission coefficient associated with the use of commodity i of pollutant p.

The first term represents emissions related to the output of the sector. The second term represents emissions related to the use of intermediate inputs. These have three components: intermediate consumption, household final demand and other final demands. Short- to medium-term elasticities, representing effects in the one- to three-year range, are used.

43 For a detailed discussion of the model, see O'Ryan *et al.* 2000 and Beghin *et al.* 1996.

44 Different production and consumption processes are modelled, generating different amounts of emissions for the same quantity and type of fuel.

The main source of information is the Chilean social accounting matrix (SAM). The SAM was built based on information provided by the Chilean Central Bank (see Venegas 1995; Alonso and Roland-Holst 1995), using the input–output matrix for the year 1992 and reduced to 18 commodities. Labour is divided into skilled and unskilled, and households into five quintiles of income. The matrix is measured in billions of real pesos converted using purchasing power parities (PPP). The emission coefficients for particulate matter (PM10), SO_2, NO_x, CO and volatile organic compounds (VOCs) used in the model are from Dessus *et al.* 1994.[45] The coefficients for CO_2 emissions are from Dessus and O'Connor 1999.

11.6 Impact of eliminating energy subsidies

11.6.1 Effects of eliminating coal subsidies

The effects of eliminating the coal subsidy in 1995 are evaluated using the model. This allows the model to be validated by comparing the results with the economic effects actually observed in the sector. The environmental, distributional and other social effects of this move are also estimated, assuming that the savings of eliminating the subsidy are used either to reduce public debt or to increase transfers to households.

The results are presented in Table 11.2. The overall macroeconomic effects are very small. Investment increases when the savings are not used to increase public spending. Total consumption falls slightly. Other macroeconomic variables also change very little. When the savings are used to increase transfers to households, the effects are even lower.

For most sectors the impact on output is small or negligible. The model estimates that domestic coal production fell by around one half solely as a result of the elimination of the subsidy. Output falls most in the electricity sector, which still relies partly on coal, followed by road transport and manufacturing. On the other hand, the construction industry—in the case where the savings are used to reduce public debt—benefits the most. This is because of an increase in investment, which increases construction activity. However, when the savings are used to increase social spending, output in the hydraulic sector (dam building, water treatment and irrigation) increases most.

The removal of the coal subsidy has a slightly positive impact on income distribution when transfers are used to compensate households. Income increases for all income groups with the exception of the richest, but aggregate income is unchanged. When the savings are not used to pay for increased public spending, income for all groups falls slightly, but the distribution of income is not affected.

46 These were calculated for the United States using information from the IPPS database of the World Bank.

	Variable	*With transfers to households*	*No compensatory increase in public spending*
Macroeconomic	Real GDP	0.0	0.0
	Consumption	0.0	–0.1
	Investment	0.1	0.5
	Exports	0.0	0.1
	Imports	0.1	0.1
	Government savings	0.0	6.2
Sectoral output	Coal	–43.2	–43.3
	Electricity	–0.5	-0.5
	Manufacturing	–0.3	–0.1
	Road transport	–0.2	–0.3
	Construction	0.1	0.4
	Other transport	0.1	0.1
	Oil refinery	0.1	0.1
	Hydraulic	0.3	0.1
Income distribution	I quintile	0.7	–0.1
	II quintile	0.3	–0.1
	III quintile	0.1	–0.1
	IV quintile	0.0	–0.1
	V quintile	–0.1	–0.1
Environment	SO_2	0.1	0.1
	NO_2	0.1	0.1
	CO	–7.8	–7.8
	VOC	0.0	0.0
	PM10	–0.8	–0.9
	CO	–1.2	–1.3

Table 11.2 **Effects of raising oil product prices (% change)**

Source: CNE 2002

The elimination of coal subsidies generates several positive environmental effects. CO emissions fall by nearly 8%. Particulate and CO_2 emissions also decline slightly. SO_2, NO_x and VOC emissions remain broadly unchanged in both cases.

In summary, the policy of eliminating coal subsidies appears to have been beneficial for most sectors. Furthermore the positive effects were enhanced to the extent that the savings were used to boost public spending on social programmes.

11.6.2 Effects of eliminating oil product subsidies

The effects of eliminating existing subsidies on oil product sales were modelled by carrying out two simulations. Both are based on the average subsidy of 12% that prevailed between August 1999 and June 2000. The first simulation assumes that domestic prices rise by an average of 12% in line with the assumed increase in import prices to international levels. The second simulation assumes that the government directly subsidises domestic prices so that they remain stable. There is no change in other types of public spending.

The short- to medium-term results are presented in Table 11.3. The macro-economic effects of raising prices depend on whether a direct subsidy is introduced or not. If so, there is a smaller impact on almost all the macroeconomic variables examined compared to the case with no direct subsidy. The exceptions are the public-sector budget and investment. The latter falls because of a fall in the budget surplus that reduces the overall level of savings and, therefore, investment in the economy. On the other hand, consumption and exports increase. The results are broadly similar across sectors. Were no direct subsidy is introduced, output falls in most sectors. However, with a direct subsidy, output is little changed. The incomes of better-off households are higher with a direct subsidy. By contrast, the environmental effects of raising prices are strongly positive only when a direct subsidy is *not* introduced. This is largely because consumers switch from oil to less-polluting fuels.

It is important to point out that the parameters of the model used allow only short-run effects to be simulated. In the longer run, subsidies may have important negative economic effects since lower investment will have an effect on long-term economic growth. A static model such as ECOGEM does not capture this phenomenon. If subsidies are not eliminated, there is less incentive for the introduction of cleaner energy sources. Furthermore, technological changes involving more-efficient energy use are also discouraged.

These results suggest that there may be significant short-run economic benefits when a subsidy is used to offset increases in oil product prices. Because the economy is generally highly dependent on oil products, a sudden increase in the price of oil products raises production costs in all sectors and, therefore, will tend to depress output and, through lower wages and employment, household income in the short run. However, higher oil prices also bring important environmental benefits through lower consumption.

11.7 Conclusions

Analysing the effects of removing energy subsidies, in this case for oil products and coal, requires careful consideration of the complex interrelations between the various economic actors and sectors, and of the time-horizon considered. Different policies will result in different 'winners' and 'losers'. Policy-makers need to bear this in mind in reforming energy subsidies in order to handle potential conflicts. The simulations presented here show how these complex relations can be analysed

	Variable	*With direct subsidy*	*Without direct subsidy*
Macroeconomic	Real GDP	–0.1	–0.3
	Consumption	0.1	–0.6
	Investment	–1.6	–0.4
	Exports	0.2	–0.8
	Imports	–0.7	–1.5
	Government savings	–21.4	–3.2
Sectoral output	Coal	–4.7	–4.4
	Electricity	–1.4	–0.3
	Manufacturing	0.0	–1.2
	Road transport	0.0	–10.2
	Construction	0.0	1.3
	Other transport	0.1	0.4
	Oil refinery	0.1	–1.2
	Hydraulic	2.2	–1.4
Income distribution	I quintile	0.0	–0.5
	II quintile	0.0	–0.5
	III quintile	0.0	–0.5
	IV quintile	0.1	–0.6
	V quintile	0.1	–0.7
Environment	SO_2	0.0	–5.3
	NO_2	0.0	–5.2
	CO	0.0	–1.6
	VOC	–0.1	–2.1
	PM10	0.0	–4.7
	CO_2	–0.1	–4.6

Table 11.3 **Major effects of eliminating coal subsidies (% change)**

in a systematic and consistent economic framework using a computerised general equilibrium model.

How subsidy reform affects the macroeconomy, economic sectors and the distribution of household incomes depends on how energy subsidies are financed and how the proceeds used when they are eliminated. In many cases, the differences are quite significant.

A key conclusion of the analysis for Chile is that removing oil subsidies could have bigger economic and distributional effects than removing coal subsidies. This is mainly because consumption of oil is much larger than that of coal. Not surprisingly, the effects on the sectors concerned—namely, oil refining and coal production—are much bigger in each case. The environment clearly benefits from the removal of both coal and oil subsidies. Emissions of CO, PM10 and CO_2 are much lower in both cases.

Another important conclusion is that there may be significant short-run economic and social costs from removing oil subsidies that have to be traded off against the short-run environmental benefits. There are also trade-offs between the short-run costs and the long-run economic, environmental and social benefits of subsidy removal.

12

Analysis of the findings of country case studies

This chapter summarises and analyses the findings of the country case studies contained in Chapters 3–11. It draws out generic conclusions about the economic, environmental and social effects of subsidies. The country case studies illustrate the pervasiveness of energy subsidies and the need for policy-makers to consider their full implications for economic development, the environment and social welfare—the three pillars of sustainable development. Most subsidies still go to fossil fuels. The scope for environmental improvement and for enhancing economic efficiency by removing those subsidies is often considerable. In many cases, the economic costs of subsidies, manifested, for example, by inefficient energy use and supply, the burden on public finances and the trade balance, and rationing are high. The main environmental costs are increased air and water pollution and higher emissions of climate-destabilising greenhouse gases. But removing subsidies can involve significant short-run economic and social costs, notably in the form of job losses and income effects. These need to be addressed from the outset in the design of any subsidy reform package.

12.1 Types of subsidy

The country analyses illustrate the diversity of energy subsidies with respect to the types of energy subsidised, the mechanism used and the policy goals they are intended to support. In the OECD, most energy subsidies are still concentrated on the production of fossil fuels and nuclear power, although the amount of these subsidies is thought to have declined in recent years. In many European countries, subsidies to oil are often offset by special taxes and levies intended mainly to raise money for the national treasury and increasingly for environmental purposes such as in the case of Ecological Tax Reforms. Remaining subsidies are aimed at protecting local industries from competition from imports for reasons of employment and/or energy-supply security. The coal industry still benefits from large subsidies in a small number of countries, notably Germany, although they are being reduced gradually in most cases. At the same time, subsidies to renewables and energy-efficient end-use technologies are growing in response to environmental concerns, particularly climate change and local air pollution, with the aim of achieving a more diversified energy mix. The biggest and most common forms of subsidy are favourable tax treatment, grants and soft loans, regulations that favour a particular technology or fuel and funding for R&D. Price controls, which used to be the favoured approach to subsidising energy, have been largely abolished with the liberalisation and restructuring of energy markets.

Energy subsidies in most of the developing and transition countries considered here, which are generally much larger net of taxes than in OECD countries, take markedly different forms. The bulk of them are aimed at consumers. Government price controls, which hold prices below the full economic cost of supply, remain the most widespread type of subsidy. They are most common for electricity, but are still important in some countries for oil products, coal and gas. The extent of under-pricing is generally bigger in countries where the energy sector is state-owned. State companies are usually treated as public-service entities and are not required to maximise profits. Subsidies to fuels supplied mostly by private firms usually have to be provided through more transparent mechanisms, such as a compensation fund (as with oil products in Chile). Energy subsidies are especially pervasive in Iran and Indonesia, where the prices of almost every type of energy are well below competitive markets. India has taken important steps to raise oil and coal prices to economic levels in recent years, but massive electricity subsidies remain.

12.2 Measuring subsidies and assessing their effects

The country analyses illustrate the enormous practical difficulties in measuring subsidies and their effects. It is hard to compare the size of subsidies across countries because the way in which they are measured and the scope of analysis vary so much from country to country. Few countries systematically attempt to compile data on or monitor energy subsidies. The United States, for instance, updated a 1992 study of federal energy subsidies in 1999 and 2000 (US DOE/EIA 1992, 1999, 2000), although some of its findings have been questioned (see e.g. Koplow 1993). The bi-yearly subsidy report by the German government is also a source of valuable information as it regularly reports on all types of subsidy (see Bundesministerium der Finanzen 2001). International organisations, non-governmental bodies and academics have carried out most other studies that have tried to quantify energy subsidies.

Quantifying the different effects of subsidies, both costs and benefits, is even more difficult and subjective. A subsidy by its very nature involves a complex set of changes in economic resource allocation through its effect on costs and/or prices. These shifts inevitably have interrelated economic, social and environmental implications. Indeed, the reason why any of the subsidies described in the preceding chapters exist at all is to support some economic, social or environmental goal.

Economic theory says that social welfare is maximised when the price of each good and service is determined by the intersection of producers' willingness to supply and consumers' willingness to pay (see Chapter 2, Section 2.2). When price deviates from this point of static equilibrium, resource allocation is economically inefficient since the benefits to consumers from the last units of energy consumed are smaller than the costs involved in supplying the energy service.

In practice, however, free markets in energy services left to their own devices do not work perfectly so that social welfare is not maximised. In particular, they do not take account of any social and environmental benefits and costs that might be associated with certain types of energy activity. So there is a justification for governments to intervene in energy markets in pursuit of environmental and social objectives and to fix any problems in the way those markets operate. Any subsidy can be justified if overall social welfare is increased, when the social gain or environmental improvement exceeds the economic cost. However, measuring these effects, especially the social and environmental costs and benefits, is extremely difficult.

Energy markets can malfunction in various ways. A market is said to fail when it does not put a price on a 'public good': that is, a good or service that is freely accessible by everyone but which carries no explicit charge. Air is a classic example of a public good and one that directly concerns energy. Deterioration in air quality is said to be an external cost, because there is no market in the supply of air. Governments have a responsibility to intervene to protect air quality by regulating emissions from energy-related and other activities, since individual polluters would otherwise not pay for the environmental damage. Levying charges on polluting activities is one important way of making the polluter pay for that damage. This concept is known as the 'polluter-pays principle'. In this way, external costs are internalised in the final price to consumers. A carbon tax, which has been introduced in a number of OECD countries, particularly in Europe, is an example of this approach.

Taxes or levies—the opposite of subsidies—on the fuels responsible for causing external costs are, in principle, the appropriate response to this type of market imperfection. But subsidies directed at less- or non-polluting activities can achieve similar end-results and are often considered a more practical solution where raising or introducing taxes is seen as politically awkward.

Social considerations such as concern for the poor, sick or otherwise disadvantaged may also, in principle, provide a reason for subsidising energy. Society as a whole benefits from everyone having access to modern energy, but the market does not reflect that 'social good'. Again, this benefit is external to the market. If some people are too poor to afford to pay for that energy, then the market again is failing. Most governments consider that access to a reasonably priced minimum supply of modern energy services is socially desirable. Subsidies, however, may not be the most cost-effective means of achieving this goal in practice.

The existence of barriers to market entry, another type of market imperfection, might also justify subsidising energy. The high initial cost of developing cleaner energy technologies and the acute technical and financial risks associated with those new technologies, which might deter investors, are examples of such barriers. Governments can help to compensate for this by subsidising a particular energy source or technology so as to encourage investment either in new capacity or in research and commercial development. Reducing the unit costs of production of emerging renewable technologies such as solar photovoltaics and wind requires experience, which comes from building and operating plants. The time needed to gain this experience may be too long for private investors without a degree of government support. The facts bear this out. Few energy technologies have reached maturity without substantial public-sector investment.

Because of market imperfections, the distortions that energy subsidies engender do not *necessarily* lead to less-desirable outcomes when external costs and benefits are taken into account from the standpoint of overall social welfare. But experience in those countries analysed in the preceding chapters provides evidence that, in many instances, the effects of subsidies are negative. In other words, overall social welfare would be higher without subsidies. This may be because the rationale for the subsidy is invalid: for example, because too much emphasis is put on a particular policy goal to the detriment of others. The way in which the subsidy is applied may also be ineffective. Even where the net benefits are positive, energy subsidies may not be the most efficient way of achieving policy goals (see Section 12.4 below). Evidence of the kinds of economic, environmental and social effects from the country analyses is summarised in Table 12.1. These effects are discussed in more detail below.

12.3 Economic effects

The country case studies demonstrate that the economic effects of energy subsidies and their removal depend very much on their type and size as well as the structure of the economy. The effects also vary over time. But there is ample evidence that energy subsidies can involve large economic costs in the long run.

Subsidies that lower end-use prices, either directly or by lowering the cost of production, always lead to higher energy use (except where supply is rationed) and reduce incentives to conserve or use energy more efficiently. The extent of the increase in consumption depends on the price elasticity of demand. Elasticities vary across countries, fuels and over time—demand for energy responds more to a shift in price in the longer term as capital stock is replaced. The disregard for energy efficiency and conservation in housing blocks in Russia and many transition economies during the Soviet era, which resulted from a failure to price heating services properly and to meter supplies, is an extreme example. Historically, large subsidies in the Czech and Slovak Republics undermined incentives to use energy

Country/region	*Types of subsidy assessed*	*Economic effects*	*Environmental effects*	*Social effects*
OECD	All types	Studies show that removing fossil fuel subsidies would boost trade and economic growth.	Since most subsidies go to fossil fuels, removing them would reduce noxious and CO_2 emissions.	Significant short-term distributional effects, mainly due to impact on employment and household spending on energy.
Czech and Slovak Republics	All types	Subsidies have held back economic restructuring and hindered innovation, resulting in high energy intensity and low energy efficiency.	Have exacerbated the harmful environmental effects of energy supply and consumption, including local and regional air pollution and CO_2 emissions.	No detailed studies of social effects have been carried out even though household income support is primary reason for subsidising energy.
Russia	District heat	Large consumer subsidies, together with lack of metering and payment problems, cause waste and undermine investment and efficiency.	By encouraging over-consumption, under-pricing contributes to pollution and greenhouse gas emissions.	Heat is a vital service to most households. But savings from subsidy removal can finance welfare payments to the poor and improved metering and billing.
India	Electricity	Subsidies encourage waste and hold back investment in the power sector—a major constraint on economic development. Removing subsidies would trim demand in the long run by 34%.	Removing electricity subsidies alone would cut CO_2 emissions by 99 million tonnes, equivalent to a third of current power-sector emissions.	Subsidy removal would raise cost of service to households, but would improve quality of service and enhance utilities' ability to extend and expand capacity.
Indonesia	All types	Net economic cost of subsidies to kerosene, diesel, gasoline and heavy fuel oil amounted to $4 billion in 2001.	Subsidies exacerbate pollution, especially particulates and lead.	Reducing subsidies would free up resources to support the poor in more effective ways.
Korea	All types	Coal subsidies of around $500 million per year and large cross-subsidies in electricity and gas, together with the tax system, distort energy-use patterns.	Subsidies to coal and to industrial users of electricity and gas encourage over-consumption of fossil fuels and consequently boost emissions.	Removal of coal subsidies would have serious economic and social consequences for mining communities.
Iran	All types	Subsidies cause inefficient energy use, are a major burden on public finances and have resulted in poor energy-sector performance.	Excessive energy use has aggravated local and regional pollution, a major public health issue.	Mainly benefit higher-income groups, which consume larger amounts of subsidised energy. But eliminating subsidies would have a dramatic impact on household budgets.

Table 12.1 Summary of findings of country case studies: main effects (continued over)

Country/region	*Types of subsidy assessed*	*Economic effects*	*Environmental effects*	*Social effects*
Senegal	LPG	Subsidies have successfully stimulated LPG use, bringing some economic benefits but at a significant financial cost.	Growth in LPG use has resulted in savings of about 70,000 tonnes of fuelwood and 90,000 tonnes of charcoal per year, relieving deforestation pressures and reducing pollution.	Subsidies have Improved household comfort standards and safety, and have enhanced incomes.
Chile	Oil and coal	The elimination of coal subsidies in 1995 was economically beneficial. Removing remaining oil subsidies would incur short-term economic costs.	The environment clearly benefits from subsidies reform in both cases through large reductions in CO, particulate and CO_2 emissions.	Removing oil subsidies completely would have a slightly larger negative impact on richer household incomes.

Table 12.1 (continued)

efficiently and encouraged the development of energy-intensive heavy manufacturing industries. Cross-subsidies to electricity and gas used by heavy industry have distorted the pattern of economic development in Korea, too. Massive subsidies explain why electricity accounts for such a large share of energy use in the farm sector in India compared to other poor developing countries.

Removing these subsidies would reduce demand, but probably not by very much in the short term because of structural economic rigidities and the slow rate of replacement of energy-capital stock. In Russia, for example, cutting district heat subsidies would probably be effective in reducing use only if welfare payments were used to compensate for higher prices and effective metering and billing systems were installed. Otherwise, raising prices would most likely simply worsen payments problems.

A subsidy that reduces the price received by energy suppliers undermines the returns on their investments and, consequently, their ability and incentive to invest in new infrastructure. As a result, subsidies may encourage reliance on out-of-date and dirtier technology. There are many examples of this phenomenon, especially in the developing world. The dire financial condition of the state electricity boards in India is an extreme case. A failure to eliminate subsidies by raising prices to full-cost levels has severely curtailed the ability of the companies to finance new investment, which has directly contributed to the poor quality of supply and held back extending the network to remote villages.

Subsidies to producers, by cushioning them from competitive market pressures, tend to reduce incentives to minimise costs, resulting in less-efficient plant operation and investments that may otherwise not be economic. The subsidies on coal production in several OECD countries, described in Chapter 3, have hampered efforts to improve productivity in past decades. In the United Kingdom, for example, the phasing-out of subsidies in the 1980s and 1990s together with the privatisation of the industry led to a huge improvement in productivity.

Direct subsidies, in the form of grants or tax exemptions, act as a drain on government finances. For example, the IMF estimates that the Iranian government's direct spending on energy subsidies amounted to $4 billion in 1997—8% of its budget. The cost of oil product subsidies in Indonesia is even higher, at around 10% of central government spending. The special low rate of VAT that was applied to the sale of electricity and gas to households by the Czech and Slovak governments in the 1990s exacerbated those countries' budget deficit problems. Direct subsidies on oil products can lead to acute pressure on government finances during periods of rising prices. This has been a major problem in several developing countries, including Indonesia. Indonesia allocated almost $4 billion to oil subsidies in 2002. If left unchanged, the bill for those subsidies would soar to around $36 billion between 2000 and 2005 due to higher oil prices. In the long run, indirect subsidies that reduce economic growth also lead to lower government tax revenues.

Subsidies always have an impact on international trade. Consumption subsidies that increase energy use boost demand for imports or reduce the amount of energy available for export. This harms the balance of payments by increasing the country's dependence on imports. For example, the massive increase in LPG use in Senegal that resulted largely from subsidies has led to a huge increase in imports. The Indonesian government estimates that energy subsidies in total will cost the country $16 billion in lost export earnings over the five years to 2005 if they are left as they are. Iran's exports of crude oil will decline rapidly if subsidies are not removed soon, since production will be unable to keep pace with soaring domestic consumption. Subsidies in major energy-producing countries such as Indonesia and Iran also undermine global energy security to the extent that they reduce those countries' capacity to export. The removal of subsidies to oil products would lower domestic demand in Indonesia and free up more oil for export, thereby reducing the share of the dominant OPEC countries in international oil trade and reducing those countries' ability to push for higher prices.

Subsidies can also encourage cross-border smuggling of oil products and other tradable forms of energy to neighbouring countries with higher prices. This has been a major problem in some African countries, Iran and Indonesia.

Price caps or ceilings below market-clearing levels can lead to physical shortages and a need for administratively costly rationing arrangements. This is the case in India, where the state electricity boards are unable to finance investments in expanding and reinforcing the network to keep up with the rapid growth of demand that has resulted from under-pricing. Subsidised LPG is also still rationed in India.

Subsidies to specific energy technologies inevitably undermine the development and commercialisation of other technologies that might ultimately become more economically and environmentally attractive. In this way, subsidies can 'lock in' technologies to the exclusion of other, more promising ones. For this reason, the costs of subsidies can persist for a long time after they have been removed, because it can take a very long time to replace the stock of energy-supply and combustion equipment. Heavily subsidised prices caused a surge in the use of electricity for household space and water heating in the Czech and Slovak Republics in the 1990s, even though electricity is not the most economic heating option.

Subsidies have since been reduced, but households are often unwilling to switch to other heating systems because of the high initial investment cost. Similarly, large investments in additional generating, transmission and distribution capacity have already occurred to meet the increase in peak winter demand.

Some of the economic costs of energy subsidies are ultimately borne, at least in part, by the intended beneficiaries of the subsidies as well as the rest of society. Subsidies, while often intended for the poor, but largely enjoyed by the rich, deprive governments of money that could otherwise be used to pay for welfare programmes that truly target the poor. In this case, the poor would benefit from the removal of subsidies—especially where they consume little of the subsidised fuel. The main beneficiaries of LPG subsidies in Senegal are wealthy households. Poor rural households do not benefit at all since LPG is not distributed outside the main towns and cities.

The overall economic efficiency gains that could be achieved by removing energy subsidies, in some cases, could be large. The IEA estimates, for example, that the efficiency gains would amount to at least 2.2% of annual GDP in Iran (IEA 1999). Removing electricity subsidies alone in India would boost GDP by 0.2%. The studies covering OECD countries described in Chapter 3 suggest that the efficiency gains would be much smaller, since energy subsidies net of taxes are generally lower. The 2000 OECD study, for example, estimates that removing all OECD energy subsidies would raise global income by only 0.1% (OECD 2000). But it should be noted that such studies are generally based on static models. In some cases, there may be major offsetting long-term dynamic benefits resulting from technological advances that would not otherwise have occurred without subsidies. This is, after all, a major justification for some subsidy schemes, notably those aimed at boosting the development and deployment of new renewable technologies and 'cleaner' transport fuels.

Nonetheless, there is evidence that the structural upheavals caused by the removal of energy subsidies can involve economic costs in the short term as the economy adjusts to higher prices. Output in the most energy-intensive industries would normally fall initially, unless the government introduces compensatory measures that have the effect of lowering other input costs. Households' spending would also fall unless welfare payments are raised or taxes are cut. Raising energy prices to economic levels also increases the general inflation rate. This may require the government to tighten fiscal and monetary policies, dampening GDP growth, production and incomes. The results of the modelling work in Chile described in Chapter 11 demonstrate that the short-run economic costs can be significant. How subsidy reform affects different economic sectors and the distribution of income among households depends on how energy subsidies are financed and how the proceeds used when they are eliminated. These costs have to be traded off against the environmental benefits and the long-run economic and social benefits of subsidy removal.

12.4 Environmental effects

The changes in economic resource allocation brought about by the introduction, removal or change in an energy subsidy always have implications for the environment and social welfare. Indeed, the reason many subsidies exist at all is to support a particular social or environmental goal. For all the theoretical arguments in support of targeted intervention, governments are questioning more and more the validity of certain types of energy subsidy. This is mainly because of a shift in policy priorities as concerns about both the environmental consequences of encouraging energy use and the economic cost of subsidy programmes grow. A prime example is the Kyoto Protocol, which requires a reduction of subsidies that encourage greenhouse gas emissions.[46]

The preceding chapters illustrate the complexity of the environmental effects of energy subsidies. They can be both positive and negative, depending on the precise nature of the subsidy and the energy source that it supports. Subsidies that encourage the production and use of fossil fuels inevitably have some harmful consequences for the environment. Consumer subsidies that lower the price paid for those fuels or the cost of using them result in increased consumption. This can lead to higher airborne emissions of noxious and greenhouse gases as well as other forms of environmental damage such as water contamination and spoiling of the landscape. The use of fossil fuels is particularly damaging to the environment.

The environmental effects of subsidising energy are not limited to fossil fuels. Nuclear power production results in radioactive waste and the risk of contamination. Even some types of renewable may have adverse environmental consequences, though to a much lower extent than fossil fuels or nuclear energy. Dams disturb regional ecosystems and give rise to pollution during their construction and wind turbines can have an aesthetic impact on the landscape. The production of biofuels, subsidised by several OECD countries, can also be harmful for the environment, since they usually result in greater use of fertilisers and pesticides, which can damage local ecosystems and cause both soil and water pollution. Nonetheless, in comparison with fossil fuels, renewables generally give rise to very low, and in some cases zero, emissions of greenhouse gases and, by definition, are non-depletable.

But the overall impact of fossil fuel and other energy subsidies on the environment is not always negative. For example, encouraging the use of oil products can reduce deforestation in developing countries as poor rural households switch from fuelwood. This was one of the main reasons for introducing subsidies to LPG in Senegal. Public funding of fossil fuel research and development can also yield positive environmental effects if it results in the use of more-efficient, cleaner-

46 Article 2.a of the Protocol reads : '1. Each Party included in Annex I, in achieving its quantified emission limitation and reduction commitments under Article 3, in order to promote sustainable development, shall: (a) Implement and/or further elaborate policies and measures in accordance with its national circumstances, such as: . . . (v) Progressive reduction or phasing out of market imperfections, fiscal incentives, tax and duty exemptions and subsidies in all greenhouse gas emitting sectors that run counter to the objective of the Convention and application of market instruments.'

burning technologies in the long term. The United States has invested large sums of money in research and development of clean coal technology with the aim of promoting cleaner and more efficient use of coal, as coal is generally uncompetitive with other energy products under a long-term climate change policy.[47]

Furthermore, subsidies to indigenous fossil fuel production do not systematically lead to higher consumption if they result in a switch from imported to indigenously produced fuel on a one-for-one basis. This has been a strong argument to defend coal-production subsidy schemes in Germany and the United Kingdom, because they now cover the difference between actual production costs and import prices and do not involve lower prices. These subsidies do not, therefore, encourage higher consumption. Nonetheless, the financial and economic cost of keeping inefficient mines open is very high, especially when the alternative use of public money for energy conservation, efficiency increases and renewables are considered. Past agreements that mandated the burning of minimum amounts of coal in German power stations also undoubtedly held back the use of cleaner fuels such as natural gas.

Subsidies on oil products and electricity in poor countries can also reduce indoor pollution, if they encourage switching away from traditional energy such as wood, straw, crop residues and dung. Anecdotal evidence from Senegal suggests that the widespread use of LPG in urban households has greatly reduced health problems related to indoor pollution caused by burning of the traditional fuels. The incidence of fires caused by traditional fuels burning out of control and kerosene stoves being knocked over has also been reduced. Women and children, who spend more time indoors, have been the major beneficiaries. The World Health Organisation estimates that, globally, the indoor burning of traditional fuels causes around 2.5 million premature deaths each year (Goldemberg 2000).

The net environmental effect of subsidies to support renewables and energy-efficient technologies may be positive to the extent that they help to reduce emissions of noxious and greenhouse gases. But the net effects depend on how the subsidies are structured and on market conditions. If renewables replace fossil fuels and the amount of fossil fuel-based energy consumed in building the plants and equipment is not too high, then the net effect on various types of emission will generally be positive. Most OECD countries subsidise wind power to reduce emissions through switching from coal and oil in the power sector.

Throughout the OECD and in some developing and transition countries, subsidies to renewables and energy-efficient combustion technologies are increasing. This policy is being driven mainly by environmental objectives. In some cases, energy security reasons are also cited. Subsidies take various forms, including:

- Grants for producing electricity or transport fuels based on renewables or for buying energy-efficient combustion plant and equipment
- Preferential tariffs for renewables-based power
- Spending on research and development projects

47 It should be noted that the efficiency of coal power plants is lower than that of gas, operating at roughly 35% and 50% respectively.

In some cases, these subsidies need to be big to make those technologies competitive with existing ones based on fossil fuels. Wind-turbine technology is among the most competitive at present, although subsidies are still needed in most cases to encourage new investment. Solar energy technology still struggles to compete with conventional fuels.

Evidence from the case studies of the net environmental effects of introducing or removing energy subsidies is generally qualitative. This reflects the immense practical difficulties in estimating quantitatively the different effects, expressing them in consistent monetary terms and aggregating them. Nonetheless, partial analyses of the impact of removing specific subsidies—for example, on CO_2 emissions—suggest that there is considerable scope in some countries for reducing environmental degradation by eliminating subsidies. In India, for instance, power-sector emissions could be cut by over 100 million tonnes—equivalent to more than 10% of the country's total emissions—by removing electricity and other energy subsidies. Similarly, the removal of oil subsidies in Chile could lower SO_2, NO_x, particulate and CO_2 emissions each by around 5% in the short term on the assumption that prices are 12% below market levels.

12.5 Social effects

Removing subsidies that are both economically costly as well as harmful to the environment would be a win–win policy reform. Many fossil fuel subsidies fall into this category. But governments are often faced with awkward trade-offs between the economic and/or environmental benefits of reforming those subsidies and the social costs of higher fuel prices or of lower employment in indigenous energy industries.

The social implications of energy subsidies depend very much on the type of subsidy. In poor developing countries, subsidies to modern cooking and heating fuels, such as kerosene and LPG, as well as electricity, are common. They are aimed at improving poor households' living conditions by making those fuels more affordable and accessible. Where they result in switching from traditional fuels and improved access to electricity, those subsidies can bring considerable benefits to poor communities. These include less indoor pollution and a reduction in the time women and children spend gathering fuelwood and, therefore, more time they can spend on productive activities, such as farming, and education. The case study of LPG subsidies in Senegal provides a good example of these social benefits. Subsidies to district heat, electricity and gas in Russia have helped to protect the living standards of poor households: maintaining affordable energy supplies in the coldest regions can be a matter of life or death.

But subsidies that hold down prices to households do not necessarily bring social benefits, because those subsidies have to be paid for—often out of general taxation. In this case, the money spent on subsidies could be spent on other forms of social welfare support, such as direct income-support payments, health and education. The huge cost of energy subsidies in Indonesia and Iran, for example, has certainly constrained social spending. Where the energy industry has to bear the cost of the subsidy, the quality and quantity of service usually suffers in the long term—a social cost. Nowhere is this better illustrated than in India, where poor households that cannot afford backup generators have to put up with regular brownouts and blackouts. In addition, many rural households are deprived of any service at all because the electricity utilities, which make enormous financial losses, are unable to pay for grid extension.

Moreover, the poor for whom the subsidies are usually intended may benefit less than rich households, even when they receive the energy service. As a result, the poor may paradoxically end up worse off where the financial costs of the subsidy are shared by the entire population including the poor. There are two main reasons for this:

- The financial value to poor households may be very small since their consumption is generally modest. Richer households tend to benefit much more in absolute terms since they consume more of the subsidised fuel. The results of the analysis of the effects of removing oil subsidies in Chile on income distribution suggest that the richest households would see the biggest declines in disposable income.
- Consumption subsidies that involve the imposition of caps on prices below market levels may lead to a need for rationing. The richest households tend to get hold of the bulk of subsidised energy in countries where it is rationed, through petty corruption and favouritism.

Nor is it clear that there are social benefits from protectionist policies aimed at maintaining employment in domestic energy industries. The cost of those subsidies can hold back economic growth and reduce employment in other sectors of the economy. For example, subsidies to coal production that raise the price paid by power generators raise input costs to industry generally as well as energy costs to households. These social costs may be large in comparison with the direct benefits to the workers and local communities concerned, although weighing them is inevitably highly subjective and political. Moreover, there may not even be any social benefits to the local communities in the long run if the protected jobs are low-quality. This is especially the case with coal mining. Experience in Europe shows that redirecting subsidies to retraining and regional economic development aid can boost higher-paid, safer and more desirable jobs to replace the jobs lost in the coal industry. The sooner uneconomic mining activities are forced to cease, the sooner higher-added-value industries can be established.

12.6 Policy implications

The country case studies illustrate the pervasiveness of energy subsidies and the need for policy-makers to consider their full implications for economic development, the environment and social welfare—the three pillars of sustainable development. Most subsidies still go to fossil fuels, so the scope for environmental improvement by removing subsidies is often considerable. But it is hard to generalise since the effects of different types of subsidy and the way they are applied vary so much.

In evaluating a particular subsidy it is important to take into account the whole policy landscape. One cannot look at subsidies in isolation, because they interact with other government policies and measures. Subsidies often build on subsidies, sometimes working in opposite ways. In general, it is better to eliminate an existing subsidy than to introduce a new one that attempts to counterbalance the effects of the former.

Policy-makers also need to consider the long-term effects of a subsidy. Subsidies are often introduced to meet short-term goals. Similarly, politicians may be reluctant to remove a subsidy because of the short-run costs associated with the economic adjustment process. But subsidies can have a major impact on the long-term development of energy markets and on the environment. Subsidies that were introduced in the 1970s and 1980s to stimulate indigenous fossil fuel and nuclear power production might have brought some short-run energy security benefits, but undoubtedly held back the development of renewable energy sources. Building on lessons from the country case studies, the following chapter lays out important principles for the design and implementation of subsidy reform.

13 Designing and implementing energy subsidy reforms*

This concluding chapter provides guidance on the underlying principles that ought to be applied in reforming existing subsidies or designing new schemes, and practical approaches to implementing reforms. These principles draw on the lessons learned from the country case studies as well as the discussions of the UNEP/IEA workshops on energy subsidy reform. In principle, subsidy schemes should always be carefully targeted at clearly defined social groups or technologies and should not discourage the efficient use and supply of energy. They should be based on a sound analysis of all the related economic, social and environmental costs and benefits and should be practical and affordable, transparent and limited in time. Reforming existing energy subsidies requires strong political will to take tough decisions that benefit society as a whole. Phasing out subsidies in a gradual fashion and compensating financially the social groups that would suffer unduly can make implementing reforms easier. In any event, governments should always communicate to the general public the reasons for reform, demonstrate the net benefits to society as a whole and actively involve stakeholders in the process of formulating policy.

13.1 Principles of subsidy reform

In most instances, governments are faced with complex and politically difficult trade-offs, both between the economic, environmental and social effects of reforming subsidies and between those consumers or producers who stand to lose out and those that stand to gain. But, in many cases, removing or reforming energy

* This chapter draws on UNEP/IEA 2002, which also formed the basis for UNECE guidelines on reforming energy pricing (UNECE 2002).

in combination with other policy measures, such as those aimed at rationalising the tax system, could bring important net overall economic and environmental benefits. Governments should place priority on removing or at least reducing the size of those subsidies that are clearly harmful to the environment as well as being economically costly. Subsidy removal, in this case, would be a win–win policy reform. Many subsidies that encourage fossil fuel consumption fall into this category.

There may, nonetheless, be a good case for retaining subsidies in specific instances, especially where they are aimed at encouraging more sustainable energy use. Examples might include temporary support for new renewable and energy-efficient technologies to overcome market barriers, and measures to improve poor or rural households' access to modern, commercial forms of energy. But the way in which a subsidy is applied is critical to its cost and to how effective it is in meeting policy objectives.

There is no single right approach or model to designing or reforming subsidy policies. Every country needs to take account of national and local circumstances. These include the country's own policy objectives and priorities, its stage of economic development, market and economic conditions, the state of public finances and the institutional framework. But there are a number of basic principles that countries need to apply in designing subsidies and implementing reforms to existing programmes.

Experience shows that subsidy programmes and their reform should meet the following key criteria:

- **Targeted.** Subsidies should go only to those who are meant and deserve to receive them.
- **Efficient.** Subsidies should not undermine incentives for suppliers or consumers to provide or use a service efficiently.
- **Soundly based.** Subsidies should be justified by a thorough analysis of the associated costs and benefits.
- **Practical.** The amount of subsidy should be affordable and it must be possible to administer the subsidy in a low-cost way.
- **Transparent.** The public should be able to see how much a subsidy programme costs and who benefits from it.
- **Limited in time.** Subsidy programmes should have limited duration, preferably set at the outset, so that consumers and producers do not get 'hooked' on the subsidies and the cost of the programme does not spiral out of control.

Each of these principles and how they should be applied in practice are considered below.

13.1.1 Targeting

Targeting subsidies effectively so their benefits are limited to a clearly defined targeted group should be the first consideration in reforming or designing a subsidy programme. The targeted group would normally be a certain type of producer or category of consumer: for example, the operator of a wind turbine or poor households. The country case studies demonstrate clearly how many energy subsidies end up helping other categories of producers or consumers, too, resulting in significant economic distortions and costs. Subsidies that are enjoyed by all types of producer or all consumers regardless of their income or the form of energy should, therefore, be avoided. A special low rate of sales tax applied to heating fuels benefiting all consumers—the largest consumers most in absolute terms—is a good example of such an untargeted subsidy.

Generally, consumer subsidies should be restricted to the poorest households and to the environmentally cleanest energy sources. Subsidies that are intended to alleviate poverty should normally be restricted to energy services provided through fixed networks, i.e. electricity, natural gas or district heat. Subsidies to non-network forms of energy, such as oil products, can never be properly targeted at poor households, because those fuels can be freely traded. Policy-makers also need to define the 'poor' in narrow terms so that it captures no more than a small proportion of the population. Moreover, the mechanism for subsidising a particular fuel should not allow richer households to benefit from the subsidy. Where this is not possible, it is preferable to eliminate the subsidy and address the problem of poverty directly through social welfare policies.

As demonstrated for India in Chapter 6, lifeline rates—special low rates aimed at small users—can be an effective way of reducing the cost of service for poor households. Energy consumption is usually strongly correlated to income level, so limiting subsidised rates to small consumers targets the subsidy at the poor. How lifeline rates are applied affects how well the subsidy is targeted:

- A **capacity** subsidy can be applied to the standing charge covering the fixed monthly cost of maintaining a connection to the network. To limit the subsidy to poor households, this rate should be applied only to households subscribing to the lowest capacity: for example, less than 3 kW for electricity service. Richer households, which usually consume more energy, subscribe to higher capacity, for which subsidised rates should not be made available. Abuses can occur, however. For example, richer households may try to obtain more than one subscription for the same address, especially if the potential savings are large. This has been a problem with social tariffs for electricity in Italy.

- A **commodity** subsidy can be applied to the tariff for each kWh of energy consumed. Where the subsidised tariff is applied only to a small tranche of consumption, those households consuming small amounts of energy would profit most. Better still, the subsidised tariff can be applied solely to households subscribing to the lowest capacity, so that richer households have to pay full-cost rates for all their consumption.

In practice, however, neither approach results in perfect targeting. Consumption is not just a function of income: large, poor families may consume more energy than small, rich families. In addition, secondary residences, usually owned by the richest households, might also benefit from the subsidy where they are rarely occupied. For these reasons, capacity subsidies are often more effective at targeting poor households. Moreover, they are less likely to encourage waste than commodity subsidies and they do not require metering. A lack of metering is a major problem in Russia and other transition economies.

Subsidies to energy producers should normally be restricted to energy sources and technologies that bring real environmental benefits. This would primarily concern energy efficiency and renewables. Subsidies to renewables should normally be targeted at those technologies that are closest to being competitive with conventional fuels and technologies.

13.1.2 Efficiency

Energy subsidy programmes should always be designed in a way that does not undermine incentives for consumers to use energy efficiently or for producers and suppliers to provide a service efficiently. With consumer subsidies, the size of the subsidy and the mechanism by which it is provided affect end-use efficiency. The bigger the subsidy, the less incentive consumers have to use energy efficiently—especially where the cost to the consumer at the margin cost is lowered through a commodity subsidy.

Price controls that keep prices below the full cost of supply should not penalise financially the energy service provider. Nor should those companies bear the cost of policies that allow consumers to avoid paying their energy bills—a form of subsidy. Subsidies that cause energy companies to lose money undermine its ability to maintain a reliable service and upgrade and expand the network to meet demand. They will also discourage new investors from entering the industry. This is a major problem in India and many other developing countries. Cross-subsidies that favour households should also be avoided, since they can undermine the international competitiveness of industrial and commercial firms that are forced to pay above-cost tariffs. Where subsidised capacity or commodity tariffs for small consumers are considered necessary, they should be financed out of public funds. This approach would help to minimise economic distortions and protect the financial health of service providers.

The issue of whether to subsidise capacity or output also applies to producer subsidies aimed at encouraging output of a particular fuel. The right approach will depend on the type of fuel or technology and the phase of development and commercialisation of renewables. For certain types of renewable energy source, such as wind power and solar photovoltaics, subsidies to new capacity may provide a stronger incentive to investors than subsidies on each unit of energy produced, because of the high initial cost of capital. This approach has been effective in boosting investment in wind and photovoltaics in several countries, including Austria, Denmark, Germany, Japan and Sweden. But capacity subsidies may not encourage construction of the most efficient technologies. Moreover, they do not always ensure that the systems, once installed, are run optimally. Fixed, subsidised commodity tariffs for renewables-based power give a stronger incentive to invest in the most efficient technologies, since the amount of subsidy a producer receives depends on output. In practice, a combination of capacity and commodity subsidies may be the most cost-effective approach. Several OECD countries, such as Germany and Spain, have adopted this strategy.

13.1.3 Rationale

Because subsidies can result in serious market distortions and adverse environmental, social and economic effects, it is essential that a decision to introduce or retain a subsidy be soundly based. Many of the subsidy programmes described in this report were introduced to support specific social or environmental goals without thorough analysis of all the consequences. The onus should be on the authorities to present a convincing case for the subsidy based on a comprehensive and coherent analysis of *all* the associated economic, environmental and social costs and benefits. The burden of proof should be on demonstrating the net benefits of both new and existing subsidies. Since market conditions and policy objectives change over time, this type of exercise must be carried out on a regular basis to ensure that the case for maintaining a subsidy remains valid. A subsidy may make sense today, but changing circumstances may mean that it no longer makes sense a year or two later.

Carrying out this type of analysis is easier said than done. In reality, it requires reliable data, such as market assessments and customer surveys, and effective analytical capacity. Where that capacity is lacking, which is often the case in poor developing countries, governments can develop training and education programmes and make use of external expertise—for example, from international organisations or consultants. Where it is not possible to properly assess the full implications of a subsidy because of a lack of data or expertise, it is usually best not to proceed with the subsidy at all.

13.1.4 Practicality

Practical considerations may mean that a subsidy that looks good on paper may not be cost-effective—often because the financial costs of providing the subsidy outweigh the benefits. There are two aspects to this. First, the country may simply not be able to afford the subsidy if it involves large financial transfers from the national treasury or loss of income to a state-owned utility. Second, it may not be feasible to administer the subsidy in a way that does not involve large administration costs including the cost of preventing and dealing with abuses. Subsidy programmes involving cash payments to producers or consumers are notoriously expensive to administer, since the authorities need to verify that each recipient is entitled to the money. Cheating can be commonplace. For example, subsidised kerosene and LPG have been diverted to transport uses in several countries, including Ecuador and India, causing major safety problems as well as depriving the poor of fuel.

13.1.5 Transparency

Transparency is essential to good governance. The goals of a particular subsidy policy, the associated financial costs, the channels through which financial transfers are made and assessments of their impact should always be made fully transparent. Reporting this information to parliament and publishing it on a regular basis would help to prevent abuse as well as enable the authorities and the public to monitor the cost of the programme. Germany has, since 1967, a regular reporting system on all subsidies. If developed further, this could serve as an example for a reporting system likely to emerge under the Kyoto Protocol to monitor the reduction of subsidies that run counter to the goal of reducing greenhouse gas emissions. Where a subsidy programme is justified, it should be kept on-budget, to make it more visible and easier to monitor. On-budget costs should be properly accounted for and the results made available to the public.

13.1.6 Duration

When introducing a subsidy, it often makes sense to establish a time limit or a 'sunset clause' for ending the programme. This ensures that producers and consumers do not get permanently 'hooked' on the subsidy and can prevent the financial cost of the programme spiralling out of control. It also forces policymakers to actively question the need to maintain the programme. Ideally, temporary subsidies should be linked to clearly defined targets, such as the penetration of a particular fuel or cost reductions. Once a technology or a distribution network is established and economic, the subsidy would normally no longer be needed. The short-lived reintroduction of coal subsidies in the United Kingdom in 2000, designed to give the mining industry a chance to further improve competitiveness, was accompanied by a commitment to remove them in 2002. The subsidy was duly removed after two years. Many other subsidy programmes described in this report remain in place because of political inertia and vested interests regardless of whether the original rationale for them is still valid.

13.2 Implementing energy subsidy reforms

13.2.1 Barriers to reform

Even when there is general agreement that the cost of a particular subsidy outweighs its benefits, it can be very difficult to reform the subsidy in the face of hostility from those who benefit from it and politicians who champion their cause. By its very nature, the costs of an energy subsidy are usually spread throughout the economy, while its benefits are usually enjoyed by only a small segment of society—not necessarily the targeted group. Those beneficiaries will always have an interest in defending that subsidy when their gains exceed their share of the economic or environmental costs—a phenomenon known as **political mobilisation bias** (IEA 1999). It is easier to lobby political support for the clear interests of small, homogenous groups than for the comparatively vague 'public interest'. This helps to explain why subsidies are as popular in practice as they are unpopular in theory.

The resistance to cutting subsidies can be very strong. Plans to raise electricity prices in India in 2000 led to mass demonstrations and rioting, which left dozens dead. The German coal-mining industry has been remarkably successful in garnering public support for maintaining subsidies, despite the large economic costs and determined claims from the green lobby that those subsidies boost coal use and exacerbate pollution. Indeed, it would be cheaper and the effects would be less distortionary if subsidies were paid to workers directly without linking them to coal production. Resistance to reform is particularly acute in the economies in transition. In these countries, the general public often still considers energy to be a basic social good, like food and housing, the pricing of which should not be left solely to market forces.

The majority of the population, who bear the net cost of the subsidy, are typically less inclined to support political action to remove the subsidy since the cost is likely to be much smaller in per capita terms than the benefit to the recipients. Furthermore, it can be difficult to demonstrate the economic cost of subsidy in terms that the public can understand. Those that want to keep a subsidy often find it much easier to provide concrete examples of their social benefits: for example, in terms of jobs supported or financial savings to poor people. Information about economic efficiency losses is much harder to document and explain to the general public. The problem is even bigger when the environmental costs of a subsidy are global, as with greenhouse gas emissions. Most people in poor developing countries have less concern for such matters, though they are likely to be affected most by climate change.

These barriers to reform help to explain why it is so hard to remove subsidies once they have been introduced. This inertia makes it all the more important for policy-makers to be extremely cautious in devising new subsidies. As a rule, a new subsidy should only be introduced if the immediate net benefits are demonstratively large and likely to persist for a long time.

13.2.2 Overcoming resistance

Reforming existing energy subsidies requires strong political will to take tough decisions that benefit society as a whole. Politicians are often more willing to tackle difficult subsidy issues immediately after elections in the hope that opposition to reform will have diminished by the time new elections come around.

The following approaches can help policy-makers to overcome resistance:

- Reforms may need to be implemented in a gradual, programmed fashion to alleviate the financial pain of those who stand to lose out and give them time to adapt. This is likely to be the case where removing a subsidy has major economic and social consequences. The pace of reform, however, should not be so slow that delaying its full implementation involves excessive costs. Financial support for coal mining in France, for example, has been gradually reduced under a 20-year programme agreed in 1986. This made the removal of subsidies politically easier and eased the pain of social adjustment, although the financial burden of coal subsidies was reduced only slowly.

- If reforming an energy subsidy reduces the purchasing power of a specific social group, the authorities can introduce compensating measures that support their real incomes in more direct and effective ways—if that goal is considered socially desirable. It may, in any case, be the price that the government has to pay to achieve public support for reform. Such a move, however, depends on systems and structures for distributing welfare payments to the needy.
- Politicians need to communicate clearly to the general public the overall benefits of subsidy reform with respect to the economy, the environment and society as a whole. They also need to involve stakeholders in the process of formulating subsidy reforms to counter political inertia and opposition. In most industrialised countries, for example, the public is becoming familiar with the environmental advantages of renewables and natural gas over coal, making it harder for politicians to maintain support to ailing coal industries.

Multilateral lending institutions, other international organisations and aid providers have an important role to play in devising and implementing addressing energy subsidy reforms. They can provide advice and expertise on subsidy reform and broader aspects of energy policy-making. They can also impose well-reasoned conditions on subsidy reform for lending and development aid. Indeed, countries trying to cut subsidies may find it politically safer and easier to have their hands tied by such conditions. These organisations should, nonetheless, take account of environmental and social considerations in formulating their strategies for developing countries and transition economies even if the primary aim should be to eliminate costly and ineffective subsidies. For example, at a Ministerial Meeting in July 2001, the G8 Task Force on Renewable Energy committed to help developing countries strengthen institutional capacity and national strategies aimed at removing subsidies on conventional energy and attracting private investment in renewables.

13.3 Conclusions

Energy subsidy reform can play a vital role in moving countries onto more sustainable development paths. Many of the subsidies described in this study—especially those that encourage fossil fuel consumption—are clearly harmful to the environment as well as being economically costly. Removing them would, therefore, be a win–win policy. However, there may be a strong case in principle for retaining or even introducing subsidies in specific instances to address a particular social or environmental policy goal. Nevertheless, how such a subsidy is applied in practice has a big impact on how successful it is in meeting policy objectives and on its cost. By following the principles described in this chapter, policy-makers can limit harmful side-effects and greatly improve the cost-effectiveness of energy subsidy programmes. The country chapters provide numerous examples of this. For instance, the targeted use of lifeline rates in India could greatly reduce the cost of ensuring a minimum level of service to poor households. And structural and regulatory reforms in OECD countries, the Czech and Slovak Republics and Chile demonstrate how market-based approaches to energy pricing can bring about more-efficient energy resource allocation and use. The gradual shift in subsidies away from fossil fuels towards energy efficiency and renewables in many countries reflects a genuine attempt to question the rationale for established subsidy schemes and a growing recognition of the damage that many of them do to the environment, to the economy and to social welfare. In many such cases, considerable progress has been made in overcoming resistance to reforms by communicating the potential benefits to the general public and implementing them in a way that minimises the impact on particular social groups.

Understanding the effects of energy subsidies is crucial to designing appropriate reforms. Considerable progress has been made in developing methodologies for identifying the relationships between subsidy polices and broader economic and social indicators, although quantifying those effects in practice remains highly complex. Various methodological approaches that can be used to assess quantitatively the economic, environmental and social effects of energy subsidy reform in an integrated way are reviewed in more detail in the annex that follows this chapter.

Annex
Methodological approaches to analysing energy subsidy reform

This annex describes various methodological approaches to examining the economic, environmental and social effects of energy subsidy reform in an integrated way. In principle, the volume of pollution associated with energy use under a subsidised regime would be reduced if support were removed since the level of energy supply would normally fall. Economic gains are also possible as a result of reduced government expenditure on subsidies and improved efficiency in the economy. Any economic or environmental effects resulting from subsidy reform will also have a social dimension, affecting some socioeconomic groups more than others. Integrated assessment of different effects requires measuring the welfare effects in the same way. The assessment needs to be carefully tailored to the local context. Involvement of stakeholders in assessing the effects of energy subsidy reform in an integrated manner and gaining support for policy action is critical.

A1 Assessing economic effects

Various methodologies for assessing the economic impact of reform of energy subsidies exist. Data availability and other institutional constraints may limit their applicability to particular countries and regions. The range of methodologies presented here is by no means comprehensive but is intended to reflect those that are well established as well as some that remain in development.

Established methodologies that are appropriate for the assessment of economic impacts of energy subsidy reform are based on models of the economy that detail the relationships between key economic variables within a market or markets. Such models are built using theoretical and empirical estimates of these relationships. To a large degree, the sophistication of the analysis depends on the number of market interdependencies that are considered. It should be emphasised in the context of energy subsidy reform that a reliance on market-based economic analysis limits our depth of understanding in economies with widespread state ownership. Equally, application of this type of analysis is inappropriate in areas such as sub-Saharan Africa, where non-market transactions make up a significant part of the economy.

A1.1 Partial equilibrium analysis

The simplest type of analysis, known as partial equilibrium analysis, considers only the market directly impacted by the proposed subsidy reform and identifies price and output changes in that market. The analytical framework is known as demand and supply analysis. It is most often illustrated in diagrammatic terms, as in Figure A1.

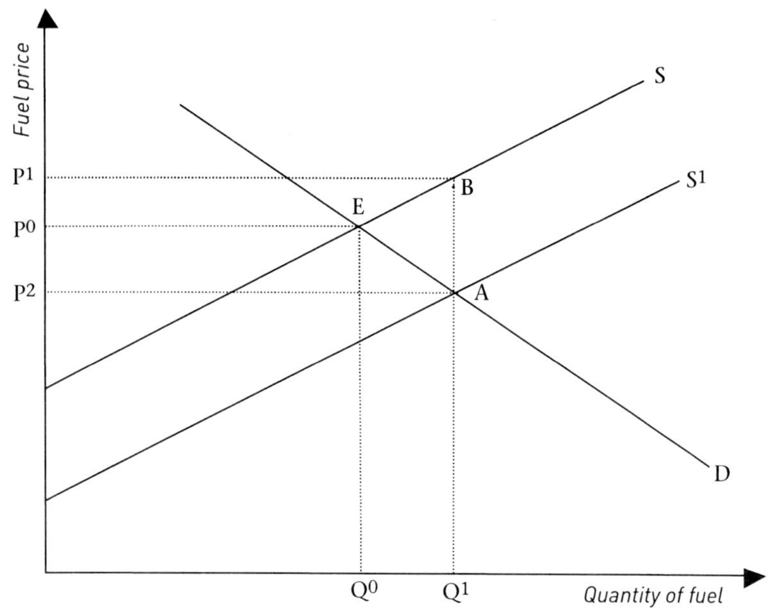

Figure A1 **Impact of subsidy removal on output (example of a consumer subsidy in a closed economy)**

The removal of an energy subsidy will directly impact the equilibrium price that holds in the particular energy market that is affected. For example, in a number of developing countries and former centrally planned countries, energy prices to consumers are held below the market equilibrium price. In Figure A1, this subsidised price is represented by price P^2 below the market equilibrium price of P^0. In this market the demand function, relating the quantity of energy that will be demanded at different prices, is represented by the curve D. The original supply function, relating the quantity supplied by producers at different prices, is given by the curve S. The subsidised supply function, where the government is in effect paying the producers to supply more, is given by S^1.

In this example, the subsidised price of P^2, the quantity demanded by consumers, is greater (Q^1) than that demanded at the equilibrium market price (Q^0). If the subsidy is removed so that the market price rises to the equilibrium level of P^0, consumers' welfare will decline, represented by the loss in consumer surplus. This is the difference between what consumers are willing to pay for a given quantity (given by the demand curve) and what they actually pay (the market price). It is represented by the area P^2P^0EA. Producers, too, will suffer a reduction in their producer surplus—the difference between what they receive for each unit of output (the market price) and what it costs to produce (given by the supply curve). This is represented by area P^1P^0EB. However, the combined consumer and producer losses are outweighed by the fact that, when the subsidy is no longer given, there is a saving in government expenditure, represented by the area P^2P^1BA. The resulting net welfare gain to society is EAB.[48]

The slopes of the demand and supply curves will determine the precise results of a partial equilibrium analysis of the type outlined above. The steepness of the curves indicates the degree to which a change in the price brings about a change in the quantity supplied by producers and the quantity demanded by consumers. These degrees of responsiveness are known as the price elasticity of supply and demand. If the response in quantity, in percentage terms, is greater than the percentage change in price that brought about the response, the price elasticity is said to be elastic. The curve will be relatively flat. Conversely, if the quantity response is less than the price change in percentage terms then the price elasticity is known as being inelastic, and the curve will be steeper. These elasticities will determine the magnitude of the impact of energy subsidy removal or reduction on output and, therefore, employment.

This formal analysis can be understood intuitively. If a subsidy is removed, the price of the good rises and consumers are not able to buy the same quantity as before. Hence they will be worse off in real terms. For producers, Figure A1 shows that, without the subsidy, output is lower, which is likely to be reflected in reduced employment. These losses, as highlighted in this partial equilibrium analysis, may be less than the gains that the state (and therefore society) makes as a result of not having to allocate resources away from other productive uses and to subsidised production. These gains can only be picked up through the use of general equilibrium analysis. The net social welfare gain also masks a pattern of gains and losses by different groups. As is evident above, it is those parties that suffer losses that are most likely to argue against energy subsidy reform. It is the role of general equilibrium analysis to demonstrate the broader gains that society makes as a result of the reduced burden on the public finances of the economy.

Indicative estimates of price elasticities of demand for different energy sources in OECD and developing countries are presented in Table A1. It notes that the values are negative, reflecting the fact the quantity response is in the opposite

48 This analysis has been shown for only one market. When supply and demand in different markets are related, the analysis has to be extended to several markets. In practice, this would require more data on the effects of changes in prices in one market on demand and supply in others.

	Gasoline	*Gas*	*Coal*	*Electricity*
Developing countries	−0.5	−0.5	−0.5	−0.5
OECD	−0.5	−0.7	−1.3	−0.5

Table A1 **Typical price elasticities of demand for different energy sources**

Source: Anderson 1995

direction to the price movement. Furthermore, elasticities also change over time as technology changes and as technical endowments change. The price elasticities of demand shown are—with the exception of coal in OECD countries—inelastic. In this case, any reduction in output and the accompanying fall in employment in the energy sector resulting from a reduction in subsidies would be expected to be relatively small.

These indicative values clearly give only a first estimation of the market relationships that exist in the country or region of concern to the analyst. It is preferable to gather actual data on the market affected by the reforms in order to get an accurate measure of the economic effects. In many cases where an energy subsidy reform is under consideration, data is likely to be either unavailable or incomplete. In this case, the analyst has to rely on his or her understanding of the structure of the market or broad generic estimates of price elasticities and output–employment relationships.

A number of studies have used partial equilibrium models to assess the impact of the introduction or removal of energy subsidies. A 1994 study by DRI on behalf of the OECD used a partial equilibrium model to estimate the potential effects of removing coal subsidies on the world coal market in a group of countries including France, Germany, Spain, UK, Japan and Turkey (DRI/McGraw-Hill 1994). In part because the analysts were modelling only the effects of going *beyond* already-announced reforms, the study concluded that the price effect would be very small, since the global supply curve for coal was assumed to be very elastic. Consequently, the effect on demand for coal was small and the macroeconomic effects limited. However, there would be significant regional employment effects hidden within a total employment loss of 174,000 in these countries between 1990 and 2010.[49]

A 1995 study of the macroeconomic impact of phasing out producer subsidies in oil-exporting developing countries by Birol *et al.* used an econometric partial equilibrium model to estimate price- and non-price-induced energy savings. The domestic oil savings were estimated at 13% in Algeria, 20% in Iran and 19% in Nigeria for the year 2005. The study assumed that oil saved would be sold on the world market, resulting in substantially increased export revenues. Including the increased domestic revenues, the total increase in revenues was estimated to be $9.5 billion in Algeria, $4.5 billion in Iran and $14.9 billion in Nigeria.

49 These conclusions have been challenged in a study by Anderson and McKibbin (1997), which argues that the supply effects would be much larger.

A 1999 study by the International Energy Agency asks the question, *what would happen to energy consumption, exports/imports and CO_2 emissions if all subsidies for energy end-use were removed?* (IEA 1999). The study looked at eight countries: China, Russia, India, Indonesia, Iran, South Africa, Venezuela and Kazakhstan. It uses a price-gap measure of subsidies. The results are shown in Table A2.

	Average subsidisation (% of reference price)	*Annual economic efficiency gains (% of GDP)*	*Reduction in energy consumption (%)*	*Reduction in CO_2 emissions (%)*
China	10.89	0.37	9.41	13.44
Russia	32.52	1.54	18.03	17.1
India	14.17	0.34	7.18	14.15
Indonesia	27.51	0.24	7.09	10.97
Iran	80.42	2.22	47.54	49.45
South Africa	6.41	0.1	6.35	8.11
Venezuela	57.57	1.17	24.94	26.07
Kazakhstan	18.23	0.98	19.22	22.76
Total sample	21.12	0.73	12.80	15.96

Table A2 **Results of 1999 IEA study on energy subsidies**

Source: IEA 1999

In these IEA country studies, those that focused on oil and not coal often set the reference or market price as the international price of oil. This would establish a 'horizontal' supply curve for oil in Figure A1 and any subsidy would lower that curve, yielding a loss of welfare. Critics have pointed out, however, that the international price is not really a free-market price and so the real welfare loss could be different from that calculated on this basis. While this is true at the global level, at the national level oil is available at the international price and so this can effectively be taken as the relevant supply price, giving a welfare measure for the country of any removal of subsidy that is correct (we assume the country is not in a position to be able to change the price it pays by altering its level of consumption, which is generally a correct assumption).[50]

A1.2 General equilibrium analysis

Partial equilibrium analysis of this type makes the economic impacts of subsidy reform in the sector directly affected more transparent. However, it cannot provide

50 One reviewer has also noted that the estimated welfare effects will depend on the exchange rate, which is often out of line with the correct rate. In a proper estimation of welfare benefits a shadow rate should be used, which corrects for this distortion, thus defining the market rate to allow for this fact.

answers to certain questions. For example, price increases in the energy sector will affect the input mix in other sectors of the economy that use energy as an input to production. If no substitution is possible, these higher prices will be passed on to some degree. In the absence of similar reforms in other countries, the international competitiveness of domestic industries will also be affected. There may also be upward pressure on domestic inflation. These sectoral and macroeconomic effects are not addressed in partial equilibrium analysis, nor are efficiency gains in resource allocation throughout the economy. These effects therefore need to be identified and quantified using a wider framework. Computable general equilibrium (CGE) models are the most common such approach for analysing the impact of subsidy reform. The CGE model incorporates a set of behavioural equations describing economic behaviour of the agents identified in the model as well as the technological and institutional constraints that they face. The model is in equilibrium because a set of prices and quantities exists such that all excess demands are zero. This is a counterpart of a Walrasian equilibrium and has its roots in welfare economics.

General equilibrium analysis involves a complex set of calculations to determine market prices using a set of demand and supply equations. The analysis is therefore most frequently undertaken using a computer. Computable general equilibrium models essentially simulate markets for production factors and goods using systems of equations specifying supply and demand behaviour across all markets. There are many examples of CGE models, each 'tailor-built' with a specific purpose in mind.[51] It is not, therefore, possible to present a generic methodology here. However, in all cases the main tasks for the modeller are to:

- Specify the demand and supply equations and to determine the values of the parameters of these equations; and
- Solve the system of equations, which will almost invariably be non-linear.

This exercise is first undertaken for the economy with the subsidy in place. The proposed subsidy reform is then modelled by shifting the supply and demand curves. The model is then re-solved, yielding a new vector of output and consumer prices. The overall net cost or benefit of the policy is determined by examining the difference between the pre- and post-policy vectors of prices and outputs.

The data and resource requirements for the construction of CGE models are very substantial. However, this drawback should be weighed against the gains in accuracy of simulation to actual market changes that such modelling allows.

Results of three CGE studies that have attempted to estimate the economic effects of energy subsidy reform are presented in Table A3. The conclusion that can be drawn from these studies is that the welfare effects from subsidy reform—as measured by changes to GDP—are likely to be positive at an aggregate level. This is primarily due to the enhanced price incentives to allocate resources efficiently. For example, one consequence of reform may be that the savings in government expenditure are reflected in lower marginal tax rates on labour, thus encouraging more labour to be supplied to the market. Another key finding is that the economic

51 An overview of such models is provided in OECD 1997b.

Study/author	*Geographical area*	*Time-period*	*Support measure removed*	*Model specifics*	*Economic effects*
Burniaux *et al.* 1992	OECD and non-OECD countries	1990–2050	All consumer subsidies	Multi-region dynamic general equilibrium model	Real income increases per annum: • World: 0.7% • OECD: 0.1% • Non-OECD: 1.6%
Larsen and Shah 1992	Sample of non-OECD countries	1990–2020	All consumer subsidies	Multi-region dynamic general equilibrium model	Non-OECD income increases by $35 billion (1.8% per annum)
Clarke and Edwards 1997	Western Germany	1990	All producer subsidies	Single-country static general equilibrium model	GDP increases by 0.35% (0.55% including environmental benefits)

Table A3 **Economic effects of energy subsidy reform: results from CGE models**

gains are likely to be much bigger in non-OECD countries, mainly because subsidies there are bigger.

The coverage and findings of these studies differ substantially. These differences reflect less their authors' differences in opinion about the nature of the markets concerned and more the differences in model capacity, data availability and the time-periods considered. One lesson for future CGE development and application is that every aspect of the model's design and scope should be made as transparent as possible in order to explain differences in findings. This would promote harmonisation of approaches to analysing subsidy reform.

A1.3 Extended partial equilibrium analysis

An alternative to CGE modelling is for the partial equilibrium analysis to be extended to several linked markets. This approach requires data on the effects of changes in prices in one market on demand and supply in others. This option may be better suited to the context of some developing countries where the development of interconnected goods and factor markets is not as advanced as is assumed in most CGE models. In extended partial equilibrium analysis, the analyst can judge for him- or herself which markets should be included in the study in order to capture the majority of the welfare effects. Figure A2 illustrates the distinction between partial, extended partial and computable general equilibrium modelling. To take the example of changes in subsidies on electricity and gas, we could look at the impacts of these in the markets for the two commodities. In the 'micro-level' case, this would be done independently for each market, rather as illustrated in Figure A1. At the sectoral level, the analysis would look at the energy sector as a whole, so account would be taken of the cross-effects between electricity, gas and other sources of energy, which arise when the prices of electricity and gas are changed as a result of the subsidy removal. Finally, there is the full general equilibrium analysis at the economy-wide level, which takes account of the linkages between all markets, including the markets for labour, and the commodities that are produced using the different forms of energy. For example, more energy-intensive production will increase in price, which will have an impact on the welfare of consumers.

A1.4 Input–output modelling

An alternative approach, if there is insufficient data to build one of the above models, is to make a more general characterisation of the economic system in terms of input–output flows. These provide an estimate of the quantity changes that would result from energy subsidy reform. Input–output analysis, as it is known, is based on linkages between economic activities. Each production activity acts both as a 'supplier' and a 'buyer'. Each activity sells its output to other sectors and to final consumers, while also buying outputs from other sectors, as well as labour, capital and raw materials (primary inputs). The total value of output from any one activity comprises both the value of intermediary goods and services acquired from other sectors and the value of primary inputs consumed directly in the production process.

Input–output analysis is essentially a method of systematically quantifying the linkages between various sectors in an economy. Although there are no examples of the application of this modelling approach to the assessment of energy subsidy reform, there seems to be some potential for its use in the future since the data requirements are less severe than with CGE modelling.[52]

A1.5 Indicators of economic effects

Measures of economic well-being are generally expressed in terms of income and, at a national level, GDP. The methodologies outlined above allow changes in these indicators to be used. Intermediate economic indicators, such as reduced competitiveness in international markets as a consequence of higher prices resulting from the removal of a subsidy, may also be used. However, these indicators can also be converted to GDP. For example, the net loss in export revenues is reflected in lower national income levels and lower total economic welfare, expressed in monetary terms.

52 See EC 1996 for further details of how this technique can be applied. It should be noted, however, that input–output data can require some degree of sector-based averaging in values, which may affect the reliability of the results.

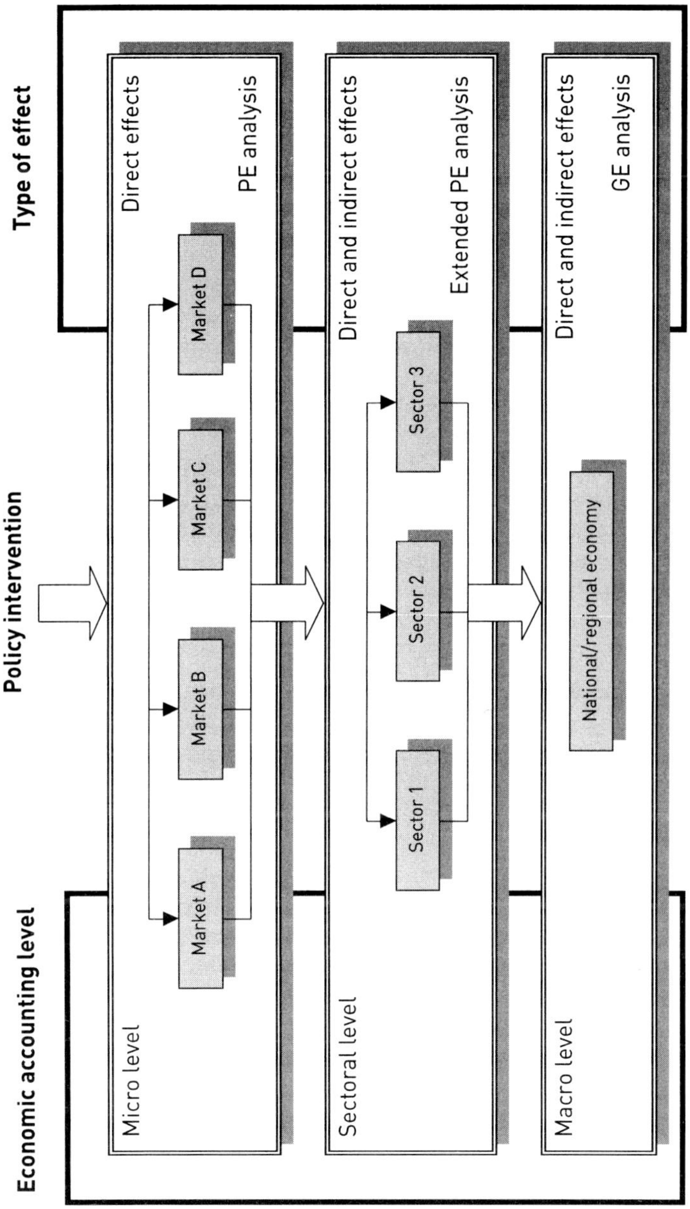

PE = partial equilibrium GE = general equilibrium

Figure A2 Partial equilibrium, extended partial equilibrium and computable general equilibrium modelling

A2 Assessing environmental effects

Energy subsidy reform is likely to have two principal types of environmental effect. First, if the effect of a subsidy is to lower the price of a fuel to the consumer or the cost of production to the supplier, a subsidy will tend to increase demand for that fuel. With higher demand, more fuel will be consumed, which will, in turn, affect the quantity of polluting emissions to the environment. The precise nature of this relationship is itself determined by the amount of substitution that occurs between highly polluting fuels and less-polluting fuels.[53] Pollution can be local, such as toxic airborne or water-borne emissions; regional, such as acid rain; or global, such as climate change brought about by emissions of greenhouse gases. We focus in this section on pollution from emissions to air. While there are a number of models relating to water and land pollution, the effects of energy subsidy reform on the environment has received more attention in its relation to air pollution.

The second form of environmental and social impact is on the depletion of natural resource stocks. In the case of fossil fuels, stocks are non-renewable. Once used, they are not directly replaceable and so the long-term capacity to provide energy from this source is depleted. In the absence of a substitute, future levels of welfare will be reduced. However, as natural resource accounting methodologies suggest, substitution between natural capital and other forms of capital can offset this welfare effect.

A2.1 Local air pollution modelling

Local air pollution modelling aims to identify the change in pollution that results from a change in energy use that, in turn, results from a change in an energy subsidy. Figure A3 presents a framework for air quality assessment. It should be noted that the modelling requirements are high if the analysis is undertaken from scratch because of the complexity of the interrelationships between economic activities and pollution. One starts with the changes in *emissions* resulting from the change in subsidies. These are then dispersed geographically and generate changes in concentrations of pollution in different locations. The *dispersion modelling* module deals with these changes. Individuals and non-human assets are affected by these changes, which are evaluated in the *exposure assessment* module. From these exposures one can make a *damage assessment* in physical terms (e.g. change in number of restricted activity days for the population). The data from this assessment is fed into the *economic assessment* of the damages, as well as the changes in environmental expenditures required to address these damages. This whole environmental effects assessment interfaces with the economic assessment shown below the dashed line, which looks at the economic and social effects of the environmental and other changes.

53 The removal of a subsidy may increase or reduce pollution, depending on how the fuel mix is changed. The removal of a subsidy on solar power may, for example, result in higher pollution as demand switches to more-polluting fuels.

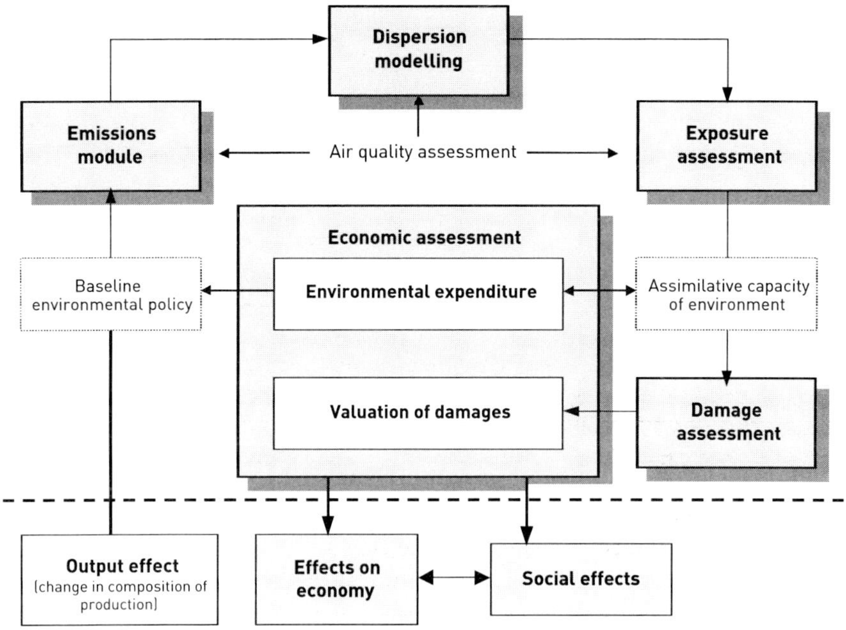

Figure A3 Key components of air pollution assessment

The starting point is to estimate the output effects associated with subsidy removal: namely, the changes in the volume of activity in the recipient sector that will determine changes in emissions. Using the partial equilibrium methodology used to quantify economic impacts, a larger change in the quantity of production will lead to a larger change in incomes, and therefore emissions and resource use.[54] It follows that the economic and environmental quality effects of subsidy removal will be greater the more elastic is supply. The effects of different price elasticities on emissions and resource use are summarised in Table A4.

In general, the magnitude of the change in production levels induced by subsidy reform and the subsequent change in environmental effects depend on:

- The characteristics of the support measure being removed. These might include among others, how the subsidy:
  - i affects the marginal costs of the recipient sector relative to its competitors;
  - ii protects the recipient sector from competition by other means;
  - iii forces consumers to use the subsidised fuel; and
  - iv affects the total amount of energy consumed.

54 Assuming the same technologies and level of environmental protection.

		Price elasticity of supply	
		High	**Low**
Price elasticity of demand	**High**	Large	Moderate to small
	Low	Moderate to small	Small

Table A3 **The effect of elasticities on potential emissions and resource use with producer subsidies**

Source: Adapted from OECD 1998

- The characteristics of the recipient sector. For example, how supply and demand conditions in the recipient sector affect choices open to that sector, including substitution possibilities.
- Existing and expected environmental policy. For example, how environmental regulations affect baseline emissions and resource use.
- Autonomous technological and economic change. For example, how developments in the relative costs of different types of energy and other factors affect market penetration, baseline emission and resource use.

The effects of subsidy removal on downstream industries may also have important economic and environmental consequences. In particular, energy subsidy reform may lead to substitution of material inputs in industries, which could impact the economy or the environment. A 1998 study by Normann *et al.* investigated the potential impact of subsidy removal on the use of energy-intensive and less-energy-intensive processes in the newsprint industry in Sweden. The study concluded that subsidy removal might lead to the loss of competitiveness *vis-à-vis* other countries, leading to a fall in energy demand by this sector and, therefore, lower emissions in Sweden. The overall environmental impact of a shift in newsprint production would depend crucially on the emissions levels from energy generation and the process used to produce the newsprint. If less-energy-intensive production process were used and the energy were generated using less-polluting technologies, then overall pollution would fall. Several factors determine the environmental impact of subsidy reform on downstream industries. These include the effect of a smaller subsidy, or increased taxation, on the marginal effective tax rate on energy use and the difference between the energy intensity of alternative production processes. The impact on competitiveness of reducing subsidies depends on the extent to which other countries follow suit in reducing energy subsidies.

These factors reinforce or counter the effects of subsidy removal. They must, therefore, be taken into account in the analytical framework. The purpose of the emissions module in an economic model is to calculate a spatially distributed (or 'gridded') emissions inventory,[55] with and without the support measure. The gridded emissions inventory provides the input to a dispersion model, which allows air pollution concentrations in an area to be calculated as a function of time and location. It also provides the basis for calculating the effects of subsidy removal on air quality. Environmental damage assessment yields information on the impact of air pollution on human health, ecosystems and buildings.

The purpose of the economic assessment is to place a monetary value on the damaging effects of air pollution and the cost of environmental protection. This can be done using various methods. These include valuing losses in productivity losses or expenditures on averting damage. Another approach involves evaluating people's willingness to pay (WTP), or willingness to accept (WTA) compensation for changes in environmental quality. This can be achieved by studying behaviour in similar markets where a value has been placed on environmental quality or by surveying people's WTP and WTA.

In practice, two main approaches have been adopted to assessing the effects of energy subsidy reform on air quality. The more sophisticated of these approaches relies on the so-called 'impact pathway' approach adopted in the European Commission's ExternE project (see e.g. EC 1995, 1999), and subsequently applied in countries such as Brazil, Russia and China. An impact pathway identifies the sequence of events linking the emission of a specific pollutant such as SO_2 to a specific impact such as reductions in crop yields, allowing a value on the environmental costs to be calculated. The methodology therefore proceeds sequentially through the main elements shown in Figure A3. The total costs and benefits associated with a change in the energy mix are calculated by adding up all the values associated with each pollutant.[56] Table A5 provides estimates of environmental damage for all the countries in the European Union from the ExternE project. The estimates are for one or more sites rather than national averages. As a result, most country estimates are shown as ranges.

A simpler approach relies on fixed damage-cost coefficients for individual pollutants: for example, in the form of euros per tonne of pollutant. These coefficients reflect the economic effects of the pollutant on some combination of human health, crops, materials and ecosystems. They are usually derived from the application of the impact pathway approach in a specific geographical context. This approach requires far less information than impact pathway analysis, but is less flexible and transparent. Aggregate costs and benefits are calculated by multiplying the standard coefficients by changes in emission levels in a specific context. In analysing the effects of reforming energy subsidies, the geographical dispersion

55 An emissions inventory is a list of all the relevant air pollutants in a geographical area, broken down by activity sector (for example, power generation, energy-intensive industries and transport).

56 Valuation exercises such as this can only ever capture some of the benefits and costs. For example, valuation of the health effects of air pollution using the impact pathway technique cannot capture lifestyle changes, minor physical and mental discomfort or some of the more chronic intangible effects.

Country	SO_2	NO_x	Particulates
Austria	9,000	16,800	16,800
Belgium	11,388–12,141	11,526–12,296	24,536–24,537
Denmark	2,990–4,216	3,280–4,728	3,390–6,666
Finland	1,027–1,486	852–1,388	1,340–2,611
France	7,500–15,300	10,800–18,000	6,100–57,000
Germany	1,800–13,688	10,945–15,100	19,500–23,415
Greece	1,978–7,832	1,240–7,798	2,014–8,278
Ireland	2,800–5,300	2,750–3,000	2,800–5,415
Italy	5,700–12,000	4,600–13,567	5,700–20,700
Netherlands	6,205–7,581	5,480–6,085	15,006–16,830
Portugal	4,960–5,242	5,975–6,562	5,565–6,955
Spain	4,219–9,583	4,651–12,056	4,418–20,250
Sweden	2,357–2,810	1,957–2,340	2,732–3,840
United Kingdom	6,027–10,025	5,736–9,612	8,000–22,917

Table A5 **Unit damage costs of air pollutants from the ExternE project (1995 €/tonne)**

Source: De Nocker *et al.* 1999

modelling that the impact pathway analysis requires will generally not be possible, so that a fixed-coefficient approach may well be more appropriate in many cases.

Some recent studies have examined the local benefits associated with a reduction in air pollution brought about as a result of action to meet a target for reducing climate-destabilising greenhouse gas emissions. A 2000 study on China by Garbaccio and Jorgensen estimated that reductions in carbon emissions of 5% per annum, compared with a base case, would cut premature deaths by around 4% and reduce hospital visits and days lost from sickness. Using standard valuation methods, these benefits were converted into a gain in gross domestic product of 0.2% per year, equivalent to about $2 billion in 2000. A 1995 study by Larsen and Shah estimates that removing subsidies to energy production in China would reduce carbon emissions by about 7%. Therefore, energy subsidy removal would be expected to yield an environmental health benefit of around 0.3% of GDP. The results for China can be applied to the world as a whole to give a rough figure on the potential local environmental gain from energy subsidy removal. Larsen and Shah estimated that global subsidy removal would reduce carbon emissions by 5%. That equates to local air quality benefits of roughly 0.2% of world GDP, or $56 billion for 2000. These estimates, however, depend critically on the assumptions made about the monetary value of health improvements. A 1995 IEA study estimated that eliminating all subsidies in Russia would reduce NO_x emissions by 40% over 20 years compared with 1990 levels. SO_2 emissions would fall by 65% and total suspended particulates by 75%. These would generate substantial air quality benefits.

A2.2 Global climate change modelling

For global pollutants such as greenhouse gases from energy combustion processes, the overall impact of energy subsidy policies on emissions can be assessed using global climate integrated assessment modelling. This approach may draw on the results of economic modelling.[57]

Two major studies estimated the effect of fossil fuel subsidies on global carbon levels. In both cases, the effects are expressed in terms of physical units. The 1992 study by Larsen and Shah, described in Table A3, estimated the size of fuel subsidies in every country by comparing the domestic price of each type of fuel with its world price. The impact of the removal of subsidies on greenhouse gases was estimated using the relationship between energy prices and energy consumption and carbon emission factors for each fuel. The study concludes that subsidy removal would reduce emissions by around 9% of global emissions. Because unsubsidised fuel prices on international markets would fall as consumption in countries with subsidies falls, consumption would rise in other countries. The net reductions in global emissions would therefore be lower, at around 5%. The bulk of the reductions would come from countries that consume large quantities of subsidised coal: notably, the former Soviet Union, China, Poland, South Africa, the former Czechoslovakia and India.

A 1998 study by the OECD shows that the methodology employed and assumptions made crucially affect the results of analyses of the potential for reducing carbon emissions. The study reviews two studies, one by Anderson and McKibbin in 1997 and the 1994 DRI study. Anderson and McKibbin conclude that subsidy removal in the countries considered would reduce coal production, but that coal imports would rise. This would drive up the world price of coal, resulting in lower coal use in all countries. The resulting falls in carbon emissions would be substantial, at around 13% from the baseline. The DRI study also predicted increased coal imports in the countries that remove their subsidies, but no significant increase in world prices. As a result, global carbon emissions would be hardly affected, falling by a mere 0.3%. The large differences in the results of these two studies are explained by different assumptions about the price elasticities of supply[58] and the amount of subsidy removed,[59] and by different methodologies.[60]

Using a slightly different approach, Steenblik and Coroyannakis (1995) showed that, even assuming a one-for-one substitution of imported for domestically produced coal, elimination of subsidies to coal production in Europe could result in fewer emissions in greenhouse gases. For example, methane emissions from Europe's deep underground coal mines are much greater than from the mines from

57 A detailed description of this methodology can be found in Tol 1996.

58 DRI assumed a very flat or elastic supply curve compared with Anderson and McKibbin.

59 The level of subsidy removal in the DRI study was only half that of the level in the Anderson and McKibbin study.

60 DRI used partial equilibrium techniques, while Anderson and McKibbin employed a multi-country dynamic general equilibrium model of the world economy.

which imports would be sourced. And, because imported coal tends to be lower in sulphur, emissions of CO_2 would be saved through reduced scrubbing requirements. However, the authors suggest that reform could lead to *reduced* consumption of coal in Europe—at least in the medium term—as many old, inefficient coal-fired power plants were being kept in operation simply to meet obligations to consume domestic coal. Once those obligations are removed (as happened in the UK), much of this capacity would be decommissioned and not all of it would be replaced by new coal-fired capacity.

A2.3 Natural resource depletion

Assessing the value of depletion of fossil fuel resources requires an approach based on capital stocks, as changes in the stock of capital available for future use affect its potential for generating welfare for future generations. Valuing the future welfare change simply by multiplying the market price of the resource by the volume sold in the last period does not yield the true cost of over-depletion due to subsidies in terms of loss of welfare. Applying the approach in this manner does not give an indication of whether the revenue has been used to fund investment in alternative capital stocks for generating future welfare (sustainable income) or whether it has simply been spent on current consumption. So, appropriate methodologies must assess how much current production results in sustainable income. A number of studies have been carried out in this area, though none of them specifically addresses the issue of energy subsidy reform.[61] The effects of government policies on natural resource stocks are usually assessed in physical units, such as tonnes per year or the proportion of total remaining proven reserves.

A3 Assessing social effects

The assessment of the social effects of energy subsidy reform must address two principal concerns:

- First, how different social groups are affected by changes in energy prices. Changes in real income distribution result both from changes in the pattern of economic activity and changes in environmental conditions. The former is generally more significant. An understanding of the winners and losers from subsidy reform is essential to a full assessment of the potential welfare benefits.
- Second, how subsidy reform affects people's access to and use of different types of energy and consequently their health and well-being. This in turn affects their comfort levels and their ability to generate income. For

61 See e.g. Repetto *et al.* 1989 for Indonesia; Solorzano *et al.* 1991 for Costa Rica; van Tongeren *et al.* 1993 for Mexico; Bartelmus *et al.* 1993 for Papua New Guinea; and World Bank 1997b for 103 countries.

example, a shift of industrial subsidies to those that promote rural electrification can have a major impact on livelihoods and poverty alleviation in rural areas.

The relevance of the two sets of concerns will also differ considerably between developed and developing countries, with the latter being much more interested in the second set of issues. Within this category the results will also depend critically on the types of fuel used as well as the urban–rural distribution of population.

A3.1 Measuring income distribution effects

An extension of the partial and general equilibrium methodologies outlined above can be used to identify distributional effects. The price and quantity changes derived from equilibrium-based economic modelling provide a starting point for assessing changes in employment, consumption patterns and real incomes for different income groups within society. A matrix of the distribution of gains and losses can be generated in this way. This analysis can be extended by applying weights to the welfare losses identified in the different income groups. For example, lower-income groups could be given higher weighting to reflect the fact that income changes affect them proportionately more than richer people. To take a concrete case: if a scheme to remove subsidies reduces the real income of both a poor person and a rich by one euro, society may value the first loss greater, by giving it a weight of 2, and the second loss less, by giving it a weight of 0.5. In this way the total loss would add up to $(1 \times 2) + (1 \times 0.5) = 2.5$, instead of simply 2. Techniques for doing this have been developed some time ago and used in cost-benefit analysis.[62]

This also allows the changes to be expressed in monetary terms and the welfare losses to be aggregated on an equity-related basis. This method is based on converting changes in income into changes in welfare, assuming that an addition to the welfare of a lower-income person is worth more than that of a higher-income person.

Two recent studies used partial equilibrium analysis to identify the changes in real disposable income and welfare in different income groups that result from energy price increases. A 1995 study by Hope and Singh analysed the economic and social effects of energy price reform in Colombia, Ghana, Indonesia, Malaysia, Turkey and Zimbabwe. The study used survey data on household spending to estimate the effect of energy prices on spending patterns. The results depended on assumptions about demand elasticities, budget shares and the size of the price change. An inverse relationship between income and the share of energy in household budgets was found for kerosene and electricity—the two largest commercial energy sources used by households in these countries. In other words, rich households spend a lower proportion of their income on energy than poor income households do. The maximum loss in income was very small, ranging from 1% to slightly over 3%. In all cases, the biggest losers were poor urban households—the

62 For a recent study using such weights, see Markandya and Halsnaes 2002.

largest users of commercial fuels. However, this group is not typical of the poorest population groups, which comprise mainly rural households using non-commercial fuels. Furthermore, recipients of gasoline subsidies were primarily car owners, who are among the richest people in these countries.

A 1995 study by Freund and Wallich analysed the welfare effect of energy subsidy reform in Poland by estimating the changes in consumer surplus that would result when different price elasticities of demand are assumed. The welfare loss of higher energy prices is greater for the non-poor than for the poor.[63] Assuming a zero elasticity of demand, the welfare of the poorest quintile declines by 5.9%, while that of the richest quintile declines by 8.2%. For all consumers taken together, the welfare loss associated with an 80% increase in prices is between 4.6% and 7.6 % of their total budget, depending on the price elasticity of demand that is assumed. The more elastic the demand, the lower the welfare loss. In this study, among the different socioeconomic groups considered, farmers and families are hurt the least by higher energy prices, largely because they do not consume district heat for which prices increase the most. Assuming a zero elasticity of demand, their welfare drops by about 5.2%. That of pensioners drops the most, by 9.4%. Workers are also hurt significantly, their welfare falling by 7.1%. These results suggest that the 'constituency' for keeping prices low—primarily workers and pensioners—is quite large in Poland and demonstrates that reforming energy subsidies can face stiff political resistance.

A3.2 Assessing the wider social impacts of changes in use and access to different fuels

In developing countries one needs to look particularly closely at how the changes in prices affect the use of different types of energy by vulnerable groups and how the mix of fuels they use changes. For example, a reduction in subsidies to commercial fuels (gas, kerosene, LPG, etc.) has been known to make them so expensive that households resort to non-commercial fuels, such as wood, which can cause deforestation and increase exposure to indoor air pollution. The reduction of subsidies on kerosene in South Africa in recent years has prompted many households to switch to traditional biomass. Biomass is relatively cheap, but gathering can lead to deforestation and soil erosion. Estimates of worldwide premature deaths due to indoor air pollution are put at 2 million a year (Smith and Metha 2000).

Other important social impacts include:

- First, reduced demand for the less-subsidised energy could result in loss of employment. The strongest case of this has been with respect to the removal of coal subsidies, not only in the OECD countries but also in Eastern Europe. The shrinking of the coal sector as a result of these changes, as well as increased competition from other sources, has been remarkable, with serious impacts on employment in the coal -mining

63 'Poor' is defined here as the lowest income quintile. Preliminary results from the *poverty assessment* for Poland indicate that the poverty headcount is less than 20%.

areas. To alleviate this, countries such as Ukraine and the Russian Federation have developed programmes to retrain workers as well as to provide social protection to their families, with some help from the international community.

- Second, a World Bank study has shown a strong correlation between low indoor winter temperatures and illness of elderly people in Eastern Europe. For example in Sevastopol, Ukraine, it was reported that in 56% of households somebody had become ill because indoor temperatures were too low; in Moldova many households are subjected to indoor temperatures of only 5–10° Celsius in the winter months. Similar problems have been encountered in many other countries, especially in the last winter (2002–2003), which was exceptionally cold. Such effects are often not picked up in the energy indicators; indeed, an increase in 'energy efficiency', which is much lauded, may be evidence of an increasing problem of access (World Bank 2002).
- Third, another recent World Bank study looked at demographic and health data from over 60 low-income countries and found that, in urban areas, linking households to electricity is the only key factor reducing both infant mortality rate and under-five mortality rate, and that this effect is large, significant and independent of incomes (Buys *et al.* 2003). This may seem surprising, given that water supply is generally thought to have a bigger effect. Access to sanitation and piped water do of course have an impact, but it does not dominate that of electricity when the latter is also included in the regression.
- Finally, a lack of electricity increases the drudgery of work for women and could reduce their quality of life significantly (Reddy 2000). At the same time, proper education might be impeded by a lack of electricity in poor households, so that children cannot use enough of it for homework.

These impacts, especially related to health, are clearly important and have major social implications, especially in developing countries. Indeed, any programme of subsidy removal would need to track them with great care, in order to develop measures that offset these negative social effects, including through the rechannelling of financial resources to those who are in most need of them.

A3.3 Potential social advantages of subsidy removal

The above has focused mainly on the potential negative social consequences of removing subsidies but there are positive effects as well. If, for example, the reform programme proposes the dismantling of economy-wide energy subsidies, coupled with better targeting of subsidies on rural electrification projects, the net result could be that more people in the countryside gain access to electricity. This would increase opportunities for these people to undertake productive activities and so increase their incomes. Changes in future incomes can be measured using the sustainable livelihoods methodological approach.[64] This approach aims to answer the following questions:

- How are energy needs currently met, and what role does electricity have for those already connected?
- How does subsidy reform affect livelihoods?
- Will the reform have an equal effect on the welfare of men and women?
- Will the changes brought about by reform increase economic disparities within communities?

The results of sustainable livelihood studies are generally expressed either in physical units, such as the number people affected, or in a qualitative way, such as which gender is affected the most. In principle, however, it is possible to express the change in monetary terms if the present value of the change in future earnings resulting from the energy subsidy reform can be estimated. This assumes that market values can be assigned to the changes in production of goods and services brought about by the reform.

The implementation of the rural electrification master plan for Namibia,[65] launched in 2000, is an example of retargeting of energy subsidies towards a specific social group: in this case, the rural poor. The scheme plans to connect 52,000 customers to the electricity grid in 2,157 localities over the next 20 years. The benefits in present value terms are reportedly significantly above the cost of nearly NAD50 million. The development of the master plan by the electricity company involved wide consultation with stakeholders, including local and regional authorities and the central government.

A3.4 Integrated assessment

The three building blocks for integrated assessment are the economic, the environmental and the social. In this annex each of these has been discussed in some detail but each by itself is not enough.

Economic analysis is best undertaken as the first part of the integrated assessment process, since subsidies are economic instruments and, as such, are designed primarily to bring about economic changes. Data on changes in GDP that result from subsidy reform masks the fact that different groups within society will benefit or lose out to differing degrees. Analysis of the distributional effects of subsidy reform is essential, since well-targeted compensatory schemes for those made worse off may need to be introduced in parallel. Partial and general equilibrium analysis can help in this regard. The methodologies outlined above can be extended to incorporate some of the environmental effects of energy subsidy reform.

The partial and general equilibrium methodologies applied in the economic analysis carry over to the environmental analysis as well. As in the economic case,

64 See UNDP 1997 for a detailed discussion of this methodology.
65 See www.nampower.com.na/NamPower/lpr_show.asp?r=60.

it is essential to adopt an approach that is sufficiently disaggregated to assess how changes in economic activity affect different groups through changes in environmental conditions. The environmental effects of subsidy reform are most easily expressed in physical terms. Converting them into monetary values is problematic and controversial, since markets for these effects do not exist.

Finally the assessment of the social effects of subsidy reform are often seen as flowing from analysis of economic effects but involve more than just the narrow interpretation of these effects as measured in terms of changes in expenditure on energy. There are strong direct linkages between energy use, health and social development, including through the environmental impacts. It is critical that these be addressed in any integrated assessment.

A4 Conclusions

This discussion has shown the steps that need to be taken and the kinds of analysis that need to be conducted for an effective integrated assessment of energy subsidies. The methodology is still evolving, however, and at present all the different components cannot generally be put into one single analytical framework. This leaves a lot of room for judgement on the part of the researcher on how best to combine different techniques.

Abbreviations

APM	Administered Pricing Mechanism
BMU	Bundesumweltministerium für Umwelt, Naturschutz und Reaktorsicherheit (German Federal Ministry for the Environment, Nature Conservation and Nuclear Safety)
boe	barrel of oil equivalent
CEA	Central Electricity Authority (India)
CENEf	Centre for Energy Efficiency (Russia)
CERC	Central Electricity Regulatory Commission (India)
CGE	computable general equilibrium
CILSS	Comité permanent Inter-états de Lutte Contre la Sécheresse au Sahel (Interstate Committee for Drought Control in the Sahel)
CMIE	Centre for Monitoring the Indian Economy
CNE	Comisión Nacional de Energía (National Energy Commission, Chile)
CO	carbon monoxide
CO_2	carbon dioxide
CORFO	Corporación de Fomento (Chile)
CSE	consumer subsidy equivalent
CZK	Czech Republic Koruny
DM	deutsche mark
DTIE	Division of Technology, Industry and Economics (UNEP)
EC	European Commission
ECLAC	Economic Commission for Latin America and the Caribbean (UN)
EEA	European Environment Agency
EEC	European Economic Community
EFR	Environmental Fiscal Reform
EIA	Energy Information Administration (USA)
ELES	extended linear expenditure system
ENAP	Empresa Nacional del Petróleo (Chile)
ENDA-TM	Environment and Development Action–tiers monde
ERA	effective rate of assistance
ESI	electricity supply industry
ETB	Economics and Trade Branch (UNEP DTIE)

ETR	Ecological Tax Reform
EU	European Union
fcfa	CFA (Communaute Financiere Africaine) franc
FEPP	Fondo de Estabilización de los Precios del Petróleo (petroleum price stabilisation fund, Chile)
GBR	Green Budget Reform
Gcal	gigacalorie
GDP	gross domestic product
GE	general equilibrium
GJ	gigajoule
GW	gigawatt
GWh	gigawatt-hour
IEA	International Energy Agency
IMF	International Monetary Fund
IPP	independent power production
IPPS	Industrial Pollution Projection System (World Bank)
kcal	kilocalorie
KEPCO	Korea Electric Power Corporation
KOGAS	Korea Gas Corporation
kV	kilovolt
kW	kilowatt
kWh	kilowatt-hour
LNG	liquefied natural gas
LPG	liquefied petroleum gas
mb/d	million barrels per day
Mboe	million barrels of oil equivalent
MCA	multi-criteria analysis
mkl	million kilolitres
MOE-CR	Ministry of the Environment of the Czech Republic
Mt	million tonnes
Mtoe	million tonnes of oil equivalent
MW	megawatt
MWh	megawatt-hour
NAD	Namibian dollar
NO_x	nitrogen oxides
OECD	Organisation for Economic Co-operation and Development
OMVS	Organisation pour la Mise en Valeur du Fleuve Senegal
OPEC	Organisation of Petroleum Exporting Countries
PJ	petajoule
PM10	particulate matter 10 microns in diameter and smaller
POP	persistent organic pollutant
PPP	purchasing power parity
PSE	producer subsidy equivalent
R&D	research and development
REC	Rural Electrification Corporation (India)
RENES	Programme de Redéploiement Energétique du Sénégal
RSEB	Rajashtan State Electricity Board (India)

SAM	social accounting matrix
SAR	Société Africaine de Raffinage
SEB	State Electricity Board (India)
SERC	state electricity commission (India)
SEVEn	Energy Efficiency Centre (Czech Republic)
SKK	Slovakia koruny
SO_2	sulphur dioxide
SO_3	sulphur trioxide
SPM	suspended particulate matter
tce	tonne of coal equivalent
TERI	The Energy and Resource Institute
TFC	total final consumption (of energy)
toe	tonne of oil equivalent
TPES	total primary energy supply
TWh	terawatt-hour
UN	United Nations
UNCTAD	United Nations Conference on Trade and Development
UNDESA	United Nations Department of Economic and Social Affairs
UNDP	United Nations Development Programme
UNECE	United Nations Economic Commission for Europe
UNEP	United Nations Environment Programme
UNFCCC	United Nations Framework Convention on Climate Change
US DOE	US Department of Energy
UTM	unidad tributaria mensual (monthly tax unit, Chile)
VAT	value-added tax
VOC	volatile organic compound
WEC	World Energy Council
WLPGA	World LP Gas Association
WSSD	World Summit on Sustainable Development
WTA	willingness to accept
WTP	willingness to pay

References

Alam, M., J. Sathaye and D.F. Barnes (1998) 'Urban Household Energy Use in India: Efficiency and Policy Implications', *Energy Policy* 26.11.

Alonso, E., and D.W. Roland-Holst (1995) *A Detailed Social Accounting Matrix for Chile* (Working Paper, Department of Economics, Mills College).

Amous, S. (1992) *Dégradation de l'environnement au Sénégal: Le rôle de l'énergie* (Dakar, Senegal: PEEA/ENDA-TM).

Anderson, K. (1995) 'The Political Economy of Coal Subsidies in Europe', *Energy Policy* 23.6: 485-96.

—— and W. McKibbin (1997) *Reducing Coal Subsidies and Trade Barriers: Their Contribution to Greenhouse Gas Abatement* (Seminar Paper 97-07; Centre for International Economic Studies, University of Adelaide, Australia).

Bartelmus, P., E. Lutz and S. Schweinfest (1993) 'Integrated Economic and Environmental Accounting: A Case Study of Papua New Guinea', in Lutz 1993.

Bashmakov, I. (2000a) 'Energy Subsidies and "Right Prices" ', *Energy Efficiency* 27 (April–June 2000).

—— (2002b) 'Heat, Money, and Housing Reform', *ZhKX* 7 [Russian language].

—— (2002c) 'Development and Implementation of Regional Energy Efficiency Programmes', *ZhKX* 8 [Russian language].

——, V. Papushkin *et al.* (2000) *The System of Fast Reaction in Emergencies in Heat Supply Systems* (Moscow: CENEf [Russian language]).

Beghin, J., S. Dessus, D. Roland-Holst and D. van der Mensbrugghe (1996) *General Equilibrium Modelling of Trade and the Environment* (Technical Paper; Paris: OECD Development Centre).

Birol, F., A.V. Aleagha and R. Ferroukhi (1995) 'The Economic Impact of Subsidy Phase-out in Oil Exporting Developing Countries: A Case Study of Algeria, Iran and Nigeria', *Energy Policy* 23.3: 209-15.

Böhringer, C. (1996) 'Fossil Fuel Subsidies and Environmental Constraints: A General Equilibrium Analysis of German Coal Subsidies and Carbon Emission Restrictions', *Environmental and Resource Economics* 8.3: 331-49.

Bundesministerium der Finanzen (2001) *Bericht der Bundesregierung über die Entwicklung der Finanzhilfen des Bundes und der Steuervergünstigungen gemäß § 12 des Gesetzes zur Förderung der Stabilität und des Wachstums der Wirtschaft (StWG) vom 8. Juni 1967 für die Jahre 1999 bis 2002 (18. Subventionsbericht).*

Burniaux, J.-M., J.P. Martin and J. Oliveira-Martins (1992) 'The Effect of Existing Distortions in Energy Markets on the Costs of Policies to Reduce CO_2 Emissions: Evidence from GREEN', *OECD Economic Studies* 19: 141-65.

Buys, P., K. Bolt, K. Hamilton, L. Wang, S. Dasgupta, C. Meisner, K. Pandey and D. Wheeler (2003) *Measuring Up: New Directions for Environmental Programs at the World Bank* (World Bank Policy Research Working Paper 3,097; Washington, DC: Development Research Group and Environment Department, World Bank).

Cavard, D., and Y. Sokona (1992) *La consommation de l'energie des ménages à Dakar: Changements de structures, Évolution des Équipements et des comportements des consommateurs* (Dakar, Senegal: COPED/IEPE/ENDA-TM).

CEA (Central Electricity Authority) (1998) *Fuel Map of India* (New Delhi: CEA [Planning Wing, IRP Division], Ministry of Power, Government of India).

Clarke, R., and T.H. Edwards (1997) *The Welfare Effects of Removing the West German Hard Coal Subsidy* (Discussion Paper 97-23; University of Birmingham, Department of Economics).

CNE (National Energy Commission of Chile) (2000) *Petroleum Products Parity Price Data 1991–2000* (Santiago: CNE).

—— (2002) *Balance de Energía 2000* (Santiago: CNE).

De Nocker, L., R. Saez and P. Linarez (1999) 'ExternE: National Implementation Programme', http://externe.jrc.es/nletter6.html.

Dessus, S., and D. O'Connor (1999) *Climate Policy without Tears: CGE-Based Ancillary Benefits Estimates for Chile* (Technical Paper 156; Paris: OECD Development Centre).

——, D. Roland-Holst and D. van der Mensbrugghe (1994) *Input-Based Pollution Estimates for Environmental Assessment in Developing Countries* (Technical Paper 101; Paris: OECD Development Centre).

Direction de l'Energie (1991) *Plan RENES 2000* (Dakar, Senegal: Direction de l'Energie).

DRI/McGraw-Hill (1994) *Effects of Phasing Out Coal Subsidies in OECD Countries*, in OECD 1997a.

EC (European Commission) (1995) *Externalities of Fuel Cycles, ExternE Project. Report Number 2: Methodology* (DGXII, Science, Research and Development, JOULE Programme).

—— (1996) *Methodologies for Impact Assessment* (DGVII, Transport Research APAS Strategic Transport).

—— (1997) *Proposal for a Council Directive Restructuring the Community Framework for the Taxation of Energy Products* (COM[97]30 final).

—— (1999) *Externalities of Energy, ExternE Project. Volume 7: Methodology 1998 Update* (DGXII, Science, Research and Development, JOULE Programme).

EEA (European Environment Agency) (1996) *Environmental Taxes: Implementation Issues and Environmental Effectiveness* (Copenhagen: EEA).

—— (2000) *Environmental Taxes: Recent Development in Tools for Integration* (Copenhagen: EEA).

Florian, M. (1999), *Analýza dotací v energetice* (*Analysis of Subsidies in the Energy Sector*) (Prague: SEVEn [Energy Efficiency Centre]).

Freund, C., and C.I. Wallich (1995) *Raising Household Energy Prices in Poland: Who Gains? Who Loses?* (World Bank Discussion Paper 1,495; Washington, DC: World Bank).

Garbaccio, R.F., M.S. Ho and D.W. Jorgenson (2000) 'The Health Benefits of Controlling Carbon Emissions in China', *Expert Workshop on Assessing the Ancillary Benefits and Costs of Greenhouse Gas Mitigation Policies*, Washington, DC, 27–29 March 2000.

Goldemberg, J. (ed.) *World Energy Assessment: Energy and the Challenge of Sustainability* (New York: United Nations Development Programme/United Nations Department of Economic and Social Affairs/World Energy Council).

Government of India Planning Commission (2001) *Annual Report on the Working of State Electricity Boards and Electricity Departments* (New Delhi: Government of India Planning Commission).

Greenpeace (1997) *Energy Subsidies in Europe* (Amsterdam: Greenpeace International).

Hope, E., and B. Singh (1995) *Energy Price Increases in Developing Countries: Case Studies of Colombia, Ghana, Indonesia, Malaysia, Turkey and Zimbabwe* (Policy Research Working Paper 1,442; Washington, DC: World Bank).

IEA (International Energy Agency) (1995) *Energy Policies of the Russian Federation* (Paris: IEA).

—— (1999) *World Energy Outlook Insights. Looking at Energy Subsidies: Getting the Prices Right* (Paris: IEA).
—— (2001a) *Energy Policies of IEA Countries: 2001 Review* (Paris: IEA).
—— (2001b) *Coal Information* (Paris: IEA).
—— (2001c) *Energy Balances of OECD Countries 1998–1999* (Paris: IEA).
—— (2001d) *Energy Subsidies in India* (Economic Analysis Division Working Paper; Paris: IEA).
—— (2002a) *Coal Information* (Paris: IEA).
—— (2002b) *Energy Prices and Taxes, Second Quarter* (Paris: IEA).
—— (2002c) *World Energy Outlook 2002* (Paris: IEA).
—— (2002d) *Electricity in India: Providing Power for the Millions* (Paris: IEA).
—— (2002e) *Energy Balances of Non-OECD Countries* (Paris: IEA).
—— (2002f) *Key Energy Statistics* (Paris: IEA).
—— (2002g) *Energy Policies of IEA Countries: Republic of Korea 2002 Review* (Paris: IEA).
IMF (International Monetary Fund) (2002a) *Czech Republic: November 2002 IMF Staff Visit Concluding Statement* (Washington, DC: IMF).
—— (2002b) *Slovak Republic: November 2002 IMF Staff Visit Concluding Mission Statement* (Washington, DC: IMF).
Iranian Ministry of Energy (2000) *Energy Balance Book 1378 (1999/2000)* (Teheran: Ministry of Energy).
—— (2001a) *Energy Balance Book 1379 (2000/01)* (Teheran: Ministry of Energy).
—— (2001b) *Time Series of Energy and Non-energy Expenditures of Urban and Rural Households* (Energy Planning Department; Teheran: Ministry of Energy).
Jilkova, J., P. Malkova and O. Potluka (2001) *Domestic Emissions Trading System in the Czech Republic: Options for an Implementation Framework* (OECD/IEA Report; Paris: OECD; www.oecd.org/dataoecd/5/38/2467371.pdf).
Koneko Marketing Co. Ltd (2001) *Energy Economy: Czech Republic 1996–2000 in Numbers* (Prague: Koneko).
Koplow, D. (1993) *Federal Energy Subsidies: Energy, Environment and Fiscal Impacts* (Washington, DC: Alliance to Save Energy).
—— and A. Martin (2000) *Fueling Global Warming: Federal Subsidies to Oil in the United States* (Washington, DC: Greenpeace).
Krivosik, J. (2001) *Dotácie v Energetike Slovenskej Republiky* (*Subsidies in the Energy Sector of the Slovak Republic*) (Prague: SEVEn [Energy Efficiency Centre]).
Larsen, B., and A. Shah (1992) *World Energy Subsidies and Global Carbon Emissions* (World Bank Research Paper 1,002; Washington, DC: World Bank).
—— and —— (1995) 'World Fossil Fuel Subsidies and Global Carbon Emissions', in L. Bovenberg and S. Cnossen (eds.), *Public Economics and the Environment in an Imperfect World* (Norwell, MA: Kluwer Academic Publishers).
Lutz, E. (ed.) (1993) *Toward Improved Accounting for the Environment* (An UNSTAD/World Bank Symposium; Washington, DC: World Bank).
Markandya, A., and K. Halsnaes (eds.) (2002) *Climate Change and Sustainable Development* (London: Earthscan Publications).
Ministère de l'Energie et de l'Hydraulique du Sénégal (2000) *Documents de présentation des journées de réflexion sur le secteur de l'energie* (Dakar: Ministère de l'Energie et de l'Hydraulique du Sénégal).
MOE-CR (Ministry of the Environment of the Czech Republic) (2001) *The Czech Republic's Third National Communication on the UN Framework Convention on Climate Change* (Prague: MOE-CR).
Myers, N., and J. Kent (2001) *Perverse Subsidies: How Tax Dollars Can Undercut the Environment and the Economy* (Washington, DC: Island Press).
Normann, Fritz and Springfelt (1998) 'Effects of Government Subsidies on the Environment: The Case of Electricity and Paper Production from a Swedish Perspective', in OECD 1998.
O'Ryan, R., C.J. de Miguel and S. Miller (2000) *Documento Técnico Modelo ECOGEM-Chile* (Documentos de Trabajo CAPP, 63; Santiago: Universidad de Chile).

OECD (Organisation for Economic Co-operation and Development) (1997a) *Reforming Energy and Transport Subsidies* (Paris: OECD).
—— (1997b) *Environmental Policies and Employment* (Paris: OECD).
—— (1998) *Improving the Environment through Reducing Subsidies* (Paris: OECD).
—— (2000) *Environmental Effects of Liberalising Fossil Fuels Trade: Results from the OECD Green Model* (working paper; Paris: OECD).
Okugu, B.E., and F. Birol (1994) 'Market-Based Carbon Abatement Policies: The Case of Coal Subsidy Phase-out', *OPEC Review*, Autumn 1994: 359-76.
Oosterhuis, F.H. (2001) *Energy Subsidies in the European Union* (IVM report W-01/21; Amsterdam: Institute for Environmental Studies, Vrije Universiteit).
Pearce, D., and E.B. Barbier (2000) *Blueprint for a Sustainable Economy* (Sterling, VA: Stylus Publications).
Reddy, A.K.N. (2000) 'Energy and Social Issues', in Goldemberg 2000.
Repetto, R., W. Magrath, M. Wells, C. Beer and F. Rossini (1989) *Wasting Assets: Natural Resources in the National Income Accounts* (Washington, DC: World Resources Institute).
Rogat, J., and T. Sterner (1998) 'The Determinants of Gasoline Demand in Some Latin American Countries', *International Journal of Global Energy Issues* 11.
RSEB (Rajashtan State Electricity Board) (1999) *Revised Rates* (New Delhi: RSEB).
Russian Ministry of Energy (2001) *Energy Strategy of the Russian Federation to 2002* (Moscow: Ministry of Energy).
Saaty, T.L. (1980) *The Analytical Hierarchy Process* (New York: McGraw-Hill).
Schlegelmilch, K. (1999) *Green Budget Reform in Europe. Countries at the Forefront: Prospects in Central and Eastern Europe* (Berlin/New York: Springer).
Smith, K., and Metha (2000) 'Estimating the Global Burden of Disease from Indoor Air Pollution', in D. Kay, A. Pruss and C. Corvalan (eds.), *Methodology for Assessment of Environmental Burden of Disease: Report on the ISEE Session on Environmental Burden of Disease* (WHO/SDE/WSH/00.7).
Solorzano, R., *et al.* (1991) *Accounts Overdue: Natural Resource Depreciation in Costa Rica* (San Jose, Costa Rica: Tropical Science Centre; Washington, DC: World Resources Institute).
Sow, P.A. and C.R. Sagna (1999) *Etude portant sur les coûts d'approvisionnement, de conditionnement, de transport et de distribution du gaz butane au Sénégal* (Transafricaine de Technologie; Dakar: PROGEDE [Composante Demande], January 1999).
SRI Consulting and Korean Energy Economics Institute (1998) *Energy Conservation Study for Korea: Phase II* (SRIC Technical Assistance Project 7426).
Steenblik, R.P., and P. Coroyannakis (1995) 'Reform of Coal Policies in Western and Central Europe: Implications for the Environment', *Energy Policy* 23.6: 537-53.
Svejnar, J. (ed.) (1995) *The Czech Republic and Economic Transition in Eastern Europe* (New York: Academic Press).
TERI (The Energy Research Institute) (2002) *Energy Data Directory and Yearbook 2001/2002* (New Delhi: TERI).
Tol, R.S.J. (1996) 'The Damage Costs of Climate Change: Towards a Dynamic Representation', *Ecological Economics* 19: 67-90.
UNCTAD (United Nations Conference on Trade and Development) (2002) *Review of Status of Emissions Trading Activities in CG11 Countries (Country Profile: Czech Republic and Slovak Republic).*
UNDP (United Nations Development Programme) (1997) *Productive Employment and Poverty Reduction: How Can Livelihoods be More Sustainable?*
UNECE (United Nations Economic Commission for Europe) (2002) *Draft Guidelines on Reforming Energy Pricing and Subsidies* (Task Force on Energy and Environment, Geneva, 19 November 2002, www.unece.org/ie/se/pdfs/Reform_Guidelines_E.pdf 2002).
UN ECLAC (UN Economic Commission for Latin America and the Caribbean) (1995) *Establecimiento de una Política Energética Basada en el Funcionamiento de Mercados Competitivos y en la Participación Privada: La Experiencia de Chile* (Santiago, Chile: UN ECLAC).

—— (1999) *Panorama Social de America Latina 1998* (Santiago, Chile: UN ECLAC).
—— (2000) *El Fondo de Estabilización de Precios del Petróleo (FEPP) y el Mercado de los Derivados en Chile* (Santiago, Chile: UN ECLAC).
UNEP (United Nations Environment Programme) (1997) *Economic Values and the Environment in the Developing World* (Cheltenham, UK: Edward Elgar).
—— (2004) *The Use of Economic Instruments in Environmental Policy: Opportunities and Challenges* (Geneva: United Nations).
——/IEA (International Energy Agency) (2002) *Reforming Energy Subsidies* (Paris: UNEP/IEA).
US DOE (US Department of Energy)/EIA (Energy Information Administration) (1992) *Federal Energy Subsidies: Direct and Indirect Interventions in Energy Markets* (Washington, DC: US DOE/EIA).
——/—— (1999) *Federal Energy Market Interventions 1999: Primary Energy* (Washington, DC: US DOE/EIA).
——/—— (2000) *Federal Energy Market Interventions 1999: Energy Transformation and End Use* (Washington, DC: US DOE/EIA).
Van Tongeren, J., S. Schweinfest, E. Lutz, M. Gomez Luma and F.G. Martin (1993) 'Integrated Economic and Environmental Accounting: A Case Study for Mexico', in Lutz 1993.
Venegas, M.J. (1995) *Matriz de Cuentas Sociales 1986: Una SAM para Chile* (Serie de Estudios Económicos 39; Santiago: Banco Central de Chile).
World Bank (1989) *Urban Household Energy Strategy* (Washington, DC: World Bank).
—— (1997a) *Expanding the Measure of Wealth: Indicators of Environmentally Sustainable Development* (Washington, DC: World Bank).
—— (1997b) 'The Economic Toll of Pollution's Effects on Health', in *Pollution Prevention and Abatement Handbook: Part II* (Washington, DC: World Bank).
—— (2000a) *Energy Services for the World's Poor: Energy and Development Report 2000* (Washington, DC: World Bank).
—— (2000b) *Indonesia: Oil and Gas Sector Study* (Washington, DC: World Bank, June 2000).
—— (2002) *Coping with the Cold* (World Bank Technical Paper 529; Washington, DC: World Bank).
——/WLPGA (World LP Gas Association) (2001) *West Africa LPG Market Development Study* (Washington, DC: World Bank).